BY ANY OTHER NAME

a lesbian's journey out of west virginia

ROSE WALTON

ISBN: 5-800114-892615

For Marjorie

My wife, my best friend,
the love of my life

My Precious Treasure

ACKNOWLEDGEMENTS

Marjorie E. Sherwin has been my life partner for thirty nine years, my wife for ten. She has been my main support throughout the years of work and writing. I am blessed by her caring love.

Martin J. Sherwin, a Pulitzer Prize winning American historian, and Marjorie's brother, for his advice and support from the first draft. While Marge and I were visiting him and Susan, his wife, we had a very productive discussion about the title. The outcome was the subtitle: *a lesbian's journey out of west virginia.*

Lucy Field Goodman for her insistence that I finish the manuscript, her support, and her inspiration. She is a best friend with all that goes with it. Can't do without her guidance. And for our many discussions, one of which created: *BY ANY OTHER NAME.* Lucy's is the author of the beautifully written book, *On the Way to Wonderland.*

Kathy Collins awakened my desire to write and continued her encouragement during the years of my work. Thanks for that first writing workshop and your steady prodding and motivation. I enjoyed your books: *Lovers in the Present Afternoon* and *Risk of Change.*

Joan Casamo and Linda Clarke worked tirelessly to dot the i's and cross the t's. I give you my eternal gratitude; a regular thank you is in order. You two are very special and are deep in my heart forever. Your thoughtfulness makes our community a better place. *On a Planet Sailing West*, and your RAVINGS at jlblue.com, keep us aware of our natural world.

The cover painting was created by a very dear friend, Ann Allen. She is a master goldsmith and a very talented artist. She and her wife, Mary Jane Winstead, have created jewelry with a message, especially for women, for forty five years.

My sister Nancy left us much too early. Her four children, Jeff, Jennifer, Randy, and Robin, their spouses and children, Kristie, Mickey, Natalie, Nick, Trevor, Tori, Josh,

Katie, Abbie, Michael, Amanda, Zach, Alex, Chloe, Nicki, and Marco, have given my wife and me much joy and love.

I have enjoyed the last fifty Christmases with a very dear friend: Jo and her husband, children, their spouses and their children. They keep the joy of the holiday alive and well. Thank you, Jo, for those early sensitive readings, and for your steadfast support and love.

The design and technology experts, Barry Dingman and Joel Cohen, were always there with the right answer immediately. Their creativity and sensibility began the book cover discussion.

There are many others, too many to include, but you know who you are. I thank you from the bottom of my heart.

BY ANY OTHER NAME is my version of life with memory and emotional truth. Some of you may remember it differently but this is MY story to the best of MY recollection.

A bright and sunny day   most important   significant
biggest day   *my name on a building*
at the hospital   only know one other lesbian with her name
on a building...an elementary school   they did not know she
was a lesbian or it would not have happened   everyone here
knows   proud   excited   don't believe it   just doing my job
just doing my job   oh my god, look at all those people   here
for me   thank you   overwhelming   the president of the
hospital comes to the car   congratulations Rose and thank
you.   everyone is moving toward the car   can't get out
can't walk   this damn disease   where is my scooter?   here
now   thanks Marge   we move to the auditorium   nervous
sweaty hands   nose running   they are still coming   I
haven't kissed this many people for a long time   Tom opens
the gathering   such good words   deserving   your work
East End   did so much   so early   how did you know?   I
won't remember all these speakers   so much appreciation
compliments   such praise   tears start   can't cry all day
then hospital administration   happy to have your name on
the HIV/AIDS clinic   you deserve the honor   hope I am
smiling, I know I'm crying   Nancy's children will hear all of
this   last night, Marge's family and mine together for the
first time   exceptional   talk about tears   of joy   and love
hard to talk   voice is quivering   Natalie sings   beautiful
chills   Larry Kramer   oh boy   the first leader in the
response to this epidemic, plague   crisis   I honor his
willingness to say it as it is with no sugar coating   now   my
turn   can't thank them all   try   don't forget my precious
treasure   and the family   so much love   so blessed   and the
sign on the building

ROSE WALTON CARE SERVICES
at DAVID E. ROGERS, MD CENTER
SOUTHAMPTON HOSPITAL

1

Mrs. Easton, my third grade teacher, leans over my shoulder and whispers, "Just write deceased in the blank for your father's name." She quickly moves to the front of the room.

She doesn't whisper to any other kid. Why to me? Am I the only kid in the classroom whose father is deceased? How does she know? I left it blank last year. I don't know when he died. Did he really die? No one ever talks about him at home.

I write DECEASED and walk up to her desk and lay the card on her desk. I turn it over so DECEASED doesn't show.

I remember the first morning of school. I was prancing all around, wearing a new blue dress, even if it was a hand-me-down from my big sister, Nancy, and new shiny white shoes. Then momma came to spoil the day.

I hear her yell as Nancy and I run down the front steps. I'm so big. I'm going to school even if I'm just five years old. I'm jumpin up and down inside and I can almost hear my heart beat. Momma comes out and yells at me. "Now Rose Ann, remember what I told you yesterday about your father. If anyone asks anything about him you just say he's dead. He died right after you were born."

"I remember, momma." How could I forget? It's the only thing I know about him. I jerk away from her and run to catch Nancy. Why'd she say anything? I kick dirt and now my white shoes and socks are dirty. I'm not pretty or even clean anymore. Nobody will wanna talk to me. They'll just make fun.

"Hey, Nancy, wait. What'd you say last year?" She doesn't answer. Just runs ahead. I'll be alone all day.

Billy and Joe are mad at me because I'm winning all their marbles. We play marbles often in their backyard. We draw a big circle and each of us puts in five marbles and then take turns shooting with our special marble to hit them out. We keep the ones we hit out and now I have five. It's Billy's turn. I watch as he leans on one knee. His bony knee is like mine, real skinny. I turn to look at Joe's big knee and wonder if Billy's or mine will ever be that big. He's older and plays with us cause he thinks he can beat both of us. He never does. Billy holds three marbles in his left hand and shoots with his right. He misses. Joe holds two marbles and misses all of the ones in the circle. I shoot and hit one marble that hits another one out so I win. I'll leave the rest for them. I jump up and say, "I gotta go."

Billy says, "That's not fair. You cheat."

"I do not." I go toward the street and hear Billy mumbling behind me. I turn and say, "What?"

"You cheat. Cause you don't even have a father."

I keep going and he yells behind me, "Rosie has no daddy. No daddy. No daddy." He's right behind me. He pushes me and keeps on yelling. Hot tears start down my face and I run down the hill, around the corner, home. I sit down hard on the ugly, broken, wooden front steps. I hang my head. I know no one will talk to me about what Billy said. Everybody has a daddy. Don't I?

I'm almost eight and I don't want anybody to tease me, I always cry. How can Billy say I have no father? If I don't know, how can he know? I've always wanted to know about my daddy. I look down at myself, skinny little kid with dirty shorts and muddy knees. My T-shirt's dirty, too, where I cleaned my special marble before each shot. My marbles are always clean when I start to play. I wash them at the hose near the barn almost every day.

I look through the front door screen. I see momma sittin in the bedroom readin the paper. Our bedroom, where momma, Nancy, and I sleep, is just behind the living room and I can see straight through both rooms. I go in and let the screen slam. Momma yells, "Why do you always slam that goddamn door?" She doesn't even look up.

I slide to the bedroom floor at her feet. The cold linoleum is a funny brown and white mix, old and faded with scratches all over. I still have tears in my eyes but she doesn't notice. She looks down at me and asks, "What the hell do you want? Can't you see, I'm reading the paper?" She is very tall, dark- wavy hair and always sits very straight

4

in any chair. She's in a desk chair now with the paper on one bed and her feet on another. She has her shoes on too. She'd yell if I did that.

I look up at the paper and say, "Yes, momma, but Billy said I never had a daddy. He got mad when I won all his good marbles. He hit me and yelled at me. Is it true? Where is my daddy? Everybody has a daddy, don't they? You do." She lowers the paper and I see those mean black eyes staring down at me. If I were bigger, she'd pay attention. I'm skinny and the youngest. Nobody listens to me. My heart speeds up and more tears come. I hang my head as she points her finger at me.

"Shut your goddamn mouth and don't ask me about him again. He's dead. I told you that when you started school. Now go change those dirty shorts and put on a clean blouse for supper."

I move away from her feet and sit on the edge of my bed. I think she's gonna hit me. She shakes the paper toward me like she's getting rid of a bug. Maybe she'd like to stamp me out like my daddy. "But momma, I just want to know." Am I peein my pants?

"I SAID SHUT YOUR GODDAMN MOUTH. IT'S NONE OF YOUR GODDAMN BUSINESS. And stop that everlasting crying. Now get out of here and let me read the paper."

I jump up; throw my arms around and run to the back porch. I hate her. I don't care if she is my mother. I have to find someone to tell me about him and where he is. We; my mother, Nancy, and I, live with Deh Deh and Granny, mother's father and mother. None of them will tell me anything. Someday someone will. Mother's always mad at someone, usually Granny or me. Deh Deh has his own house, really a shack, out back so he doesn't bother with any of us much. He and I have long talks about everything and nothing when he's just sittin in the back yard. He only comes in the real house to eat supper.

The pantry is just off the kitchen and I love to look at things in here. When I want to be alone and not dust or

5

sweep; I hide from Nancy and Granny. These shelves are full of old dishes and bowls, some look like they were cut from chunks of glass that Granny used in her kitchen and dining room before Nancy and I came along. She says she put everything away to save for us. She probably thinks we'd break them. The dishes are beautiful but I like the red, double globe glass lamp best. I look out the window and see Deh Deh poundin the husk off our black walnuts.

He's sittin in front of his shack in his sling-back chair. That chair's been patched so many times I can't tell what color it was. He uses old feed sacks to patch it. They're scratchy so I don't sit there much. I open the window and wave with both hands. He finally sees me and smiles. I sneak out through the kitchen, jump down the back steps, run under the grape arbor, and then take thirty-three giant steps to get to the barn. Then I turn to the left and go past the funny-looking room with a dirt floor and open sides like a cage, where Deh Deh keeps tools and junk. The chicken feed's there too in a big bin. Sometimes I go in there and get a handful of the feed and eat it. Tastes like dry oats and makes my mouth sticky. From the turn, it only took me eighteen steps today; took twenty last week. I'm getting bigger.

Deh Deh puts boards on the ground where he lays the black walnuts to dry. Last week, I helped him pick up the big green balls from under the tree. They were pretty then but now they've turned black and wrinkly; ready for pounding the husk off each one. Then they have to dry again and finally we can crack them with a hammer to eat the nut. Black walnuts are the best. I try to get the nut out of the shell in two pieces like I do with pecans, but walnuts have more little pieces of shell inside that hold the meat very tight.

"Can I help? I'll be careful."

He looks at me over his glasses and sees my old jeans and a clean shirt. He shakes his head. "No, you just sit over there on that log and stay out of trouble. You have no damn business with a hammer. And if you get too close, the walnut juice will get all over your good clothes."

His clothes are the same every day. I guess it doesn't matter to him if they get dirty. He wears old overalls over one or two pairs of other pants and they're always dirty-looking to me. But I don't say anything about his clothes. He always has on a blue long-sleeved shirt that Granny calls his railroad shirt. He works three days a week at the local train station. He's a freight agent at the depot. He talks about retiring sometimes and says he'll buy a newsstand in town to make some money. I've never seen a newsstand in town. He wears a blue and white-striped railroad hat when he goes to work, and when I go to the station and see that hat I know it's my Deh Deh. I always run to where he is even if he tells me not to run near the tracks or on the platform.

"They're my old pants. They're already dirty. Please, can I shuck just one?"

"I said NO, and I mean it, damnit. I'm not telling you again. Now if you want to stay here, you'll have to sit over there." I go sit on the log that's on the other side of his boards. I wish he'd let me help but it's no use getting mad or pouting cause he's made up his mind. I start askin questions about the walnuts. *"How many walnuts this year? Have you counted them? I can if you want me to. I'll count the ones you've done. OK?"*

He keeps on shucking and doesn't bother to answer me. So I start rambling about everything else on my mind. "When will the grapes be ripe? I think the blackberries are all gone. I couldn't find any yesterday when I was in the patch."

"You just have to look closer. Don't be in such a damn big hurry."

"Then the briars scratch my arms and momma gets mad. She tells me not to go to the patch." I go on counting. Ninety, ninety-one, . . . one hundred. "I wanna go live with someone else. She hates me."

"Hush! She does not. She loves you."

"She does not. She loves Nancy."

"You're not goin anywhere so get that crazy thought outta your head. Anyway who'd help me?" He looks up and smiles.

"Do you want me to go to the store? Granny'll need sugar when the grapes get ripe." Granny never asks for anything. Just cooks and cleans.

"Your grandmother uses too damn much sugar in everything. I'll make the grape jelly. She won't need sugar."

I don't say anything cause I know that tomorrow or the next day he'll send me to the store to get sugar for her. He just sits there hammering the covering off each nut. His hands are that ole yellowish orange color and they get darker as time passes. We have a lot of black walnuts from this one big tree right in the back yard between the house and the barn. There's a little hill under the tree where Nancy and I lie on our backs and watch the clouds go by. Every cloud looks like something. We make up stories of where we'd go if we were in that cloud. I always go far away but Nancy goes to visit her friends. Maybe that's why everybody says she's a good girl.

Granny's goin to see Mrs. Atkins and Lucy today. I hope she asks me to go with her. She almost never asks me to do anything with her, but Nancy won't go there so maybe I'll get lucky. She walks into the living room where I'm dustin. "Ann, come to Mrs. Atkins with me. You can finish that later. OK?"

"Really, Granny, can I go?" I don't wait for an answer. I go put the dust rag away and run back to the front porch where she's waitin for me.

Nancy acts like she's afraid of Lucy. I feel sorry for Lucy. She can't hear very well and can't talk like everybody else. I try to make her laugh. She really can't laugh but she makes sounds and gets this really big smile on her face when I show up. I know she likes me and thinks I'm funny. We carry on a real conversation even if she can't talk. I make motions to let her know what I'm talking about. I hear Mother talk about her being deaf and dumb. She might be deaf, but she sure isn't dumb. She's different and I think I am too. I just don't fit in with anybody. But Lucy and I get along just fine.

8

They live in a really little house about two blocks from our house. It's in an alley behind some bigger houses. It's the smallest house I've ever been in except Deh Deh's shack. There's a kitchen just big enough for one person to move around and a living room and bedroom with a curtain between them. Two little beds, like the cots that just fit with about a foot between them. Don't know where they keep their clothes; I've never seen a closet. The bathroom, just a commode, is on the back of the house like an add-on. It looks like somebody took an outhouse like ours and nailed it to their wall. It has a flush john though. They seem happy and I like them. I go to visit them sometimes by myself but nobody knows 'cept Mrs. Atkins and Lucy.

"Com'on Ann, if you're going. I have to hurry to get back to make dinner. We won't be gone long. I just want to say hello."

I hate the name Ann and Granny always calls me Ann. She never calls me Rose or Rosie. She says it's the name of one of Deh Deh's girlfriends. Probably before they were married but like all the other questions, there are no answers. "OK OK. What's the big rush? I want to take Lucy something. What can I take?" Granny doesn't walk very fast. She broke her hip last winter and now she walks with a limp. She's short and bent over. I notice that more when she's at home and walkin in her slippers.

"Just go with me. I have a little something and you can give it to her. She loves you. You'll be enough."

"OK." I skip down the street in front of Granny and then turn and skip back. Walk a few steps with her and then skip ahead and back.

"Say, Granny, did you ever see my Daddy?"

"Hush, Ann, you know better than to ask me those questions. Ask your Mother."

I skip ahead and turn around and stop right in front of her. She stops, puts her hands on her hips and gives me one of those "Now what?" looks. "Why won't anybody tell me about my Father?"

"Ask your Mother. Now let's go." She moves past me and walks a little faster.

9

"Maybe I'll just run away." I skip far ahead and hear her call me. She thinks I'm really gonna run away. I can't do that now. No clothes, no money, no place to go.

Granny catches up, tells me to "settle down" and hands me a package to give to Lucy as we go up the two little steps to their back porch. Actually it's their front and back porch. Mrs. Atkins comes shuffling to the door. She's so tiny and so old. She has a big smile on her face and that makes more wrinkles. I bet she's almost 80. Poor Lucy has to live with this old woman without any brothers and sisters. But she's a lot older than I am too. I think she's thirty-five. That's pretty old, but compared to Granny and Mrs. Atkins I guess that's not old.

I hug Mrs. Atkins. I'm almost as tall as she is. Then I run to Lucy. She's sittin on the couch and I fall into her lap. She's fat and doesn't walk too much so I just go wherever she's sittin. "Here, Lucy, a present." I hand it to her and hug myself to show it's made with love and then point to Granny. "She made jelly last week and we brought you a little jar."

Lucy smiles and makes her usual happy sounds. Her eyes light up and sparkle. She likes to hold my arm so I move close and go on yapping about the end of summer and goin back to school as she smiles and coos and slaps her other hand on her knee. I can tell she's happy and glad to see us. She likes Granny too, and reaches out a hand to say hello to her. Granny and Mrs. Atkins go back in the kitchen and Lucy and I just keep goin on. I want to tell her I'm going to run away but I can't make her understand. Granny calls me. I kiss her hand and say, "Bye."

That's the biggest wasp's nest I've ever seen. It's hanging in the peak of our roof like a giant silver balloon that just blew out of my hand. I lie on the ground, under the big walnut tree, in the back yard, watching the wasps fly in and out like a busy parade of ants. The nest is beautiful with little ridges all around like wrapping a giant balloon with ribbon that has lace on each side. They build the nest bigger and bigger. Maybe they're adding space for new wasps. I think there are already thousands.

I showed it to Nancy yesterday and sure enough, she told Deh Deh. Today, he's going to knock the nest down and probably kill the wasps. They aren't bothering anybody. Why destroy their home and kill them? He told us to stay inside and out of the back yard today.

I'm standing at the pantry window right under the nest. Nancy's trying to get at the window, but there's not room and I keep goin from side to side so she can't see.

Deh Deh's puttin his longest ladder against the house, but I can't see how close it is to the nest. He's goin up the ladder with a long pole. I hope he doesn't get stung. He's not afraid of anything. He wears his usual overalls over other pants. Maybe the wasps can't sting through all those layers. His old straw hat sits funny on his head, but his face is not covered and neither are his hands. The wasps can surely sting through that old shirt. Now I can't see him.

I turn to go tell him to be careful. Too late! The nest falls. "WOW, LOOK AT ALL THOSE WASPS." They're like a trail of black smoke following the nest as it crashes to the ground and breaks into about ten pieces. Beautiful. I want to pick up the pieces and put them together. It looks like there are tiny rooms all in rows. Maybe tunnels around and around if the pieces were together. The wasps dart in and out of the nest. What would I do if our house fell apart?

Nancy pushes me away from the window. "Let's go out so we can see them better"

"Go ahead. I'm not gettin stung." I hope she does. Deh Deh will really yell at her.

"Sissy." "Chicken." She leaves the pantry, and I follow her. When we start out the back door, Deh Deh is standing right there, on the porch, brushing the wasps off his clothes. "I told you girls to stay the hell out of the back yard today. You don't listen to a damn thing. Now get back inside and stay away from this door."

Nancy hits me and runs through the house and out the front door. I chase her but as the screen door slams in my face I see that she's going across the street to the Epperleys. I don't wanna go there so I head up the street, across the creek and to the garden. I don't want to be anywhere near the back of the house. I'll pick some flowers for Granny. Deh Deh plants lots of flowers near the vegetable garden but he doesn't think they should ever be picked. He says that if the man upstairs, that's what he calls God, wanted flowers to be inside he would have had us put dirt in at least one room.

I've checked the wasps three times and most of them are still there. I'm surprised Deh Deh didn't kill them this morning. Maybe too many. I watch them from the pantry window. They fly between the crushed nest and the overhang of the roof. They act scared and lost. I try to watch one wasp but they all look alike flying up and down and down and up, over and over. There seem to be thousands of them but I don't think the nest's that big. It's huge though and broken open so the little cells show. Deh Deh called them paper wasps. The inside looks like honey comb but nothin's dripping from this nest. Dry as a bone. They're not honeybees. I have to go closer so I can really see them. I run through the house and go outside to the corner of the house closest to the nest.

I yell, "Nancy, come here. Look at this beautiful nest."

"Deh Deh told us not to go back there."

"I'm not in the back yard, stupid. I'm in the side yard looking around the corner. You wanna see it or not."

She comes toward me and hides behind me to look around the corner. She's such a goody two-shoes. I have to find a way to get her to break the rules.

"Hey, Nancy, let's see who can go closest to the nest without gettin stung."

"No!"

"C'mon, Chicken. Now who's a sissy?" That'll get her. She thinks she's so tough and better than me, cause she's older.

"I know I can get closer because you're too slow. They'll get you for sure", says Nancy.

12

"Betcha." I could push her.

"And you'll get punished."

"Says, who?"

"Deh Deh said. . . . ."

"He's not even here now. He said he was going to kill them but he didn't. He'll never know unless you blab." We're both in shorts and short-sleeved shirts. My shirt's big so a wasp could fly under it. I'll tuck it into my shorts. I have on shoes and socks but Nancy just has on sandals. The wasps will get her feet.

"OK, Rosie, you go first."

Oh boy, here I go. I run as fast as I can, half way between the house and the walnut tree. I was about six feet from the nest. Nancy follows but she's about a foot closer. Now I run within two feet of the nest and very close to the back porch steps. I can feel the wasps around me but none land on me or sting me. I get to the corner of the house and hope Nancy won't run again. "Game's over, I win."

I look back and see her hiding her eyes. She thinks I got stung. She's too scared to run.

"Do I win, Chicken? Cluck. Cluck."

"No! Just wait a minute. You'll see." She runs very fast, close to the steps and hits me as she reaches this side of the house. I knock a wasp off her shirt. She turns and tells me we better quit.

"So you think you win and now we have to quit. Oh No, you don't. Watch this." I run right beside the nest and have to go around the porch steps to keep from falling. The wasps swarm all over me. I scream and brush them as fast as I can. I'm being stung all over. I try to get away from them but more of them keep flying at me. I run toward the front of the house and see Granny coming to find out what has happened.

"Help me, Granny." I'm sobbing. It's like a million hot needles going into my skin all at once. They're everywhere. I'm scared. I'm really in trouble. Deh Deh will be very mad. I keep yellin and sobbin at the same time. I see bumps all over my arms.

Granny puts her arm around me and tells me to settle down, that the wasps are all gone. I still feel one on my leg. It's under my sock. I see bumps on my legs, too. I can't stop crying enough to tell her but I keep dancin wildly, jumping up and down, pointing to my foot. She keeps trying to get me into the house. She tells Nancy to open the door and help bring me inside. I want to stay outside till the wasp is out of my sock. Nancy finally sees me point to my foot. She pulls my sock down and the wasp flies away. I go inside and Granny helps me get to her bed. I hurt all over.

"Now, Ann, just lay still. I'll get some baking soda to stop the stinging.

Nancy comes over and whispers that she won. Says she'll tell Deh Deh that we were just looking at the nest and the wasps came around the corner. I know better. She'll tell him that she tried to stop me but I ran past the nest anyway. She always tells on me. I hide my face and tell her to go away.

Granny comes back with a dish of soda and cold water. It feels better as she puts it on my arms and legs. I want to stay here in Granny's bed so Mother and Deh Deh won't yell at me when they come home. Maybe I won't be able to get up.

Mother comes in and I act like I'm asleep. "Are you alright?"

"Uh huh."

"Good. You should stay here until supper time. I'm glad you feel OK. Nancy said the bees just swarmed around you. I'm sorry." She bends over and pats my shoulder.

"Thanks." Boy, I never thought she'd say that. I feel better. I turn over toward the wall and curl up in a little ball.

I see Deh Deh sittin in his favorite chair, in the back yard, peeling apples. He sits like that for hours. His pipe hangs out of one side of his mouth but I can't tell if it's lit. I don't see any smoke. His baldhead is smooth as glass. I touch it sometimes when I pass by; he doesn't do much touching, so I'm careful not to get too close. I think he likes for me to sit with him and I like to be with him.

14

I sure don't want to be in the house with Nancy. Granny's always doin housework and I hate that. Dustin's a waste. It just gets dusty again tomorrow. Nancy'll make fun of my cut off shorts and flowered top. Her clothes always have to match. She gets up early to choose the clothes she wants or hides them the night before. We wear the same things, but she claims some are hers.

I go through the kitchen, grab a couple of paper bags and head for the orchard. I'll eat apples for breakfast cause I didn't get up before Granny gave **MY** oatmeal to the stray cats. Darn stray cats. They're everywhere; they all come here to have their kittens. I hate them. I bet Nancy had her oatmeal but she didn't call me. She doesn't like me either. She's mother's good little girl.

I go to the side of the house where four of the six apple trees are early transparent cause I know they're ripe. I've been eatin them for weeks green and hard but I like them. Deh Deh taught me the names when I was little. We have Grimes golden delicious, red wine sap, Jonathan, and rusty coat. The rusty coat tree has less than ten apples that won't be ripe till October. I check em and count em every day to make sure they're all still up there. If they fall early I'll get them first.

In the first bag, I pick a dozen early transparent apples from the biggest tree; pick some from the ground, and add a few from another tree for the other bag. I take the good apples to Granny in the kitchen and take the other bag to the back steps where I sit to eat and watch Deh Deh. I'm not sure he can see me. I'm behind a post under the grape arbor.

He sits in front of his shack in that old sling chair that he patched last week with a scratchy burlap sack. Nobody else sits in it. It's low to the ground so he's in the right position to drop the apples in one bucket and peelings in another. The peelings get fed to the chickens and the apples get cooked into applesauce, stewed apples, or apple-butter for canning. We have apples on our supper table every day. I don't think he'd come in the house to eat if that wasn't true. He does most of the canning in this family. He

15

always complains about how much sugar Granny uses when she makes apple butter and even when she makes an apple pie for him. But, I know he still wants her to make the pies. We have apples, beans and cornbread every night. Even if we have chicken, we still have apples, beans and cornbread. When I grow up, I'm never going to eat another bean. Especially the terrible soybeans.

At the end of the early transparent apple season we'll make cider. I love homemade cider and Deh Deh makes the best. I think it's because he throws everything in the cider mill. He uses rotten apples, good apples from the tree that are perfect and delicious, but mostly the ones from the ground, that bees eat. Sometimes I think the bees get in the cider mill. He'll let me help pick up the apples if he thinks I've been good. I'm always afraid I'll get stung but I don't tell him that.

I watch him get up with a bucket of peelings and walk to the path between his shack and the storage cage. His one-room shack is made of wide rough boards with little strips of wood on it every few inches. It looks black but not painted, just old wood. The storage cage is just across the narrow path. I guess he's taking the peelings to the chickens as a midmorning treat. Maybe he goes back there to go to the bathroom. I don't know where he goes to pee, I never see him go to the outhouse. He comes back with an empty bucket. I can tell cause he's swingin it higher now. He looks toward the house, sees me, smiles, and waves.

He puts the bucket down and turns to go into his shack. I see him take his keys out of his pocket. He keeps them tied to a very long shoestring that's also tied to his pants. It's long enough for him to reach the lock without ever dropping his keys. They are always attached to him. I don't know why he keeps his shack locked when he's right there. He even sleeps in that old shack, not in the house with Granny. It's like he lives there, except for supper. Everybody calls it Mr. Walton's place. Seems strange to me, but I sure don't ask questions. Nobody answers them anyway.

16

I know what his shack looks like inside. Sometimes he gives me the key to go get something for him. I can hardly reach the big padlock. There's a black pot-bellied stove in the middle of the room and a black iron bed with messy sheets and an old army blanket in the corner. High shelves cover one wall and half the next. A beautiful roll top desk sits below the shelves to the left of his bed. One time when I was in his shack with him he showed me how the desk worked. The top slides up in groves and uncovers the desk. It's really a beautiful desk. I hope it'll be mine someday. The floor is mostly old boards but some of it's hard, black dirt. He has Granger tobacco cans sitting everywhere. He saves stuff, maybe money, after he smokes the tobacco. He always has a pipe in his mouth except when he comes to supper. It smells good all the time, lit or unlit. He cooks on a two-burner gas stove. He always tells me not to touch it. I'd like to have my own shack where no one else could go unless I told them they could. Someday, I'll have my own house. I don't ever want to live with anybody.

I see him coming back to his peeling. I get up, grab my bag of apples and take them to him.

"Thank you, I was about to go pick some. Now I can keep peeling." He motions for me to sit near him.

I sit on a three-legged stool about eight inches off the ground. Deh Deh usually puts a bucket on it for whatever he's gonna cook. As usual, I want to help but I'll have to wait for him to get tired of my rambling and give me his pocketknife. He taught me to peel apples and potatoes with one piece of peeling and it's so thin you can read a paper through it. With all the apples we have, I think that's a waste of time. I have to be real careful to do it right.

I hope he lets me use his pocketknife today. I love that little brown and silver knife. It's sharp as a razor. He sharpens it on the grindstone. I start askin questions. "Do you need more apples? Do you want me to go to the store? Can I wash the jars? Are you making cider today or tomorrow?" I don't give him time to answer.

"Can't you be still for a damn minute? Are those good clothes?"

"No, they're old."

"Here, use this pocketknife and keep quiet."

"Oh! WOW! Thank you." My heart races and I hope I don't cut my finger or drop the knife in the dirt. I sit very still and peel very carefully. Now he starts with the questions. I guess he thinks I can't or won't talk while I peel.

"Have you made your bed? What's your sister doing? Should you be helping? Did you help your grandmother clean the house before you came out here?"

I answer with a grunt or "uh-huh" or just shake my head and go on peeling just like he's doing. When I get tired, I wipe his knife off on my shorts and give it back to him. "Thanks for lettin me help"

"OK. Remember we have vegetable plants to put in the ground after lunch."

"OK." I'd forgotten about the big package of plants that arrived yesterday. He sells most of the plants and then we plant the rest of them. I like to help him. I skip toward the house but stop to eat some red and black raspberries on the way. I leave the yellow ones for Nancy. She likes them best, but they're too sweet for me. I hear Granny calling me for lunch. Why can't she stop callin me Ann?

I go to the kitchen, wash my hands in the big sink that hangs on the wall just like at the horse barn. But this one's in our kitchen. It hangs beside the broken wooden table covered with old oilcloth that always looks dirty. When we eat breakfast, I sit in front of the shelves, covered with feed sack curtains that hide the pots and pans. Sometimes I feel dressed to match the kitchen curtains on school days.

Today, we're having lunch in the dining room. Nancy's probably made ham salad out of the baloney or Spam with Mayonnaise and Granny's canned pickles. She calls Spam spiced ham. I bet real ham tastes better. Someday I'll know.

I yell at Nancy, "Why're we in the dining room?"

"Because I want to. We're havin ham salad. You have to drink milk since you missed breakfast, Lazy Bones. Are your shorts clean?"

She has on a dress and is prancing around like she's Queen for a day. "I did so eat breakfast. I hate milk. Makes me sick. My shorts are OK too." I hate when she acts like the boss. She's not! I'll spill my milk. Or maybe I'll pour it in her glass when she's not lookin. She likes milk.

"You have to help me clean after lunch."

"Can't"

"You can so. Tell her Granny."

"Now girls, no arguments."

"Be quiet, Nancy. I'm helpin Deh Deh."

She picks up dishes and stomps to the kitchen. She knows Granny won't make me do anything if I'm helpin Deh Deh.

I find Deh Deh in the front garden across the creek. The creek comes through a very big pipe under the street and then goes past this garden to the alley behind our big garden. I can stand in the pipe under the street. It's a great hiding place. He's already made wide rows for bunches of tomato plants and points to the packages for me to bring. I try to pick up the box, it up but it's too heavy.

"How many plants did you order? They're heavy."

"Well, damnit, don't bring them all at once"

"OK."

I drag one package of tomato plants to him. "Don't give them to me. Put them in this row in bunches of twenty. You can count."

I'm ten feet tall. He never let me open the packages before. I count out twenty plants and lay them in the row. This is fun. "What other veggies do we have?"

"So far tomatoes, cabbage and green peppers. The others will be here in a day or two. Now stop playing and get them in the ground so we can water them."

Under my breath so he can't hear, I say, "I'm not playin, I'm just bein careful." I put the yellow tomato plants in first. They're my favorite and his too. After he sells most of them, we'll plant the rest. I get to keep the weeds out as soon as the plants get big enough that I won't cut them with my hoe. Deh Deh gave me a little hoe with a forked side and a flat side. I use the two-pronged side closest to the plants and the other straight side between the rows.

I knock on the garden gate, hoping Roonie and George are home. George retired from some big job in Charleston, West Virginia and knew mother there. Ronnie is a friend of Granny's. I like them, they're really nice to me, and love for me to visit. They live about four blocks from us.

I'm so short I can't see over the gate. I have warm cookies wrapped in wax paper to give to Roonie. Granny just made them and I took four when she left the kitchen. They smell so good and if Roonie or George isn't here, I'll have to eat them. I can't take them back home. I hope Granny didn't count them.

This is the most beautiful garden I've ever seen. Deh Deh has lots of flowers but they're planted all over. Roonie has hers arranged just right. She and Granny belong to the Oak Hill Garden Club. Granny's never planted a flower garden, let alone pulled a weed. Deh Deh won't let her touch a flower in our garden. They're HIS flowers and no one, especially my Grandmother, is to touch them. I wonder where Roonie is. I knock again.

Maybe I'll just eat one cookie. I can't wait much longer. The poppies weren't in bloom so I could not bring them. Flowers are always better than food.   The oriental poppies are beautiful, with giant orange petals with a black spot around a seedpod in the middle, at the top of the stem. It's a fancy lid-like cover that keeps the seeds inside till they dry up and the flower dies. I steal poppies once in a while, when Deh Deh's not around, to take to some neighbors and the teachers I like. He counts them every day. When I ask about taking one to my Sunday school teacher he really got upset. Told me not to even think about pulling flowers to take to any church thing, that churches are full of crazy people and if he had anything to do with it, I'd never go back inside a church. He told me I could learn better lessons from him.   Maybe he's right, I don't like Sunday school very much: too many rules and I don't believe all the stories.

I start to eat one of the cookies. They're so good. Oatmeal with raisins. Oops. Here comes Roonie. I quick wrap the other cookies back up in the wax paper and jump up and down. I really love Roonie. "Here, Roonie, I brought you and George some cookies. Granny just made them."

Roonie takes the little package and puts her arm around me. She pulls me close to her and we go into the garden together. She smells good and is so warm and soft. I like it when she hugs me. The garden's beautiful. The roses are in bloom all along the fence. Lots of different colors. Pink, yellow, red and white. I touch one of the big red roses and the petals fall slowly to the ground. I start to apologize when Roonie reaches over my shoulder to give me three roses she just picked. "Here, hold these while I get a paper towel. You can take them home to your Grandmother."

"WOW, Roonie, they're beautiful. Where's George?"

"He's sleeping. I'll be right back."

I walk around like it's my garden. My secret hiding place. No one ever suspects that I'm here. I never tell anyone about Roonie's garden. I even fall asleep sometimes on one of her benches. I can't today cause I told Granny I'd be right back. Some days, Roonie wakes me to go home before mother comes down the street. One day we were plantin new flowers and mother came by on her way home. Roonie told her that I was waitin to walk home with her. I wasn't; but it sounded OK and mother said it was nice for me to come that far to meet her. She didn't even yell at me that night.

"Here, Rose Ann, put these around the stems and take them to your Grandmother. You better run now. Mary will be here soon. Thanks for the cookies. I'll thank Mrs. Walton when I see her at club meeting next week. Run on now."

"No, Roonie, please don't, you don't have to thank her. I will. Tell George, I'll see him next time." I turn and skip down the street.

My Aunt Libby, mother's sister, lives just a few hundred feet up the street from our house. Deh Deh gave her property when she married Uncle Clarence. My cousin, Jimmy and I play in their front yard with other kids on the street. I'm not allowed to go in their house. Some stupid rule mother made cause she doesn't like Clarence. Or she's mad about them being married. I love Libby. She's kind and treats me like a person, takes me places in her car, and lets me go with her on walks. Uncle Clarence always grabs me or rubs my back. He scares me but he hugs me and talks to me. He owns a pinball business and lets me play the machines he's fixin in his garage. Sometimes he holds me too tight.

Jimmy and I sit with Buddy, Alton and Laverne trying to decide what to play. Jimmy's the littlest but he thinks because it's his yard he should decide. He's such a little fat kid. I want to play dodge ball but they all want to play "Guess what you're gettin for Christmas." Jimmy thinks I know what he's getting and that I'll tell him. Nancy and I found all our gifts in a closet yesterday. I'm getting a redheaded doll. I hate dolls. I want a white football.

"If you're not playin dodge ball, I'm goin home." When nobody answers, I start down the street and hear Jimmy callin me. I'm not goin back. I don't wanna play anything now. I wanna be by myself. He yells again but I keep goin.

This Christmas is gonna be awful. I gave momma a wish list: A white football, an erector set and candy. No doll. I threw my dolls away last year and the year before that, before New Year's. I don't like to play with dolls and they look silly on the bed. Nancy makes clothes for hers and has them all lined up on the bed. I have to move them to go to bed. She makes me sick. She's getting one of those dolls that you dress and give it water and it cries real tears. That's stupid, you pour water in its mouth and then it cries.

I walk home kicking a rock ahead of me. It's supposed to snow tomorrow, maybe all week. A white Christmas. So what. Christmas at my house is ugly even with white snow. We never visit neighbors or even Libby and Clarence. I wanna go to Libby's and see her house. It's probably beautiful inside with pretty furniture. This thing between Libby and mother, that no one talks about, must have happened when Libby and Clarence ran away to get married just a few days before I was born. It doesn't make sense to me. I'm supposed to love my mother no matter what she does to me.

Christmas is a good time to change all that. In Sunday school everybody talks about spreading love and joy. They say that Jesus was born that day and we celebrate his birthday. That's why we give gifts. Everybody else is happy but I'm not. I want my family to be happy. Maybe if mother and Libby make up everything will change. I'll ask Granny what happened between them when I get home. She'll be busy with cooking and cleaning before mother gets home. Granny acts like mother is the boss so if I ask her anything she'll say, "Ask your mother." I think mother hates us all, especially me, and she is never happy about anything. Not even Christmas gifts. Deh Deh helps us buy her a gift but she never thanks us or acts like she likes it. No sense askin any of them anything. I sit on the front steps and throw gravel from the walk to the street. I'll never change anything if I stay this grumpy. So I smile and go inside. It smells good.

Granny's makin cookies. I go in the kitchen, stand by her stool and stick my fingers in the dough. "Wash your hands and stay out of my cookie dough."

"But it's good, Granny.   What kind of cookies? Oatmeal?   Will you give Libby some cookies?"

"Maybe. Why?"

"I have an idea." I stick my finger in the dough again. Maybe I can get inside Libby's house.

"Stop that. Now get outta here. Go put your stuff away.   You better be good or Santa won't leave you anything."

"I'm gonna do something good. You'll see." I go see if more packages have been put under the tree. Same as this morning.

Granny gives us two cookies for supper and I hide one of mine in my napkin. I'm goin to get a plate full before Christmas and then go visit Libby and give her some cookies. I'll have to be careful that the mice don't get them. I'll hide them in the tin box with Deh Deh's pipes. Mother leaves the table to go do some work and I take another cookie without anyone seeing me.

I have six cookies. Tomorrow's Christmas Day. They'll all be surprised. I'm gonna get Nancy up early, make a lot of noise so everybody gets to the Christmas tree early and I'll announce I'm going to Aunt Libby's. Maybe mother won't stop me on Christmas. I'll ask her and Nancy even Granny and Deh Deh to go. But I can't stand around and ask or they won't let me out of the house.

Every present has been opened. My red headed doll is ugly but I don't care. Nancy's making her doll cry and it makes a whining noise just like she does. I tell her that and she throws a wad of paper at me.

"Stop. It's Christmas. Be nice." I leave the room and nobody says anything. I put on my coat and gloves and get my cookies from the tin box. When I get back to the living room everybody looks up at me.

Mother frowns and says, "Where do you think you're going?"

I take hold of the front door knob and open the door. "I'm going to Aunt Libby's. You can come if you want. I'm gonna surprise them with cookies." I run out the door and down the steps. I hear her yell. I run a few steps and then slow down. Maybe Nancy'll come. She won't unless mother says she can or comes with her. I'm almost there when I hear Nancy. "Wait, Rosie."

I turn and see Nancy and mother. I'm surprised. I really wanted them to come. I wait and take Nancy's hand. We get to Libby's front door and I ring the bell. I hear my heart pounding and Nancy is swinging my arm.

Libby has a real look of surprise when she opens the door. "Well come in here before you freeze to death. We're

24

just about ready to have cocoa. Will you join us?" I can see Jimmy and Clarence sittin at a white kitchen table.

"I brought some cookies, Libby." I hand her my little package and we begin to cry.

She bends down and hugs me like never before. She hugs Nancy and then mother. It's the best Christmas any kid could have even with an ole redheaded doll. I think my whole body's smiling.

When Granny's sister, my great Aunt Mary, is here, she always goes with me to gather eggs from the hen house. I talk to the chickens and she laughs, but I hear her call their names. This morning's muggy and hot. The air stands still holding the leaves on the trees just right. I saw a walnut on the ground as we passed the tree. I know summer's over and its back to school time. That's OK; but Aunt Mary will go home to take care of my cousins while their mother teaches school. But today, she is mine. I hold her hand to help her walk on the rough ground. She had polio when she was little and one of her shoes is built up with a big heel. She still limps when she walks. I hope I never have that much trouble walking. It's hard for her to go anywhere and she has to rest often. We stop to get water at the spigot outside the barn. I show her how I can swing a bucket of water over my head without losing the water. She tells me to be careful, but I know she thinks I'm OK.

We smell pipe smoke as we pass Deh Deh's shack and she shakes her head as if to tell him not to do that and not to stay in his shack; to go to the house with her sister where she thinks he belongs. She says things about him now and then to let me know she thinks he's a bad person. He doesn't go to church; he doesn't take Granny anywhere; he talks down to her; he doesn't give her the things she needs to keep house. He lets mother do anything and gives her money all the time. I asked him once about giving my mother money that Granny needed; he really got mad and treated Granny and her sisters terrible. I won't ever say anything like that to him again. There are too many secrets around here. Like where's my Daddy?

The chickens are expecting food when we walk in. I throw some on the floor and they jump off their nests with a flutter. Feathers fly all round us. I try to catch the little white ones before they hit the floor. Aunt Mary smiles and says, "I'll get one of these chickens for our dinner tonight."

"You better not take Gretchen or Ruth. I talk to them and they listen."

"Then you'll have to help me. You'll have to show me which one we can eat."

We gather about a dozen eggs. Some are still warm like they just came out of the hen. They feel soft. I try to mold them into different shapes but they get hard too soon. I keep trying. Aunt Mary laughs at me and says, "I'll try that tomorrow."

"Aunt Mary, do you think eggs are better when they're this fresh?"

"I don't know, never thought about it. We can make egg salad for lunch with these eggs and decide."

"Granny won't let us. She'll say we have to use the old ones first. But you could just make it and not tell her. Would you? Please. I know it'll be better."

Late that afternoon, after the best egg salad in the world, I go to sleep on a blanket in the orchard. A terrible racket awakens me. It sounds like somebody just let a hundred chickens loose right beside me. I think it's a dream until I open my eyes to see Aunt Mary trying to catch a hen in the back yard. Here she is, limping quickly after a chicken. They run this way and that, like they know she's going to get them. They run a few steps, flap their wings and fly a few feet just as she is about to grab one. I think Deh Deh should get the chicken for dinner but he won't help Granny or Aunt Mary. Do chickens have feelings? Do they hurt when she grabs them? It's a funny sight. I laugh and start to get up to help just as she grabs one and twists its head right off. It runs around and around without its head for a while before it falls. I can't tell if it's Gretchen or Ruth without her head. And she can't make any noise. Even if it is one of them I know I'll eat it for dinner.

The bike is rusty and dirty but it has a siren on the front wheel. When Buddy rides it past our house he always pulls the chain so his bike sounds like a police car. I want one for my bike, if I ever get a bike. All my friends have bikes. Deh Deh won't buy me one without buying one for Nancy. He thinks we'll get hurt. She might.

I see Buddy riding his bike toward our house. He lives on a dirt road about a block from here. He's older and likes Nancy better. He's tall with dark wavy hair. Cute, but I always think he's dirty. I run to say, "Hi." He stops. "Want to go for a ride with me?"

"Sure I do but I'm not allowed. Bring your bike in the yard so I can make the siren go. You promised."

I look around to see if Nancy or Granny is lookin out the window. I don't see either of them. And I know Deh Deh's not here. I saw him leave a few minutes ago.

"Let's take it to the side of the house where no one can see us."

"OK. Hurry. I don't have all day. I'm riding ten miles."

He pushes the bike around the corner and turns it upside down. He's very strong and has muscles everywhere. I hear the siren going very loud and see him pushing the front wheel to make it go round and pulling the siren chain at the same time. I want to do that. Oh, No, here comes Jimmy. He's such a tattletale and there's no stopping him now. He's runnin across the creek and toward us.

"Hi, Jimmy. Where you goin? Can't you see we're busy? You better go back home, NOW."

"I can watch."

"No you can't."

I turn to Buddy and say, "You better go for that ride and come back later. Jimmy'll tell everybody what we're doin."

"Oh, no he won't. He knows I'll hurt him if he does. He's just a little runt. Leave him alone. Here, you make the wheel go round while I hold the siren chain. And Jimmy, I'll put your hand between the spokes if you touch anything."

Jimmy sits down in the dirt beside the house and watches us. The siren is really goin now. WOW, this is fun. Just then I turn and see Deh Deh standing behind me. Where'd he come from? I thought he was gone.

"What in the Sam Hill are you trying to do? Cut your Goddamn fingers off on that rusty bike. STOP that right now. And get that bike out of here before you get hurt."

I put my hand on the tire to slow the wheel. I kick dirt at Jimmy. I motion to Buddy to stop making the siren go.

"Oh, Deh Deh, I won't get hurt. We're just making the siren go. Listen." I push the wheel round and round again. He shakes his pipe at me and keeps going. He turns and tells me not to come cryin to him when I cut my hand.

It's like he knew. He just rounded the corner of the house when I hit the rusty fender with my hand. I see lots of blood. I know my fingers are cut off. Buddy grabs his bike and takes off and Jimmy runs home. I stand there lookin at my hand, holdin it with my other hand. I can see the bones in two fingers and the skin looks like it will fall off any second. I scream and Nancy comes runnin. "You're really in trouble now."

I'm cryin so hard I don't hear her. She takes hold of me by my shoulder and we walk to the back yard. Deh Deh walks toward me shaking his head. "Nancy, go get some salve, some matches and a clean cloth from your Grandmother."

She lets go of me and I sink to the ground. Deh Deh sits on the ground beside me and puts his arm around me. "Now hush your cryin. We'll get this fixed in no time. Then maybe you'll listen to me next time."

He takes two bandannas out of his back pocket and tries to stop the bleeding and hands me the other one to dry my tears. He picks up the garden hose and washes my hand off with cold water. That stings. Nancy comes back with the salve and cloth. He tears the cloth into two strips and lays one on my knee. "Hold this."

I stop cryin and help him fix the bandage. He tears the ends again to tie them around my fingers. Nancy runs back into the house because she doesn't want to watch. I hold the bandage as he melts the stick salve onto the cloth. He wraps it around my middle finger and ties the two ends together. It feels better already. He does the same for the other finger and sits with me for a while. He pats my knee and says. "When I was a little boy, my daddy put the same stuff on my cuts. Those fingers will be OK in a couple of days."

The salve is the only medicine we have and it's a miracle. We call it Granddaddy Walton's stick salve. Deh Deh makes it like candy in the basement. He cooks it and pours it into a cookie sheet and lets it get hard, then cuts it into pieces like taffy. He wraps each piece in waxed paper. Deh Deh burns a corner of a piece, lets it drip on a cloth and puts it on the cut while it's still warm. It heals the cut and we don't have to go to the doctor for stitches. He told me it had whiskey in it but he didn't tell me the other things. Maybe someday he'll show me how to make it. Sometimes it leaves a little scar, like the one over my eye.

When I go in the house, Granny tells me to go lay down till supper. "Let's not say anything to your mother about cutting your fingers."

"I can't hide the bandages, Granny. She'll see them."

I'm asleep when she gets home. She sits on the bed and tells me she's sorry I got hurt. She gently rubs my back and says, "Let's go eat."

I know I'll win. I'll be a ghost with the white robe I found in the closet the other day. It's very long with red circles on each side at the top. I don't know where it came from or whose it is but it's perfect for my ghost costume. It's old and has been in that corner a long time because it's very dusty and has fold marks that didn't come out when I found it. Nobody wears it. I'll ask Granny to cut the bottom off so it's not too long.

I take it to Granny and ask her if I can wear it on Friday night for the Halloween parade. "I know I'll be the best ghost there if you let me wear this. It's perfect. Too long but you can fix it. Can I? Can I, Granny? Please."

"Where did you find that?"

"It was folded up in the back corner of the closet in the dining room."

"That belongs to Dad. You put it back right NOW."

Oh goodie! I know he'll let me wear it cause he loves me.

"Come on, Granny, I've never seen Deh Deh wear anything like this. He probably doesn't know where it is. It's in the house and he's never here to dress so why not. And why would he wear a white robe?"

"Never mind, just put it back. I'm sorry you found it."

"Why? What is it? It just looks like an old robe."

I turn and stomp back to the dining room. I put it in the closet and run out to see Deh Deh. I'll just ask him.

"Granny, Granny", I scream as I come in the back door. "He said I could wear it. Honest. I asked him. He said, "Yes". But you have to fix it. Something about the red things on it. I'll get it."

She just shakes her head and takes the robe to her room. She's not happy but I know I'll win. It'll be a great costume. The best ever. Granny's never acted this way about anything of Deh Deh's. She kept shaking her head like she didn't want to touch it. Maybe he wore it a long time ago for something she didn't want him to do. Maybe that's when he moved out of the house.

On Friday night, all the kids in the neighborhood, maybe fifty of us, parade around the horse ring again and again. I've only seen four other ghosts. I could judge quicker. I know I'm the best ghost and the best costume walking. They're giving little girls sets of dishes, but little boys get hunting knives in a leather holder. The handle looks like stone. That's what I want. It's hot tonight and this track stinks like horses. This robe is heavy and long even if Granny cut the bottom off. Hurry. Just point to me.

I can't see very well through the eyeholes I cut in the pillowcase I have over my head. But I'll see them if they point to me. I keep walking. Then I hear someone announce over the loud speaker: "Will the ghost walking near the grandstand come to the prize area?"

I jump up and down. That's me. That's me. I run toward the judges' stand. Almost trip over the bottom of this robe.

"Are you a little boy or a girl?"

I lower my head and say, "A boy." A woman smiles and hands me a knife in a leather case. I take it, thank her and hold it tightly in my hand.

As I walk home with Deh Deh, I show him my knife in its leather holder. He seems surprised that I got a knife but doesn't say anything. Tells me I'd better be careful with it. Now I can peel apples with my new knife and keep it sharp on the grindstone. It has a beautiful handle. I won't show it to Mother. She'll take it away from me.

I sit where Mother has beckoned me to be: with her on the most uncomfortable couch in the world. I never like to sit with her and this couch makes it worse. It's hard wood with thin cushions that open to make a bed. You squeeze the seat and the back together and it opens. Mice play in the space under the seat and sometimes we find little babies in there. We know they're there cause they squeak all the time. Then Deh Deh comes in, takes them out. I think he kills them. UCK! I don't like to sit here. Mother reads the paper, tries to tell me the news but I block her out with my Classical funny book. The third time she yells at Granny for rocking in her rocker in the next room, I get up and go to Granny's room, plop on the bed, and muffle my scream with a pillow. Granny shakes her head and continues to read her Bible. It's the same every night after dinner. Granny goes to her room, sits in her rocker, reads her Bible and tries to rest. She's finished cleaning the house, washing the clothes, cooking dinner and washing the dishes, pots and pans. She works all day. I start to talk to her and she hushes me. Tells me not to cause any more trouble. She sits slumped in her chair. Her head naturally bends down from the curve in her back. She has on her pink and white flannel nightgown and old bright blue and gray felt slippers. Mother fusses at her for wearing them cause they make noise on the linoleum floors as she shuffles her feet through the house. Granny can't do anything without someone swearing at her. She never answers back. She just shakes her head at them and walks away.

What would mother do if I told her to "shut up"? Granny begins to rock again and I hold my breath. I turn toward the wall, put my fingers in my ears, but I still hear mother coming this way. Her heels sound like soldiers marching. Why doesn't she just go get ready to leave? I know she's going out later like she does at least two or three nights a week.

She works for the State Road Commission and writes permits for companies to move heavy equipment on the roads. She goes out with the big shots of the companies. And she goes out with her boss. We call him Uncle Bill. Sometimes Nancy and I go with them for a picnic. He's nice but I don't like being with them.

I can't look at Granny. I don't want to see Mother's angry face. I want to push her out of this room. "I'm going to take that Goddamn rocker away from you. I'll show you what it's like to sit on a hard chair all day. It'll be the only Goddamn chair in the house. Then I bet you'll shut the hell up. Maybe I'll just nail that damn chair to the floor. That'll fix you and your constant noise. I've worked hard all day and no one here gives a damn."

I jump up and stomp toward her. What a speech. I wonder if she feels better. I shout, " SHUT UP. . . . . SHUT UP. . . ", And run outside.

I'm bored at home so I walk the one hundred fifty feet to Libby's. She's not home but Jimmy is in the garage playing the pinball machines that Clarence has for his business. He puts them in bars, restaurants, and other places. He keeps them in working condition and delivers new ones when a place wants one. He really just moves them around and he does get a new one now and then. When they break, he brings them home and works on them here in the garage. Today he's getting a new one ready. I don't like to be here when he's home but he came in after I got here. Jimmy and I play pinball machines almost every day in the summer.

Clarence says, "This machine is ready now, Rose Ann. Try it out. I bet you can't win this one."

"I can so." I walk over to the machine. It's bright with lots of lights and makes loud noises when I send the first ball. Jimmy watches for a few minutes. I like to play with him cause I always beat him. Neither of us has practiced on this new machine, and Jimmy's leaving. Maybe I should go home.

"Dad, can I go to Buddy's?"

I say, "Com'on, Jimmy. Stay. You can play the next game."

"Sure you can go. Be sure you're home for supper."

Jimmy runs out and I continue to play. I'm winning lots of points. I stand on my tiptoes to see everything as the ball goes from one bumper to another. Suddenly Clarence grabs me. "What're you doing? Put me down! I'm winning this game. You bet I couldn't." He has me over his shoulder and is going toward the house. "Where're we goin? Put me down, Clarence! STOP, You're hurting me."

"Hush. I won't hurt you. We'll play a game." He carries me into the house and bounces me on the bed like I'm a rag doll. He throws himself on top of me. He fumbles to unzip his pants as he kisses me. It doesn't feel good. I've got to get away. Squirm. Wiggle. Why is he doing this? I'm only eleven. I love him but not like this. Where's Libby? Does he care? It hurts. Why? Why? Why? Got to get out of here.

I try to get away. He's holding me too tight. "Let go of my arms, STOP."

He stops and rolls over beside me, but still holds my arm tight. "Now just lay still a minute. I won't hurt you. Just let me show you something."

He's breathing heavy, like he's out of breath. I don't want him to show me anything. I want to go home. Why is he doing this?

How can I get away? He's my Uncle. Should I let him? Am I supposed to do this? He reaches across me and puts his big hand in my pants. I know his hands are dirty. I feel dirty. Where can I go? He will always be here. He's so big. He's so strong. I yell, "STOP."

He gently moves his hand over my stomach. That feels better but why is he doing this? Where is Libby? What if she walks in? I don't want him to do this but it feels good. What am I doing? I turn toward him and he kisses me hard. His tongue goes in my mouth and I gag. He stops. Says I should go back outside and act like nothing happened. Don't tell anyone. He says he'll be back out in a few minutes. "The bet is still on. Go play that machine as long as you want."

I jump up, run out the door, down the street and hide in the creek under the street. My tears feel like fire burning my cheeks. It stinks here. It stinks everywhere.

Screeeeeeeech   That's a car right out front.

I run to the front door just in time to see a car pull away. Black marks on the road. What happened? I push open the screen door and let it slam. Down the steps fast. My heart is pounding. There he is. Lying there. Lifeless. His head is flat on the road like he's lying on his side looking to the right. He's dead. He is a piece of golden fur shaped like my dog but he looks like a deflated balloon. I love him. I feel the tears. I sit down next to him and put my hands around him. He doesn't move. I feel his heart beating very fast. He's not dead. I try to pick him up but he squirms free. He runs behind the broken fence to the side of the house, behind the honeysuckle and under the front porch. I look up and see Nancy, Granny, and Aunt Libby coming to find out what happened. I wipe away tears and tell them. Libby says if we sit on the steps he'll come out from under the porch and we can see how badly he's hurt. She puts her arm around me as we sit down.

"Will Sparky have to go to doggie heaven with your Skippy?"

"Let's just take a look when he comes to us. If he ran from you he's probably OK."

Nancy goes to the end of the porch, looks behind the honeysuckle and announces, "His tail is broken. He's licking it. It's dangling. Looks funny." She laughs.

I sure don't want her to get him first so I go to where she's standing to coax Sparky out. He looks longingly at me and I start to scoot under the porch. Nancy pulls on my shirt to stop me. "Let go!"

"No. You can't get under there."

"I can so. Let go."

Granny's sitting on the glider and starts to clap her hands like she does when she calls Sparky to eat. He stands up and dashes past Nancy and me to get up the steps to Granny.

I don't believe it. He's just fine, except for his tail. He jumps up on Granny's lap and she pushes him down when she sees a little blood on his tail. It really looks funny. Most of it's dangling from a little stump of a tail.

Granny tells us to leave him alone and he'll be OK. She says, "Ann, go wash your hands so you can help me."

She's ready to skin tomatoes and I said I'd help. I want to be with my great aunts. Her four sisters, Mary, Bess, Blanche and Ethel are visiting. They come once each summer to help Granny can vegetables and today is tomato day. I don't want to help but I want to be with Aunt Mary. I like her best. She's the youngest sister and the only one not married. She always talks to me. Aunt Blanche and Aunt Bess talk to me too but not like Aunt Mary. She's the best. Aunt Ethel's very quiet and always has tears in her eyes. They all laugh at my tricks though. Like the time I starched their underwear and mixed up their false teeth.

We all sit on the front porch around three big tubs, one with hot tomatoes and two empty. I grab a hot tomato, rub it between my hands to tear the skin off and drop it in one the tomato in the other tub. They do same but much faster. I play with the next tomato and eat it instead of putting it in the tub. They're sooooooo good.

"Do you think I can cut Sparky's tail off without hurting him, Aunt Mary?"

"Oh, honey, I don't know. You better let Mr. Walton do that." That's what she calls Deh Deh. I don't understand why, but she says that's his name. I don't call him Mr. Walton.

Sparky's lying on the porch. The end of his broken tail is hanging over the edge. I pull on it gently. He does nothing. I pull harder and he still lies there. I go to the kitchen and get the biggest knife I can find and return to the tomato skinning without a word. I sit back down; hide the knife and Sparky moves closer as if to say, "Did you move?" I wait till everyone seems intent on the tomatoes and not paying attention to me or to Sparky. In one quick move I take hold of his tail with my left hand, bring the knife down with my right hand, cut the end of his tail and throw it away. All the sisters and Granny look at me with startled faces. Sparky gives a short yelp and runs down the steps wagging his little stubby tail.

"Oh, Nancy, you are such a scaredy cat.'

"I know, but . . . ."

"But what? Don't you want to eat cherries?"

"Yes, but Deh Deh will kill us."

"He will not! I helped him cut some limbs from apple trees just the other day and so I know how. And the limbs on the apple trees are beginning to grow more than ever now. He even left the barn open today and he never does that. He'll probably be glad to get the cherries. He'll can them so we have some this winter."

"That's what you think. Call Mother. Ask her."

"You're crazy. It's none of her darn business."

I walk to the barn to get the cross cut saw. I can hardly lift it but I drag it to the yard and motion Nancy to come help me. The ends bounce like a see saw. My heart is racing. I want those cherries. I've eaten all that I can reach. I tried to get Deh Deh to let me use the ladder the other day but he wouldn't set it up for me. He said the ground was too bumpy. I look around to see if anyone is near. Only Nancy: little miss goody two shoes. I know there will be hell to pay, but there always Is, for me, so why not get Nancy to help. Share the pain. Mother will blame me anyway and spare her little angel. I pick up the saw in the middle. It's very, very long and gets heavier as I try to walk with it. Nancy finally takes one end and we get it to the cherry tree. The tree is very small only about ten feet tall and about as big at the ground as my leg. This won't take long if Nancy does her part.

We get the saw at just the right height to leave a little stump and to rest the ends of the saw on the ground when we get tired. We saw and saw, back and forth, back and forth. This is hard. I thought it would be easier. The tree is wet inside, not like the apple limbs Deh Deh and I cut last week. Those limbs must have been dead. But he said he was cutting them so the tree would grow bigger. There are no dead branches on this cherry tree. I hear a crack. "Quick, Nancy, take the saw away from the tree."

Here they come. They are bright red with a pink glow around the top, Big, juicy cherries. The tree falls and the top bounces. Nancy jumps back and I run for the top of the tree. I grab a handful and stuff them in my mouth. Just as I turn to spit the pits, I see Deh Deh coming around the house. Oh my God, he looks mad.

"What the hell do you kids think you're doing? Look what you've done. You stupid girls. Now you will never have cherries again." What does he mean no more cherries? The apple trees are growing. Why won't the cherry tree grow back?

"Now get the hell away from here and go inside. I don't want to see you anywhere near this tree. And you'll not have one cherry."

He's really mad. I've never seen him like this. I bet he'd like to whip us. I know he won't but I'm not taking any chances. I run up the back steps and in the house. I go to the pantry window and watch Deh Deh picking my cherries. Tears begin to run down my cheeks and I feel stupid. I didn't think the cherry tree would be dead but we did cut more than the limbs. We only cut limbs from the apple trees.

Granny's just getting up from her nap and wants to know what happened. Nancy's hidin in Granny's room and I hear her start to tell Granny what Rosie did. I'm stayin in the pantry.

Libby comes around the corner of the garage to say she's going to the store and asks if I want to go with her. I know I should go but I can't say anything. I shake my head. My voice is stuck in my throat. I feel him looking at me. He'll do it again. He takes every chance he gets. But he's the only one who hugs me. Libby kisses Clarence goodbye and leaves. Why don't I run now? I start to walk out when he grabs me from behind. He picks me up like a sack of potatoes, swings me across his hip and into the house we go.

"STOP!"

"Rosie, you know I love you and won't hurt you. I just want to be close and want you to feel good. Let me show you."

"NO, I'm burning up. Tears feel like hot water. He's so strong. He doesn't care. He hates me. He puts me down on the bed, pulls my shorts down and rolls over on top of me. He's so heavy. Why is he doing this? I try to scream but nothing comes out. He's holding my arms so tight, both together over my head. He fumbles with his zipper and takes his thing out. It's big and hard and he pokes it between my legs. I can't get them any closer together. It hurts. Why won't he stop? He lets go of my arms and I shove his head away from me. I wiggle loose as he moves higher. I fall on the floor and crawl to the door, get up, pull my shorts up as I run out of the room. I look back to see if he's coming after me. I see him rubbing his big ugly thing. It begins to squirt something. UCK! As I run out the door I hear him callin my name. I run   run   run.

Mrs. Blake is handing out those cards. Just like the cards in 1st, 2nd, 3rd and now 5th grades. In first grade I wrote deceased and then left it blank. After that I always wrote DECEASED. They told me just to write DECEASED. But this year I won't. I don't know if he's deceased. I know he's not here. But he may not be dead. Mother goes crazy when I ask. She says it is none of my GOD DAMN BUSINESS. I'll show them all. I'll write UNKNOWN.   UNKNOWN.   UNKNOWN.

I turn the porch light on as I open the door. A very tall woman with a very mean look on her face is standing there. "Yes Ma'am?"

"I want to see your Mother."

"Uh, she's not here." I try to close the door as quickly as I can but she takes hold of the screen door, opens it a little and puts her foot against the door. My heart begins to race and I begin to cry.

"I'll get my Grandfather."

"No. You just tell your Mother to stay away from Bill or I'll kill her."

She turns and leaves in a hurry. As she turns, I see her take something shiny out of her coat pocket. I run to Granny's room. She's sitting in her rocker. I throw myself on the floor with my head in her lap. "Granny, who was that? Why does she want to kill my mother? Does Uncle Bill have a wife? Was that her? Is he going to stop taking us places and giving us toys and candy? Granny, who is she?"

"Hush now. You just keep quiet. Forget the whole thing. I'll talk to Mary."

"But, Granny, she might see mother walkin home. She could just shoot her and keep going. No one would ever know. We better call the police."

"Now, Ann, just hush. Forget about it."

We're getting a new bathroom and two bedrooms and an office for mother. It'll be a big change. Some of Deh Deh's friends are building the addition to the side of the house. Mother will have a bedroom and Nancy and I will share the other one. It was just three or four years ago that Deh Deh tore down the outhouse and put a flush john on the back porch. When the new one is finished we won't have to go outside or use the white bucket in the bedroom. I hope they hurry.

I hated that outhouse. It always stunk and I never wanted to sit on the cold wood around the hole. At night I was really scared to go out cause there were always raccoons or possums around it. So I wet the bed or went in the pot in our room. Uck. I still think it stinks where the outhouse was. . Granny throws table scraps there and the neighborhood cats gather. Sometimes they have my breakfast cause I don't get up when Granny thinks I should.

Granny says it will be finished in a couple of months before school starts. She's already getting stuff ready to move from where we sleep now. She says Nancy and I will have to move our clothes. I hope she's right and that this will be the last picnic we have to use the outside toilet.

Today, I go outside to use the flush toilet on the back porch. It's a little room, with walls of unpainted plywood and a roof about three feet above my head with black tar paper on it. I don't know how mother or Deh Deh come in here. They're real tall. Nancy's lookin for me. I hear her callin my name but I don't want her or anybody to find me. We're havin a big family picnic for the Fourth of July and to celebrate the new addition to the house. A new back porch and the foundation for the addition are the only things that are finished. But the wood for the building part has been delivered.

Everyone's on the new back porch waitin for hot dogs and the best corn on the cob and tomatoes from our garden. Deh Deh's probably waitin for me to help him pick the corn. I want to be there but I'm afraid somethin's wrong with me. Maybe what Clarence has been doin to me has caused somethin to happen to me?

I'm bleeding and have no idea why. I'm scared and want to just sit here by myself. Nancy bursts into the bathroom, sees me, and begins to smile. I don't know why

40

she is smiling at me, she never does. She doesn't know what's wrong or about my bleeding. I hang my head lower. I don't want anyone to see me. She asks why I'm sitting there looking like I just lost my best friend. I explain to her that I'm bleeding and I don't know what's wrong.

She tells me nothing's wrong, that it's OK, that this is supposed to happen. She gets me a pad from a blue box that is hidden in the corner behind a sack. She shows me how to put it on with an elastic belt. She's kinder than she's ever been to me. I feel better now that I know what happened. How can I be so dumb? She says she'll tell everyone that I'm OK and that I should come back outside. I say OK, but I don't want anyone to know and for sure not the family. Clarence will laugh, Mother will scold, Granny'll just smile, and Nancy will tease. I'll just go lie down and act like I'm sick. I'll tell the next person who comes looking for me that I have a headache.

Mother comes in and finds me on Granny's bed. She is her usual self. "Get out of bed and go back outside. Why are you acting like a baby? You've just started having your monthly period and that means you're supposed to be more grown up. You're fourteen, act like it. No wonder Nancy calls you a crybaby. Now get back outside."

I get up but wait for her to go first. Just as I open the screen door, everyone starts to laugh. I hear Clarence say, "What'd you think, Rosie, the watermelon went through whole?"

He's so stupid. Nothing goes through whole and blood doesn't look like watermelon. I turn and go back inside.

I lie on the bed beside Nancy. She's on the outside and I'm next to the wall. It's not a big bed so we are crowded. Sometimes we kick each other in our sleep. I always have to sleep next to the wall. Right now I'd rather be on the outside cause I see Deh Deh coming in to talk with Mother. She's sittin on the other bed about two feet from ours. She's trying to get us to go to sleep so she can go out for the evening. When I ask where she's goin, she just says "Out."

Deh Deh's been cleaning his rifle on the front porch. He comes in, sits on the edge of our bed and puts his gun across his lap with the barrel pointing toward the head of the bed. He's always careful with his guns. Sometimes I ask to hold his pistol but he has never let me. Probably comin to tell Mother something about money or maybe just to say "Goodnight" to us. I like for him to come in the house, but he hardly ever does.

Granny's in her room. The kitchen is between here and her room but I still hear the squeak of her rocker. She's probably readin her bible like she does every night before she goes to bed. Mother's still dressed. If she's goin out she won't tell Deh Deh and she won't go till he's gone back to his shack. They start talking about money as usual. Nancy and I lay still and listen.

"So no need to worry, Mary, I'll find the money you need for these girls." She stands up, straightens her skirt and sits back down. He goes on. "The newsstand I bought last month is doing right well and I'm glad to have something to do. I have to be there at 3:30 in the morning to meet the paper-man but I sleep till people start knockin on the window for papers. I'm sellin a lot. Papers, candy, chewing gum and the like."

"Deh Deh, can I go with you in the morning?"

He laughs at me and as he turns to look at me there's a big explosion. Very loud and sounds like it's right here. Like a flash of lightning and thunder. We all jump. I'm standing on the bed against the wall. I can't get out. I jump up and down and scream. Mother jumped up and is standing between the beds. She's yellin at Deh Deh but I can't understand her. Nancy's real still and Deh Deh's bending over her. Oh my God, it was his gun. I see smoke comin out of the barrel. Did he shoot her? Is she dead? I start to cry and slide down the wall and sit on the bed.

Thank God, she's alive. Deh Deh is hugging her and whispering to her. I can't hear what he's saying. He's holding her head. Mother's still yellin at Deh Deh. She never does that. Now I see the bullet shell in the head of the bed, just inches from where Nancy's head was. The gun is on the floor still smoking at the end. I want out of here. I stand up again. I have to go to the bathroom

Momma screams again. "Get out of here and take that Goddamn gun with you. Don't bring it back! Get Out NOW!" She's swinging her arms back and forth like she's gonna hit him.

He takes the gun and walks out without a word. I can tell he's really upset. He hangs his head as he goes out the door.

I lie back down and hug Nancy. I listen to Granny's rocker. She didn't come to find out what happened. She's pretty deaf but she had to hear the shot. Mother sits on our bed and hugs Nancy and me. I feel her shaking inside.

I want to cut the grass in the big orchard today, but Deh Deh doesn't think that's a good idea. I'll wait a while and ask him again. Uncle Clarence gave us his power mower when he got a new one. This old one is a reel type mower and very heavy but I can control it even if I'm tall and skinny. I walk behind it and can take it in and out of gear with the lever on the handle to make it go or stop. When I need help, I just stop it and yell for Deh Deh.

I'm glad I don't have to borrow it from Uncle Clarence. I used to like him and it was fun to be with him. But he started touchin me all the time. Even when Libby was around he'd take hold of me and swing me around to be closer to him. He did things to me that I didn't like. He's quit all but hugging me tight, but I remember the first time, years ago. I was real little and scared.

Clarence comes up behind me and picks me up, throws me over his shoulder. "Put me down. Put me down." He laughs. Tells me not to be so loud. He won't hurt me. He pulls me down over his head and in front of him. Tells me to kiss him. That he's my uncle and the second most important man in my life. I don't want to kiss him now or anytime. I don't have to kiss him because he's my uncle. I never kiss Deh Deh and I sure love him more. And besides

I'm a very little girl. Why would he want to kiss me? I squirm to get away but he just holds tighter. Then he puts his arm between my legs and starts moving it. He says I'm just a kid and it doesn't mean anything. I bite his ear and he lets go. I run as fast as I can to get home and hide.

The mower's kept in the barn that's locked with a big padlock just like Deh Deh's shack. The barn is about fifty feet behind our house and connected to the storage cage. The barn has a hayloft, where I like to play. Sometimes I sneak my friends up there, if we find it unlocked, just to see the old things that are lying around. The steps going up there are old and rotten. They slant to one side. I like going up better than coming down. But today I won't go up there. I'll just get the mower out and cut the grass. I'll cut the little strip under the walnut tree first. It's the best grass and easiest to mow. I have to be careful of the rhubarb that grows under the overhang of the grape arbor. I won't eat it cause the chickens walk all over it. Granny says that's why it is so big and tastes so good. Not for me!

"Please, Deh Deh, just let me cut this side of the yard. It'll be too high soon and we'll have to use the scythe or the sickle and that's worse than the mower. Please, pretty please." I love the way the cut grass smells and the way the yard looks when it's all cut. I can see where I did something to make this place look pretty.

"OK. Damnit, here's the key. Now you be damn careful. I won't have you losing a foot."

I jump up quickly to get the mower out. I know he might change his mind in a hurry. He cusses some more before I finally get it out and ready, but I don't pay much attention. He's always cussing about something. He and Mother cuss all the time. Mostly at Granny. She never says anything back to them and never says bad words. They both yell at me when I use their words. Deh Deh doesn't mean his swearing but you have to know him to know that. He sure scares the kids who try to steal apples as they pass our place. He lets them pick up as many as they want from the ground but if he catches them pulling one off the tree, they better

44

look out. I notice that he's finished the apples and is taking them to the basement for cooking later. He dumped the peelings and bad apples into a tub for the cider mill. I hope we make cider tomorrow.

I start the mower and do the back yard and take the mower to the orchard. The sun is bright and hot. I feel sweat running down my back and the bugs are bothering me but I'm not about to stop and rest. He'll come take the mower away from me soon. A neighbor, Mrs. Kessler, is saying something to me from her backyard but I can't hear her over the mower. I'll go over there later. She likes me to cut this grass since it's close to her yard. She's probably just saying thank you. She does most of the work around her house. Mr. Kessler has a grocery store in town and is never home. Her brother is a town cop and sometimes he cuts her grass in his uniform. He must stink after that.

I cut most of the orchard before Deh Deh comes to take over. Says he'll finish the back part since it's so uneven. I watch how he moves the mower over the high and low spots, so I can do it next time. I go back and sit in his scratchy chair and watch the clouds go by. I see all kinds of shapes of people and animals, and sometimes they look like real people, like my teachers or other people in town. He finishes the mowing and takes the mower to the path by the barn.

I get up and go help him clean the mower and put it away. He lets me sharpen his knife on the big grindstone in the barn. If he starts the wheel with a little push I can make it go round with the foot petal. I want to get my little hunting knife but I know better than to suggest that now. Another day, I'll have it with me and he'll let me sharpen it. But he won't wait for me to go get it now. Says I don't need to keep it so sharp. I don't use it for anything but mumbley peg. He and I play that game once in a while. He likes to play and taught me a long time ago. Mother wasn't very happy but he told her not to worry that I only play with him. I don't, but they don't have to know that either. Both the Hodges boys have knives and so does Frankie Costello.

He's my boyfriend but we're too little to say so. He kissed me once in the hayloft.

Deh Deh and I get chicken feed from the bin near the barn. I take a hand full of feed and put it in my mouth. It makes my mouth feel dry but it's good, mostly like dry oats. I eat some every time I am here. We walk together to the chicken house. There are three wooden steps in front. He goes in first and throws the food on the floor in tin plates. The hens are sitting on nests that look like boxes piled together against the wall. Deh Deh built them a long time ago. They have straw in them and there's more straw on the floor. The chickens get off their nests to eat and we gather the eggs. He puts his eggs in my basket and tells me to be careful and take them to Granny. I know he's going to rest a while before dinner cause he does every evening. I better clean up or I won't be allowed at the table. I stink and I'm all sweaty and my clothes are really dirty. I leave him at his shack and go to the kitchen with the eggs.

Finally we are moving our stuff. The addition to our house is finished. Nancy and I have been in the rooms but today is the day we move into our bedroom and mother moves into her room. She also has an office. The bathroom is the best. A bathtub inside the house. No one says much about the addition but I'm excited to sleep in my own bed tonight. I'm in junior high school and finally my own bed. I still have to share a closet with Nancy and mother but it's much bigger than our old one.

All the rooms are in a row. The office is in front, then mother's room, our bedroom and the bathroom are in the back of the house. The closet is between the bathroom and the other part of the house. We have to enter the addition from the living room to mother's room. Then I turn right to go into her office but she probably won't allow us to go in the office. I turn left to go to Nancy's and my bedroom and on to the bathroom and closet. It means we are all going to be walking through each other's room to get to the bathroom or to go back to the living or dining room. Seems strange but it is really nice and I hope I can invite friends to see it.

Mother stomps into the office and finds me on the floor beside her desk. I have the bottom drawer open with a box out at my feet. She begins to yell. "What the hell are you looking for? You have no business being in here."

"Don't get upset. I'm looking for a picture."

"What kind of picture? Why the hell in my things? What makes you think it's here?"

"These are old pictures of me as a baby. Won't there be a picture of my father? You do have one don't you?"

"That again? It's none of your goddamn business. Put those things back. There aren't any."

"Why! Why not?"

I sit still looking at each picture in the box. I'm just waiting for her to take them from me. What's the big deal? Surely if she had two children less than two years apart, she'd have a picture of their Dad. Not in this box. I reach for the other box. She kicks the drawer shut. She goes on and on about leaving her things alone. I'm not allowed in the desk. I'm not allowed in her office. I can use the books but leave her goddamn desk and her goddamn typewriter and her goddamn drawers and her goddamn pencils and pens and all the rest of her goddamn junk alone. She raves like a mad woman. "Goddamn" is her favorite word. I think she'd get tired of cussin and screamin at the family every night but she manages to make the whole house turn on edge. My stomach begins to churn. I have to get away. I put the pictures back in the first box and hand them to her. I taste hot, salty tears on my face and know I better leave this place. Now she starts about Granny letting me go into her office. How she can yell at her mother, who cooks, cleans, takes care of her goddamn children, I don't know. I want to scream, "Shut YOUR GOD DAMN mouth." What would she do? I HATE HER I HATE HER   I HATE HER!

I stomp out of the room and go to Granny. I hug her and tell her I love her. I hide my head on her shoulder.

47

She tells me not to do things to upset my mother. Guess I could try harder. Do I really need to see a picture of him? YES YES YES But why? Cause he's my Father. If I didn't push and look she'd just find another reason or make up one to yell at everybody. "I HATE HER, Granny. I HATE HER."

"Now, Ann."

"Hey, Nancy, I have the math problems from the test for you. They're easy, but I worked them for you anyway."

"Thanks, Rosie. Did Mr. Duda see you?"

"I don't think so, but you better be careful, his room is right there. Study them before you go to class and then don't use this sheet. I'll see you at home."

I walk on down the hall to my locker. Mr. Duda comes out of his room and to my locker. He smiles and says, "You better go tell your sister that I am reversing the order of the test this afternoon. It won't be good if she has the right answers in the wrong place."

"What? I don't. . ."

"Don't worry, Rose Ann, I'll just give you both of the A's at the end of the semester. She doesn't need the course, does she?" He pats my shoulder, smiles and goes back to his classroom.

I'm spending the summer with Libby and Clarence. They moved to Virginia last year and I can work here with a special permit at fourteen. It feels a little funny but I'm not afraid of Clarence anymore and I love Libby. He hasn't touched me for three years and he treats me as I think he should. I still don't like his jokes and I try never to be alone with him. I asked mother to send my birth certificate. It arrived today addressed to Libby. She tells me she will take it to the store for me.

"Oh, Libby, that's stupid. I can take the birth certificate to Mr. Fenton."

"No, your Mother sent it to me and asked me to go with you."

"For Christ's sake Libby, I'm almost fifteen years old. What's the big secret about my birth certificate?

Just another chance for Mother to say I'm too stupid to know or think. Mother told me when I was eight that it was none of my God Damn business and every year after that she told me the same when I got bold enough to ask. But now I'm going to work and she thinks she can belittle me by having Libby go with me to show this secret document.

"Does it have my Father's name on it? I'm not stupid. Let me see." I know he was an accountant for the state of West Virginia and that he traveled around the state. She slipped one day last year and told me that much.

I grab for the paper from Libby. She turns away and then as quickly, she turns back and says, "Here, I think you should have been told a long time ago."

"But if you think that, why haven't you told me anything?" She walks away. No one talks about him. Granny says, "Ask your Mother" or "now Ann be quiet." I was always afraid to ask Deh Deh. Nancy doesn't care and says we're not supposed to talk about it. Bullshit.

I take the paper. Here at long last I can know my father's name. I don't look. I put the paper down. Folded. Hidden. As it has been all of my life.

No one has ever answered my questions and no one will answer questions now. And suddenly I'm afraid to ask more questions. Here is the answer but what will that name tell me? Nothing. Just a man's name. Where is he? Do I already know him? Is he the father of one of my friends? Does he live in Oak Hill? Did he travel from there? It's just a name, but I will know it forever. Maybe I'll change my name.

I pick up the neatly folded paper. It has a seal stamped on it. It's real. She didn't make it up. And there it is in fine print: **C. M. A.**. I sit down and look at it like I think he might appear from the paper. What does he look like? Where does he live? Is he really dead? Has he seen me? So many questions! Still no answers.

I go to the kitchen, jumping up and down. "Libby, if I change my name, I'll be in the front of the line not way back with the W's." Then I begin with all my questions. Do you know him? What's he look like? Where is he? Is he dead?

"You know I can't tell you anything about him. Are you ready to eat?"

Deh Deh isn't even smoking his pipe; not even holding it in his mouth like he always does. He's lying in the dining room on the couch. I've never seen him do that. He must be very sick. He's never been sick in his life or at least not in the sixteen years I've been around. We took a walk yesterday but it was short and he said he didn't feel good. He doesn't say much but always talks about the flowers and veggies as we pass the garden and the wild flowers when we get near the graveyard at the end of the street. I can name all the wild flowers and find the artichokes that grow near the creek and the sassafras that we dig to make tea just because he taught me. School starts soon and we won't be able to walk or have our long talks in the yard. I stand on the back porch where he can't see me but I can see him. He keeps a cloth and wipes his face now and then or just lets the cloth lay on his face. I tell God that he can't take my Granddaddy yet. I need him. I love him. I hear a knock at the door and go to see who it is.

It's Dr. Puckett. Granny must have called him. He's such a big man and pudgy too. I go behind the door of the dining room so I can hear him but not be noticed. I'm skinny enough to hide just about anywhere. Deh Deh looks like he's sleeping. Dr. Puckett asks him how he is and Deh Deh just nods. "Let me take a look. Open your mouth. Wider. How long have you had a sore throat and why haven't you called or come by the office?" He shakes his head and goes on with the questions. "What have you been able to eat? Looks to me like you might be able to swallow liquid and that's about it? Guess I'll call an ambulance and we'll go to the hospital together."

Suddenly Deh Deh is awake and alert. He halfway sits up and says, "Like hell we will. Not going to any goddamn hospital. You go straight to hell. When the Man Upstairs wants this ole pile of bones," he coughs and spits into his bandanna. "He'll just take them. But sure as hell not from a bed in any goddamn hospital." He sits up and coughs harder and spits more.

Dr. Puckett goes out to the living room looking for Granny. Deh Deh sees me behind the door and wants to know what the hell I'm hiding from.

I shrug my shoulders and go outside cause I don't want him to see me crying. He'll just tell me I'm a crybaby and that there's nothing to cry about. He told me a long time ago that when it was his time to go, the Man Upstairs (that's what he calls God when he's not cussing) would let him know. That he might be sick a short time but then he'd just go cause the Man Upstairs was in charge. He had a plan. So I knew he'd made this deal with the Man Upstairs and now it's his time. I don't like it a bit and when I talk to that Man Upstairs, I'll tell Him. I'll let Him know what a terrible time to take my only friend away, the only person in my home who even gives me time of day. How could He even think about taking my Granddaddy away?

Granny comes to the porch and tells me not to bother Dad. He needs to rest. Then says, "You can go get the eggs from the chicken house and bring them in. Dad couldn't do that this morning."

"But, I want to be with him. If he's going to die, I have to let him know that I love him. Oh, Granny, I don't want him to die. He's my best friend. He doesn't yell at me like Mama and he doesn't fight with me like Nancy. You're too busy to take time for me and he's all I have. He isn't going to die is he?"

"Now go on, get those eggs. Feed the chickens too while you are there. Hurry now before dinner."

"Rose Ann, eat your dinner, mother commands! You've been moping around since I came home. What's wrong with you? Nancy's eating, and being pleasant."

51

I hang my head and tears hit my napkin. Deh Deh isn't at the table. Don't they miss him too? What's wrong with me? What's wrong with them? "I'm not hungry, may I be excused?"

Before anyone answers, I run out to the back porch. I hear Mother coming. I sure don't have anything to say to her, so I walk around the house and sit on a bench by the flowerbed. She does not follow me. After dark, I go in, kiss him, tell him I love him and go to bed.

I jump out of bed. Is he still alive? Is he in the dining room? Or did he go to the living room after dinner? I grab my shorts and shirt. I go brush my teeth and run to the dining room. He's still there on the cot. I watch him breathing. Slow. He opens his eyes and smiles at me. I turn a chair around and sit beside his bed. I hold his hand and we say nothing.

"Now Ann, come eat your breakfast and let Dad rest."

"But Granny, I want to sit here till I have to go to the dentist at eleven o'clock. "Am I bothering you Deh Deh?'

He smiles and says, "No, but go eat your breakfast."

I know the minute she walks into the dentist's office. I know that Rita Jo, a neighbor, is here to take me home. I heard the office manager say that I was here to someone on the phone. Then the dentist took someone ahead of me. I know Deh Deh died. Why did I come to the dentist? I wanted to be with him. Before I left I picked him up even if I knew he'd rather walk on his own. But he couldn't. I carried him to the back porch and put him in the wheel chair. I kissed him goodbye.

Rita Jo walks toward me and says, "Rosie we have to go home now."

"Did he die?"

"We have to go now."

"Why can't you tell me? What's wrong with everybody? Do you think I am deaf, dumb and blind?"

"Oh, come on, Rosie."

We walk down the steps in silence. Tears roll down my cheeks and I want to run. I kick at the door at the bottom of the steps. I hit the glass in the door. It rattles. Good, maybe it will break. Everything is broken. I'll hug him even if he's dead. I want to be with him. I want to die too.

Rita Jo starts the car and does a U-turn in the middle of Main Street. She should get a ticket. I hope she does. She won't talk to me. Won't tell me what happened. I jump out of the car as she slows to stop before she gets to our house. The funeral car is pulling away. I scream. "Don't go yet."

Mother grabs me and says, "Calm down."

Who the hell does she think she is? Calm down. I will not and she can't make me. They should have waited for me. Why did she let them take him before I got here? Nancy is nowhere to be seen. Granny stands in the front door crying. She's the only one who even looks like she cares. And he treated her worse than anybody.

I run to Granny and put my arms around her. We cry and hold each other until mother tells us to go inside. I drop my arms and run through the house and out the back door. I sit looking at his shack and the barn and the yard and know that life will never be the same.

We go to the funeral home where mother works part time. Everyone greets us and tell us that Mr. Walton is in the third room on the right. Mother and Granny stay with the owner and Nancy and I go to the casket together. I burst into tears when I see him.

He looks so handsome in his suit that he only wore when he took Nancy and me to Beckley to get new glasses when I was twelve. It's probably the suit he wore for his wedding. I never saw him dressed up but that once. He should be in his overalls now. His hands are crossed over his chest. Too high and a thumb is sticking up. I move his arms down and tuck the thumb under the other one. Nancy turns, asks me how I can touch him and walks quickly to the back of the room. It's not him, just his body. But he can probably hear me. I stay with him a while. Then kiss him and walk away. I don't go back to the casket. I never want to see anybody in a casket. And I'll never be in one.

Class begins and I sit up straight. I want Mrs. Watson to call on me. Last night, when I was frantic about today's assignment, I found a copy of Nancy's writing for the same assignment last year: Write your interruption of the Christmas story in the Bible. I change a few words so it's sure to get me an "A" because Nancy got an "A+". She was the teacher's pet and I'm far from that. I can't wait for Mrs. Watson to hear it. I wonder if she'll remember.

"Nancy, let's hear your story." A minute passes and again Mrs. Watson says, "Nancy." She sounds surprised that Nancy doesn't respond immediately.

I know she means me but I am not Nancy and I'm not going to answer. She does this almost every day and I'm tired of it. I sit quietly and watch as the other students turn to see why I'm not answering. Carroll Sue and John Howard are smiling. We talked about it last week. She is the only teacher who can't seem to tell the difference. Nancy was her pet and could do no wrong. She'll figure it out soon enough.

"Nancy." Pause. "Oh you know I mean Rose Ann. Will you read your story?"

I know my face is red as I go to the front of the room to read. I read the first and second paragraph of what I think is a pretty good make over. I watch her as she frowns more and more. Finally she tells me to stop. "I've never heard anything so far from what the Bible says. Where did you get such ideas? Sit down."

I'm stunned. I can't believe my ears. I throw the paper at my desk and sit down. I want to throw it at her. I sense the class shift in their seats. She calls on John Howard and he begins to read. It sounds like he copied from the Bible and changed a few words. Maybe that's what she wanted but I know it's not what won favor last year. I stop listening and do tomorrow's math assignment. The bell rings and I wait for the class to leave. I pick up my story and place it on top of Nancy's story from last year and walk toward the front of the classroom. I drop them both on Mrs.

Watson's desk. "I know I deserve to have an "F" for today's assignment but not for the reason you told the class. I'd like to have Nancy's story back. She doesn't know I took it."

I start to walk out the door when she instructs me to come back. I turn and find her red faced, looking at the two papers. She sees that my story is word for word like Nancy's, which has a big red "A+" on top of the first page and a note, which reads: Great story! Very imaginative! I stand at her desk waiting for an apology. Who am I kidding? She hands me Nancy's story with a half-smile.

"You're right. You deserve an "F"."

I walk toward the door. "And so do you."

"Get out!"

I can't wait to get out of this car. Reverend Eastwood, our minister drives like he owns the whole road using the middle section only. I guess he thinks God will protect him since he's a preacher. He's driving Nancy and me to college. We don't have a car and he has a meeting at the college. I know some of my anxiety is about starting college. I haven't been to the campus and this is not my choice. I'd never go to a church related school. Nancy is a religious education major so West Virginia Wesleyan is best for her but mother decided I should be in the same school as perfect Nancy.

It will be different. Not like high school. I'll be on my own. No more bosses. No one will tell me what to do. I'll do as I please and try not to let anyone know that I'm her sister. I have no idea what classes I'll take. Will I be able to do college work? I seldom studied in high school. Bet I'll have to study here. But I have to pass to show Miss Kollen that she was wrong when she said I should not waste money going to college. She told me I was too lazy and not smart enough. Some counselor she was. I'll not go to any counselor here.

Reverend Eastwood drives by the campus and pulls to the curb at the Girls' dormitory. Nancy is giving directions.

I jump out of the car. We get our stuff out of the car and put it on the curb. I thank Reverend Eastwood as he drives away to get to his meeting on time. "Thank God we're here."

"Rosie, you should be thankful he drove us. I can tell you didn't like his driving."

"Maybe better than the bus but boy he is scary. You couldn't see from the back seat, but he put the emblem on the hood of his car right down the line in the middle of the road. I can't drive but I know better than to keep the middle of the car in the middle of the road."

"Well, we're here now and you need to go find out where your room is and help carry all this stuff." I go to where she tells me to find the Dean of Girls' office. The building is beautiful; it's made of old stone with pillars and a huge porch in front. I wonder what the rooms look like. I find a student at a table ready to look up my room assignment. When I tell her my name she gives me a room number and asks, "Are you Nancy's sister?" As I turn to go I mumble, "Yeah"

I hurry back to report my findings. "Nancy, I'm on the second floor and you're on the third." She has already started to carry boxes to the door. Three girls pass, she stops to talk, doesn't even introduce me. She acts like she doesn't know me, acts like I'm a stranger. Isn't that what I want? I pick up some of my stuff and walk by them like I don't know her either. Two can play this game. But I don't want them to know she's my sister so I should thank her.

The student at the table stops me in the hall to tell me that my assigned roommate will arrive tomorrow. That's great. A room of my own! I get to pick my side of the room and all the furniture I want. I'm a college student.

Audrey, Elsie and I arrive at the dorm ten minutes after the door is supposed to be locked. We thought sure it would still be open tonight. The Dean of Women is sometimes late from church on Sunday night. But this Sunday it's locked and here we are with our bags of laundry. We knock and joke about the lecture we'll get about going downtown to do our laundry. We've heard it so often. "You girls must remember that you can use the machines downstairs on Sunday after four. You should not be going out. You know. " Dean Wilson opens the door and frowns.

"This is the third week in a row that you girls are late on Sunday. Why can't you follow the rules? Most girls arrange their schedules with better timing for personal matters."

"We tried. So much traffic crossing the streets." I almost laugh out loud when I hear Elsie say this. Pretty creative. The lecture follows without a word about our excuse. We hang our heads appropriately and thank her for reminding us. In unison we promise not to be late next Sunday.

We pick up our bags of wet laundry; throw them over our shoulders like Santa's helpers and climb the five flights of stairs to the attic where we must hang our clothes. There's absolutely nothing here but a lot of dust and row after row of hanging clothes in all stages of drying. Some have been here for weeks, some maybe for years. Some just hung and others are thrown over the line without clothes pins, and are dry on one side and very wet on the other. I don't think anybody ever cleans this place. We should just throw all these old things down the steps. I see another hockey player hanging sheets in the back.

"Say Linda, you're washing clothes pretty late aren't you? Or did Dean Wilson give you special permission to use the machine after hours?"

"I washed these sheets early. I'm just late hanging them."

"Yeah. Yeah." We all laugh and look for space for our wet clothes.

Elsie and I are really angry with the Dean and want to get some revenge for her outrageous rules about washing clothes downstairs rather than going to town. There's no way the five machines in the basement can accommodate everybody in the dorm, especially when they cannot be used after midnight Saturday till four in the afternoon on Sunday. It's so much easier to go to the big laundry down town.

Elsie grabs a pillow, which has been hanging right in everybody's path at the entrance to the drying room and throws it at Linda. The fight begins in a playful mood. We each grab a pillow and run for cover. I hide in the back and pretend to be waiting for just the right moment. Truth is I don't like pillow fights. Nancy used to throw pillows at me.

Nancy hurls the pillow at me like a bomb she hopes will explode. I toss it on the floor and fall onto the bed, face down, to cry. I want her to leave. I don't want to fight. She picks the pillow up and hits me across the back, over and over, as she calls me a crybaby and a chicken. I know if I don't fight back maybe there won't be as much fuss when Mother gets home. She always finds something to fuss about.

Linda stands and throws the pillow back toward Elsie who catches it and hurls it at Audrey. She didn't expect it and falls trying to catch it. Tossing pillows continues for at least five minutes with no casualties and little effort. I've not thrown a pillow at anyone.

Elsie suggests we drape the pillows over the banister and let the feathers fall to the floors below as we go back to our rooms. She throws a pillow at the staircase and as it hits the top of the post it splits and feathers begin to float down the stairway. "Good throw, Elsie." We thought we'd have to cut the pillows. She leaps to the top of the stairway and tears the rest of the pillowcase to allow more feathers to float down. We watch as they slowly fall, sometimes up, then down and around in swirls as they make their way to level four, three, two and one. Can we get downstairs without anyone else seeing us? We make a pact never to tell and go to our rooms one by one very quietly. I hope Linda won't tell Nancy. I don't want to get in any more trouble.

The next morning, I'm the first up on my floor and as I walk toward the stairs, I see Dean Wilson sweeping feathers, nodding her head in the usual "yes, uh huh," manner. No one else is around. I want to yell for Elsie and Linda and Audrey but I know better. "Good Morning, Miss

Wilson," I say as I go past her toward the door to go for my run. I'm about to split open laughing but I hold my breath and do not wait for a reply. I almost knock Linda down as I run out the door. And Elsie and Audrey are down the steps. "How'd you get out? Did you talk with Miss Wilson?"

"No. Did you?"

"She wanted to talk to us but we ran out. Let's go to the track and keep quiet." We are all laughing and stumbling along the way. Thank goodness no one else is on the track.

I'm going to major in physical education. Miss Knepshield, the major teacher is great. She is so kind and helpful like I think a caring mother might be. I love to be in the gym. I spend a lot of free time there and she lets me do stuff for her like cleaning and putting equipment away. Then we shoot basketball. Nancy is not happy with my decision or with me spending so much time in the gym. It's none of her business.

I'm playing field hockey. I didn't make first string this year but I will next year. I want to be the goalie. Some of the seniors on the team treat us freshmen like we don't belong there but I say "you were a freshman once" to all of them. The team hasn't lost a game in three years.

Miss Knepshield gave me money for salad stuff, this morning after class, and asked me to pick up lettuce and tomatoes before coming for dinner tonight. She invited eight Physical Education majors; I think to welcome us back this semester. It's my first dinner at her house. Last semester I went to her house to study with other majors. It's very quiet. She told me today that Sharon, her cleaning person, would be there all afternoon but it's OK for me to go early to study.

That afternoon I go to the little store near the campus. I get salad makings and a bouquet of flowers and walk to her house. I'm hoping Sharon has finished. I don't like her. She's very nosey. I just don't trust her. I know she's worked for Miss K. for years but there's something about her. I look at my watch as I stop in front of her house. It's almost four o'clock.

The house is beautiful. Huge. It has a wraparound porch and white railing all around. I ring the doorbell. Sharon's still here and motions for me to come in. We exchange greetings and I go to the kitchen to fix the flowers and put the stuff in the fridge. She follows me to tell me that "Charlie," as she calls Miss Knepshield, won't be home till after five.

"I know. I'm studying. I won't be in your way. I'll go to the second floor where there's a sunroom with big windows and comfortable furniture."

She shakes her head but goes about her work. I go upstairs and settle in a big wicker chair with my history book. It's so boring. I'm sleepy and have to work hard at staying awake to read this stuff. I jump when Sharon comes to check on me. She laughs and says, "From the looks of you, you won't mess up my cleaning."

What did she expect? Does she think I'll leave wet glasses on the tables she just polished? Why did she come upstairs to tell me this? I frown and say, "Whatever."

I hear Knepshield come in downstairs. "Aren't these flowers beautiful? I hope the delivery person stayed around so I can give a proper tip."

My heart quickens as I hear her start up the steps. I'm just waiting for that tip, but as she comes in the study, I see the telltale signs of a migraine headache. She has them often. I wonder why? She'll still have dinner for eight tonight but she'll have to rest.

I greet her with a big smile that she returns with a very quick hug. My body feels warm as she touches me. It's like Roonie hugging me when I was little.

I retreat to study. I read a few pages and go to the kitchen to start dinner. I hope her headache goes away quickly so she will join us for dinner.

I'm finishing the salad when the others arrive. They came straight from class and are all bitching about the test. I'm glad I'm not taking that class. I don't think a coaching class should be that hard. Maybe Knepshield will teach it next year when I have to take it. "Hey, Rosie, is dinner ready? We're starving."

"No it isn't. You guys have jobs to do to get it ready. Knepshield has a headache. So get busy."

"Watta you think? You're in charge." We all laugh and pots and pans begin to fly. The sauce is ready, just has to be heated. It smells great. Ellen does the spaghetti, Patty the bread, while Linda and Elsie set the table. The other three just sit and wait to be served. When everything is ready, Ellen goes to wake Knepshield. When she hands me my jacket that I left upstairs, I feel everybody look at me. Probably my imagination.

Dinner is wonderful. Everything is good. We eat like we haven't had a meal for at least a month. None of us want dessert. We sing as we clean up. We thank Knepshield and run together back to the dorm just in time to get through the door before it's locked. Now I really have to study. Maybe I'll get up early in the morning.

I walk into my dorm room. Drop my books and flop on the bed. I feel something under me: a new pair of Bermuda's. Where did they come from? I pick them up. They're blue with pockets and my size. I put them on. A perfect fit. Where did they come from? I bet Nancy bought them for me. She said she made some extra money this month working for the Chemistry department. She's been very nice lately and she can get into my room.

I know I need to shower before dinner but I run to Nancy's room on the third floor and burst in. "Nancy, they're beautiful. Thanks. They fit too, don't you think? Where'd you get them?"

She's typing. She looks up at me like I'm crazy. "What are you talking about?"

"My new bermudas. They're the first I've ever had. WOW, I love them."

"Well, I didn't buy them. You better take them back and find out who they belong to cause they're probably not yours. It's a mistake."

"It's not a mistake. They were on my bed." She sure knows how to burst bubbles. To hell with her. Why do I keep trying? I turn and go to my room. Wonder who did buy them? How'd they get them in here? Nancy has a key but no one else except my roommate has one and she's away at some Christian retreat. Oh, well, I'll just wear them and someone will see them and ask me where I got them? I'll say the good fairy brought them.

I get in the shower and remember Knepshield was talking about ordering clothes the other day and ask me what size slacks I wear. I bet she put them here. I have no idea how but it's because she wants me to have them for this summer. She invited me to go to camp with her after school ends. Just two more months and we'll be there. It's a private girl's camp in Virginia. I'm to be the camp manager, whatever that means. I think I have to be a cabin counselor too. Three other girls from Wesleyan are going. Lois will do music; Patty, sports, and Linda will be in charge of all special programs. Knepshield is directing the camp for about sixty girls from age eight to fifteen. I'm not sure about being a camp counselor. I've only been to camp for a week and those counselors had their hands full. But we were in high school. What do I do if a little kid gets scared at night in my cabin?

Linda and Elsie are going home with me today to enjoy our last weekend, before finals. We arrive about three in the afternoon. I told them it was a special Sunday in our church and that they had to go with me but, didn't tell them that I'm preaching. I told Elsie that even if she is Catholic, she has to go to the Methodist church with me. I told her not to tell Granny that she was catholic because Granny, a Southern Baptist, thinks everybody but Baptists are going to hell. I guess she gives mother, Nancy and me an exception because we are Methodist. The story goes that mother had to leave the Baptist church when I was born. Two children out of wedlock didn't fit that church's rules.

I'm embarrassed when friends come home with me because the house is always dirty. I quickly begin to clean as soon as I've said "Hello" to Granny. She is cooking up a storm in the kitchen. She's over seventy and just can't keep up with all the housework. Mother certainly doesn't do any of it. She never has. I thought when I left for college this year that she'd help Granny.

In the bathroom I find a dust pile on the hot water tank that looks like a garden project. I try to make jokes about the dirt, like Mother doesn't clean for two weeks before I come home cause she knows how I love to dust and clean. My friends know better, but go along with it and sometimes help. Today, they are in the living room studying for a big test in History that we all have on Monday. I should be studying with them but the cleaning comes first. I can write my name on any piece of furniture in the house.

I run water and add Clorox in the tub and the sink and commode. It comforts me to know that Mother buys this stuff even if she acts like she has no idea what it's for. I fill the tub to just above the ring and sprinkle cleanser on the surface, as it slowly leaks out, the cleanser will stick to the sides and in a few minutes I can completely erase the ring. I dust the hot water tank, the shelf, and clean the dressing table after moving everything on it. Mother will have a fit because I'm moving her things. But so goes life. Nothing new.

The bathroom, bedroom, and office are at least presentable now and I'll give the living and dining room a lick and a promise as I go to put these cleaning things back in the pantry where they will stay till I'm home again. Dinner must be about ready and that means it's about time for good ole mother to arrive. She knows I'm coming home but I didn't tell her what time we might arrive. Nor did I tell her that I was preaching Sunday. She'll be surprised. I hope she'll be pleasant with company. Linda, Elsie and I will go to visit friends after dinner so we won't spend much time with mother.

Sunday morning is usually a mad rush and this morning is no exception. I have to be early and I don't want to tell anybody why, so I hurry, get dressed, and try to rush Elsie. Linda's been ready for half an hour as usual. I tell mother we'll walk ahead and meet her in time for church.

We're going to Sunday school first, but I have to meet with the others on the program to get everything timed just right.

My sermon is going just fine. I'm glad I decided to use James Allen's theory from <u>As A Man Thinketh</u> and combine it with a story about being the best you can be. I'm changing the <u>Man</u> to <u>Person</u> and that allows me to emphasize <u>Woman</u>. Everyone is quiet and listening and I am ready to end it. I ad-lib a little more about being what you can be drawing strength from your thoughts. Where is my shoe? I am searching for my left shoe. I always take my shoes off when I stand to speak and especially when no one can see my feet. I found my right shoe with ease, now where is that left one? I'm still talking and I notice that some people are beginning to laugh. I'm not saying anything funny. I'm very serious and about to lead everyone in prayer at the end of the sermon. Reverend Eastwood interrupts me and says out loud, "Is this what you are looking for, Rose Ann?" I am so embarrassed I want to run out of the church. How could he do this to me? I hate him. He thinks he's so cute. The sermon is ruined, everyone is laughing. I turn to see what he is doing and he just smiles at me as he holds the shoe up for everyone to see. Did he even hear any of my sermon? I grab my shoe and turn back to the congregation and say; "Reverend Eastwood will lead us in prayer." Now he's the one in shock. I sit down and bow my head.

I roll over and think my stomach is going to explode. The pain is unbelievable. I try to get up but the pain is sharper and it hurts to move. I have to go to this dance class. I've never missed a college class. Almost a year: would my high school teachers be impressed. I must go. I get up. Wash my face, get dressed and head to the gym.
Miss Knepshield'll take care of me, if I just get to her class on time. I've got five minutes. I barely make it to the gym and put my head down on my hands as I sit on the first bleacher. I hear my sister's voice. I didn't even think about her being in this class.

"Rosie, what's the matter? It can't be that bad"

"Well, good morning, Nancy. Glad you're here. I have a terrible pain in my stomach. I think I should go to the infirmary, but I don't want to miss class."

"Maybe, if you get some exercise, dancing, the pain will go away. It's probably gas. You know how you always fart."

"I don't think I can dance. I'll probably throw up on my partner. Want to be my partner?"

Knepshield comes out of her office. Whistle around her neck with that starched white blouse and hanky in her breast pocket. When I begin teaching PE that's what I'll wear. It looks great. She's pretty heavy. I wonder if it'll look the same on me, I'm pretty skinny. She walks past me; quickly turns to ask what's bothering me. I tell her I have a very bad stomach ache. She feels my forehead and tells me to go immediately to the infirmary. She tells me to walk slowly and if I want someone with me, it's OK. I shake my head and go out the door.

Maybe Nancy heard her and will follow me. I'd feel better if I had someone with me. But as usual, my big sister acts like she doesn't know me now that her friends have arrived for class.

I am very groggy. People keep coming in and out of this sterile white room. Where am I? One woman with a funny headdress comes over and tells me my mother is finally here and that we'll be going to the operating room very soon. I look around and see no one that looks like my mother. I go back to sleep. I feel movement; like I'm floating down a hill. I hear people talking in a distance, and I try to find them but they're following me and I can't see them.

I'm very thirsty. I need a drink of water. My throat feels like someone wiped it dry. I open my eyes, see no one, and ask for water. I can hardly hear my voice. Am I still in the gym? Have I just passed out? I call, "Miss Knepshield, Miss Knepshield."

Now I see my mother standing over me. How'd she get here? I realize I'm in a bed in a strange room it's very quiet. "You had your appendix removed," mother says. Oh, now I remember. They gave me something as soon as I got here. And I slept. What time is it now? I guess it's all over. I don't have the same pain. It's just uncomfortable. There's a heavy bandage on my stomach. I run my hand over the bandage. But how did mother get here? I turn to the side where she is standing and ask for water. She says she'll ask the nurse. And she wants to know if I'm OK. She tells me to keep my hands away from the bandage as she leaves the room.

I suck on the crushed ice while mother tells me about the trip in the snowstorm last night. That they wouldn't operate till she got here and that I should be damn glad she could leave work to come. "Miss Knepshield let a student use her car to meet me half way. One of the mechanics at work brought me that far. We had snow most of the trip."

"Thanks for the ice. It's good." I fall asleep.

This camp is beautiful and quiet and the people who own it are super. I am very glad to be here and I get to spend these six weeks with Knepshield outside a classroom. We might even eat together or spend a day off seeing the sites around this area of Virginia. I'll make more for the summer than if I'd gone home to work in the dime store and I'll have lots more fun I think. And best of all I don't have to put up with mother or Nancy. Tomorrow the campers arrive. Mrs. Poyser, the owner, has asked us to be helpful with the kids but to pay most attention to the parents. She has her priorities in order. I'm responsible for collecting all the outstanding monies and if a parent asks for an extension, I'm to send them to her. She'll surely take care of them.

I have collected more money than I expected. These parents hand out hundred dollar bills like they come from a tree in their back yard. Only four parents ask for an extension. Each went to see Mrs. Poyser and each one came back to give me some money and told me their extension date. I'll send them a reminder two weeks before that date.

All sixty campers checked in, met their cabin mates and counselors and wandered around the grounds checking out everything. Our "welcome to camp" dinner was the usual Sunday fried chicken.

I want to get my driver's license this summer while I'm in camp. Knepshield has promised to teach me to drive. I've never needed to know how before because we never had a car and still don't. But if I'm to run errands for camp, I need to be able to drive. Today is my first lesson. I'm doing well, but she insists I practice backing up and parking more and tells me we will go to the highway next time to learn to pass cars.

Second lesson is today and I can tell Knepshield is in a hurry. I jump in the driver's seat and say, "Let's go. We'll be back before dinner, don't worry."

We turn onto the highway and right away I'm going too fast for her. "I'm only going fifty."

"That's too fast for these curves."

I slow down. I have to practice passing cars today so I will have to go faster. . I'll speed right by every car today. I want to get my license and I'm sure she wants to end the lessons.

"Don't get so close to the car before you signal to change lanes to pass. Be sure you check the rear view mirror. And you better look to your left to be sure there is not a car in your blind spot."

"Now you slow down. Not so many directions at once."

"OK. You do have to do several things at once and you are doing well. I think today may be the last lesson except for parking."

"Great." I pass two cars and she tells me to slow down after I pass. We joke about my heavy foot as I pass a truck and head back to camp.

After the fourth lesson Knepshield approves my ability and says I can borrow her car to take the test. I have to go to Clifton Forge, a town about fifteen miles from camp. I'm not supposed to drive to town by myself but no one at camp can go today and I'm ready and I have the day off. I park the car down the street from the police station and walk to my appointment.

I try to act as nonchalant as I can. I'm not good at lying. The examiner, a state trooper, calls my number. As I approach his desk, he is looking at my application. "Have the person who drove you bring the car to the back of the building."

"She can't sir. She had an appointment in town so we parked near here. We can walk to the car. Right?"

"Does that mean you drove?"

"No sir, I didn't drive here." I repeat my lie. "A friend brought me. She's in town. The car is parked about a block away. Can't we walk to it?"

He looks at me with doubting eyes. He knows I'm lying. I guess I won't pass the test and he'll send a cop to stop me when I drive back to camp. "I suppose this time we can but if you don't pass, ask your friend to bring you here with the car next time."

I smile, say nothing and walk out the door with the trooper. I'll show him. I'll pass this time and drive the car back to camp, just like I drove it here. We get to the car and all goes well till he tells me to Parallel Park at the curb between a tree and where he is standing. I tell him I've never parallel parked a car against a curb. I try and am perfectly spaced between the tree and his foot, but am three feet from the curb. I hit the tree on the second try. He gives me "one more try."

I pull forward about twenty feet, talk to myself, and park like a pro. "If you learned to park in just three tries, I'll give you your license if you pass the written test."

I am jumping up and down inside as we walk back to the station. I answer all the questions correctly. I drive back to camp singing at the top of my voice.

Sundays at camp are fun. But today is a rainy day and the usual parade of parents didn't happen. Before dinner, Knepshield is teaching the campers to sing "This little light of mine." She can't carry a tune in a bucket. It does amaze me how she gets these kids to do anything she tries. She's very spontaneous and makes the place and time seem happier no matter what is happening. I hope I'm that good when I am in her position. She's so positive. We get through the song and have the best ever fried chicken for dinner. I go to the kitchen to thank the cooks.

I come by every morning early to get a cup of tea and talk with them. The kitchen staff is very important to camp in my opinion. They leave me a dish of chicken hearts every Sunday and that's another reason I want to thank them. And Amy, the youngest helper in the kitchen, washes and irons my clothes each week. As I get to the door, Bessie, the head cook, motions me not to come in. I'm puzzled until I see Mrs. Poyser in the back of the kitchen talking to the rest of the staff. I smile at Bessie and go back into the dining room.

Mrs. Poyser comes straight to me from the kitchen. "Rose, you must not be so friendly with the kitchen staff. Parents would not like to see you socializing with the colored help."

"I just want them to know I appreciate them." The nerve of her. I frown and start to walk away. She will not influence my thinking on this matter. People are people and the color of their skin has nothing to do with that.

"Never mind that. They aren't at your level." She walks on as though she is in a hurry to get away from me.

I'd like to see her run this camp without them. They do everything for her. I hate this racism. It reminds me of how people in my hometown treated Mr. Johnson just because he was colored. Most of the counselors from Virginia act the same. We've had some heated discussions at night. Mrs. Poyser promotes this attitude. I'm surprised she has asked me to come back next summer.

I bound down the steps into the locker room for the first field hockey practice of my sophomore year. I'll catch a few winks before the others arrive. I love field hockey but this nap on a bench in the locker room is the best. Uh oh! There's a paper in my locker. I know I locked it. It's all neatly folded under my sweatshirt. I smile as I open it to read, "A friend is a gift you give yourself." Coach is at it again. I never think of her as that but she is sentimental. I keep her notes in a special box in my room.

I stretch out on the bench and dream.

I'm running on a big green lawn. Buildings all around and a big one at the other end. I'm racing to get there. I see coach on the stage in front of the building. She has a roll of paper with a ribbon on it. She looks twenty feet tall. I run and run. As I get closer she bends down to give me the paper. Over the loud speaker I hear, "Congratulations, you are teacher of the year for our Nation."

"Hey, Walton, what do you think this is; your palace? Knepshield's really going to make you run when she finds out you're sleeping in the locker room."

I sit up with a start. My heart beats faster and I say, "No she won't." I grab my stick and race all of them to the field. I see her big smile as I round the corner of the gym. I will stop every ball they send my way today. I'm ready for that big game in Bridgewater. I like practice more this year. I'm going to be first-string goalie.

It's my first time in a Gay bar. Mary told me some things but I don't know if I should be here. I'm not sure what's proper. I see a woman I met at hockey practice the other day and she's looking at me with her watery, blue, "come here" looking eyes. I feel a slight stir as I look back to see if she is still looking. And she is. But she has someone sitting on her lap. Is it OK to flirt with someone else when you have another person that close? Well, it's OK for her, why not me? I wink this time and she smiles.

She's getting up now and that person on her lap is very nonchalant about her moving. Maybe they're just friends. I've seen her on campus but not regularly so she's not a student. She's older than most of us anyway. She's coming over this way. I'll try to be casual till I know more about her.

"Hi. I'm Pat. Please, don't get up."

"Hi. I'm Rosie." I start to get up but sit back down.

"Saw you come in with Mary, are you visiting for the weekend?"

"Yeah."

"Think I've seen you on campus. And I met you at field hockey practice last week, didn't I?"

"Yes. I play goalie."

"That's right. I've seen you play. I go to watch sometimes. Let's dance."

"I'm not a very good dancer." I get up and we walk toward the dance floor and she tells me she only likes the slow music. We stand and wait for the next song and it's slow so we dance. She's taller and slimmer than I am. Dark hair and deep blue eyes. They always look wet. She has a cute smile. While we are dancing she tells me about her school days at Wesleyan when she drank and got kicked out of the dorm and then Knepshield "Took her in tow" and she graduated and is teaching math in high school. She says she loves teaching. That's what I want to do.

We go back to the table and both sit down. She asks if Mary and I are dating. I must look shocked because she says, "Well, you came with her didn't you?"

"We're friends. I don't know if she's a lesbian."

"Are you?"

I stand up and tell her I have to go to the rest room. I quickly walk away. I'll go find Mary and see if she's ready to go home. No one ever asked me that before. Am I? I go to the other side of the room to the steps going up stairs. I see Mary with a really beautiful blond woman at the top of the stairs. Maybe she'll introduce us later. I don't want to interrupt her, so I go back to my seat at the table just as Pat comes back with two beers. I wish someone had taught me about what to do in a gay bar before just dumping me at a table. Maybe I should have a second beer to be more relaxed. Relaxed and tongue-tied is more like it. I don't drink either, or at least haven't before this weekend. Bet my sister will have fits if she finds out. I'll have to swear Mary to secrecy. She's in my sister's sorority and they tell each other everything but Mary probably won't say anything about the bar. It's as bad for her as for me.

"Thanks, but no thanks. I don't really drink. I'll get a ginger ale." I turn toward the bar but before I can move, she takes my hand and tells me to sit down and she'll get it. She goes to the bar and I sit down.

"Here's your ginger ale. Better be careful with that stuff, it'll rust your pipes."

"Yeah, like beer won't."

"Beer lubricates them so you can dance looser. Wanna dance again?"

Just then Mary comes over with her lovely blond friend. She introduces us all around and they sit down. She says she's about ready to go and asks if that's OK. Before I can say OK, Pat suggests that she'll drop me at Mary's a little later if I want to stay.

I don't want her to drop me later, nor do I want to stay here with her. There is something about the rush that makes me uncomfortable. I'm not ready to explore these feelings with her. I stand up, motion to Mary that I'm ready to go with her. She thanks Pat for the offer and invites her to breakfast in the morning. Pat accepts.

She takes my hand, gives it a squeeze and walks with us to the door. I feel all tingly inside. I like it.

Six of us pile into Knepshield's Chevy. She's taking us to town and back to the dorm in the rain. She needs something from the grocery store and we said we'd go to the store for her if she'd give us a ride. Car jokes are flying so fast laughter didn't stop about one till another had surfaced. I am absolutely wild about the new Pontiac cars. Pat just got her new one and I think Knepshield is envious. So not only do we joke about her old Chevy but every time we pass a Pontiac, we yell, PONTIAC.

Knepshield is being a sport about it all but I can tell she's not happy. When the rest of them pile out to go to the grocery store, I stay with her in the car. "You better get your friends to stop praising the Pontiac or you'll be walkin in the rain."

She can't think I have any control over them. I'll try to stop yellin but who knows what they will do. It's fun. When the others come back I say, "we have to cool it with the Pontiacs, our driver is upset."

Just then a new one goes by and I can't contain myself. **"PONTIAC."**

The car comes to a screeching halt. **"GET OUT."**

Is she serious? She'd never put me out in the rain. I don't believe it. The others open the door and start to get out. "Stop, she doesn't really mean it."

She puts the car in park and just waits. We all walk back laughing. I'll apologize tomorrow cause I don't want her mad at me. She's probably laughing too.

Audrey, Ellen, Pat and I are on our way to the movies in Clarksburg tonight. It's about twenty miles from campus and I hope we'll get back before the dorm closes. Pat is driving. We're going at least 60 when the car ahead of us moves to the right. Pat moves to the left to pass as he moves closer to the shoulder, but turning. . . . .   Oh my God!   Left.

Pat slams on the breaks and Ellen hits the dashboard. I hear glass shattering. My knee hits the front seat. The other car is on the left hand side of the road and very smashed in beside the driver's door. My knee hurts. The driver looks dazed.   Pat and Ellen jump out of the car. Audrey looks like she's in a fog. "Are you OK?"

She looks at me and nods her head.   "What happened?"

"The idiot in front of us signaled to turn right and turned left. Pat couldn't stop. I think she was going too fast as usual." How far are we from school? Can the car be driven? It doesn't look like much happened to our car but I can't see from here. The police arrive. I start to get out but Pat motions me to stay in the car. I hear Pat and Ellen both talking at once telling the officer what happened. The other driver isn't saying a word. I try to roll my window down but it's stuck. I guess we hit him harder than I thought. But a Pontiac is a very solid car. Pat says they're the best. She's always driven them and just got this one a month ago. She was upset because she couldn't get a convertible. She and Ellen are walking back to the car. She is smiling, almost laughing, and Ellen is shaking her head.

They get in the car like nothing happened. Pat says, "Don't worry, just a little bump." She starts the car. "I didn't get a ticket, he did. The officer didn't even ask him what happened. We sure fooled him. I'll get my new Pontiac now and it'll be a convertible. I'll take you back to the dorm."

I can't believe it. She laughs and thinks she's something cause she got by with speeding. She doesn't give a shit about us. Just her darned ole car. Not even "Are you OK." I slump back in the seat and think about what happens when we get back to the dorm and Nancy finds out. My knee hurts. Damn her.

Why does Beverly want to see me? She's in Nancy's sorority and already knows I'm not pledging Alpha Gam. Study. Study Study. I move paper and books so it'll at least look like I've been studying. I should've said I was too busy to see her. She hardly ever speaks. She isn't even friendly at hockey practice. She's a good forward. But she has her favorites and always passes to them.

I open the door as I hear her slight knock.

"Hi, Beverly, come on in."

"Hi, Rosie, hope you don't mind my stopping by, just to chat."

"No, why should I? But I do admit I'm surprised."

I move the chairs so she has to sit facing the window and I can see her better without the glare of the sun in my eyes. I move papers and busy myself with nothing while she walks across the room and sits down. She seems hesitant. What's this all about?

"Rosie, some of us upper-class majors have been talking and I volunteered to talk with you. You're a bright student, good athlete, and fun loving."

"What is it? Just spit it out. You don't want me to take the goalie position? You'd rather have Linda? Guess that's Knepshield's decision."

"It's not about playing hockey; you're a very good goalie. It's about being friendly with the coach."

I get up and walk to the window. I wipe the sill and pick up some papers. I turn so she can't watch my face. What the hell is going on? Is my sister in on this?

"What friendly with the coach? You guys seem friendly enough. Why me?"

"Well, just be careful. Knepshield tends to have her favorites."

Who do they think they are? I start rearranging paper and want to throw her through the window. Bet my lovely sister, sent her little flunkey. Nancy's president of her sorority and they will do anything for her. Do they follow me around? I get up and head for the door.

"So! Don't we all? And anyway, that's her privilege. She doesn't . . . "

"And we've noticed you also go off campus with Pat Mead." Jesus, how do I stop her? "She's not such a good influence. . . ."

"OK. Enough! Go tell Nancy I'm a big girl and can handle myself. I don't need her, or her sorority sisters."

"Oh, Rosie, please, just listen."

"I said, ENOUGH! Now go." I open the door. She looks at me and shakes her head and leaves. I didn't want to come to this college where Nancy had already started. I don't like following her. I had to all through school. I thought last year was enough to make my identity. I want to be ME. I know I'm different from her. I always have been.

This new Pontiac of Pat's is really beautiful. It a convertible with leather seats and a leather steering wheel. I've never seen a steering wheel like this one. Maybe it's just a cover but it looks like a molded leather wheel. I slide over to the passenger seat as she steps in to drive. We are just going for an evening drive like usual but tonight it's in a new car. I think this is great. We stop just out of town to put the top down and Pat goes into the little general store. Says she needs cigarettes but I know she'll buy beer. She drinks too much and tries to get me to drink too. I just don't like beer.

"So, where's my beer?"

"You're driving. You shouldn't drink."

"Give me a break. If I had a nickel for every time I drank a beer while I was driving, I'd be rich. Now open one."

"What's the hurry? I want to enjoy this new car."

Pat pulls off the road and grabs a beer from the back seat, opens it, takes a big drink and hands the opened beer to me. Gives me a little kiss and says, "Now isn't that better."

"Better than what?"

She pulls into our usual parking spot to watch the end of the sunset and finishes the first beer. She pulls me close to her as she reaches for the next beer. I take a drink, make a face, and slide even closer. I like kissing better than beer and I love for her to kiss my neck. I get all wet and know there has to be more to do. I don't want to find out in a car on a back road.

Miss Wilson, Dean of Girls, tells me it's OK for Pat to stay in the dorm tonight. She is driving some of the hockey team to our game in Virginia tomorrow and my roommate is away. I know she only said yes because I have two beds in my room.

Pat gets in bed with me and I turn my back to her. Not much room in this twin bed. She blows on my neck and I get goose bumps everywhere. This is crazy, she's a woman and I've never felt like this before with any boy I've dated. I squirm to move away but she holds tight. She is lying behind me. We are nude. What if Nancy barges right in looking for me? I reach up and turn out the lights. She puts her arm across me and touches my breast. I stiffen. She lets go and blows on my neck again. I don't know what to do. I tell her she should sleep in the other bed.

"But I'm not interested in sleep now."

"What are you inter. . ."

She turns me toward her and kisses me on the mouth, says I talk too much. She begins to touch me

76

everywhere all at once. My body is on fire. I kiss her back and it feels good. I'm warm and comfortable. She holds me tight.

Should I insist that we get in separate beds? Nancy or somebody is sure to come by early in the morning. I don't want to let go of her. So I won't.

I'm really focused on this game and because I'm goalie, I have to make sure the other team doesn't score. Oh my God, here comes Pat with her folding chair. Puts it down right behind the goal. I wish she'd go away. No, I want her to stay. I want to talk to her. I wanted to ride with her today but Knepshield assigned each of us to a car. I was not in Pat's. I'll change that going home. Here comes the opposing team. They are really good. Have training tables in the dorm. I scream. The ball comes flying at me. I hit it with my stick and hear it hit the goal post. Shit it bounces into the goal. Damn. Damn. The game is over. We lost by one goal. Knepshield is really mad. She told Pat never to sit by the goal again and acts like it is Pat's fault we lost. I scored the goal for the other team. I didn't mean to but, damn, when I hit the ball to clear it from the goal, it caught the front post of the goal and flipped in. What's her problem? She says I have to ride back with her and not with Pat. I don't want to and she can't make me. Usually I'd rather ride with Knepshield but today I'm going with Pat.

I walk over to Pat's car and get in the back seat. Others pile in and Pat sees where I am. She jumps in the car and yells to Miss Knepshield that she has her four passengers. She takes off before Knepshield can respond.

Everyone's upset that we lost. Big deal, it's just a game. I can hear them now, "for God's sake, it's the first time we've lost a game in three years, Rosie." So here we are at practice and I'll have to act like I care. I walk over to the goal cage and pick up my stick. I'm ready for a really hard practice. Here comes Knepshield. I love to watch her. She always has a smile on her face. Even today when I think she's going to be mad.

"OK, Walton, get to the other end of the field, NOW."

I start to walk toward the other goal and she yells again. "I mean, NOW."

"I'm going. What's the rush?"

"You ought to know. Get the lead out."

I try to run but it is very hard in these leg pads that go from my ankles to mid-thigh. They're heavy too. I stop to take them off and she yells again to move and not to take the pads off. She's really out to get me today. I'll show her.

She lines the whole team up around the striking circle and has them hit balls toward me. I'm supposed to stop every one of them without knowing where the next one is coming from. And these are my teammates. I bet she told them what she was going to do in practice while I was putting on these dumb pads. Thud thud thud against my legs. Even with these damn pads I feel every hit. It continues for at least thirty minutes and I've stopped every one. No one has scored. It seems like an hour. She finally says, "Stop."

"Now why didn't you do that Saturday?"

I hang my head and say, "I don't know."

She walks over, puts her arm around me and I feel twelve feet tall. I know deep down, she thinks it was just a game too.

This is the most beautiful garden I've ever seen. The chance to attend this national conference is my first visit to Florida. Knepshield, three other students and I are taking a break from the meetings to come see this garden. The tropical trees, flowers, and shrubs are magnificent. It's like my Deh Deh's but much bigger and not a weed to be found. I wander away from the others. I want to be alone in the serenity I feel here in this wide-open lawn with flowers around the edge, in the middle, along the walkway and almost everywhere. No one steps on this lush green carpet and it looks as though some magic hands cut each blade to match the next. I want to roll on it, take my shoes off and run across it, take my clothes off and make love on it. I sense that the others are annoyed with me for wandering off to my own space. They don't understand and I'm not about to let them know how I feel. They would laugh or scowl. They're in a hurry to go watch the water ski show. So go watch it. I won't get lost. I find a palm tree right on the edge of a path with a deep curve in its trunk. It's not smooth but I sit on it and stretch my legs up along the higher side. Like a hammock; but harder. I put my bag on the walkway and close my eyes to dream of having this kind of garden around my own home in Florida someday. I don't even have the home yet, don't live there yet, but I will. I make that vow to myself now. Maybe I'll meet someone at this conference who will promise me a job in two years.

I hear someone yell, "Get away from there."

I sit up straight and see Knepshield smiling. A squirrel is in my bag, headfirst. It reaches in, takes a candy bar and sits alongside the bag and begins to tear the paper away. It's eating my Clark bar, sitting proper, and holding it in its two front paws.

Knepshield walks over and gives me her hand to help me get out of this hammock-tree. She hands me my purse and we go to see the water skiers. I tell her she has to buy me another Clark Bar because she let the squirrel take mine. And I know she will too. She is like a Mother I always wanted. One who would be kind, protective and supportive?

"Hey, Rosie, wait up."

I turn to see Elsie coming after me, a hockey stick in one hand and a towel in the other. She's so funny, swinging her arms like a windmill and skipping along like a 5 year old.

I stop and stand with hands on my hips and wait. She can tell I am disgusted that she wants me to wait. I'm in a hurry. I really don't want to miss dinner again.

"Jesus! Rosie, why the face? I thought we were friends. What the hell's gotten into you lately? You act like you are mad at the world. "

"What'd you mean?

"Oh, I don't know, you just seem stand offish."

"Christ! Elsie, not you too. What's the damn big deal?"

I start to go on ahead and Elsie takes my arm and swings me around to face her.

"Look, Rosie, I'm on your side. There are lots of rumors about Knepshield and Ellen, that they might be lovers. They think you're next."

"Next what? And what do you mean lovers? You mean lesbians. I'm NOT so forget it. I don't care what they say. I like Knepshield and she's good to me. I'm her friend and she is mine."

Elsie looks at her watch and says she has to hurry to shower to get to dinner on time. "I'll talk to you later. Meet me in my room after dinner."

I'm no longer in a hurry. I mosey on down the walkway. Ellen and Knepshield? I don't believe it. I don't care either, it's their business. If it's true and they are really in love, I say "good" for them. It's not easy to find someone to really love and man or woman is not what's important.

Good thing I have a table assignment with friends who go slowly enough to give me time to get to the dining room. I'm last as usual.

I'm on my way out of the dorm to go to field hockey practice. I have plenty of time but I want to go early and work on some of my stops now that I'm the first string goalie. Elsie is going to meet me and drive balls at me to help me make better stops and deflect balls faster. Elsie isn't on the team. She has a very big, loud, and colorful mouth and doesn't care who she yells at or what she yells during games. Knepshield will not put up with that. After all, Wesleyan is a Christian school and she has to uphold the standards whether she agrees or not and I believe she does. Even when some of us go to her house for dinner, she makes sure no one uses foul language. We have fun but always have to watch our language. She's a wonderful coach and she's very kind to me and to most of the girls on the team. Just as I start to open the door I hear the student receptionist call my name. "Rosie, Rosie, you have a very important message."

I turn around and ask, "From?"

"The Dean; and I don't mean Miss Wilson."

Miss Wilson doesn't scare me. I'm always getting in trouble with her, so if she wanted to see me, I'd just say I had practice and I'd see her later. But this is a message from the Dean of the school, Dean Schoolcraft. I've never met him and never been in his office. He wants to see me in his office at three today. It's 2:45, so I have just enough time to get there. His office is in the administration building. I'll have to find it. I think about changing clothes and then say to hell with it. I'll go like I am. I wonder what he wants. I haven't done anything bad lately that I can think of.

I find his office and see that Miss Wilson and my sister, Nancy, are also there. "Come in Rose Ann, and have a seat. We have some questions for you."

I sit in the only chair left. It's right in front of his big desk. I notice that his desk is very neat with almost nothing on it. I look up at the very high ceiling. It is a beautiful office even if it is small. "Your sister is quite concerned about what she has heard."

What has she heard? About Pat Mead and me driving fast on the highway, me not studying, and me smoking a cigar in the dorm? Why is Miss Wilson here? What does she have to do with it? Oh my God, they heard about my drinking at the conference. I twist in my chair and feel in my pocket for a tissue. I don't have one. OH, boy.

"Rose Ann, your sister thinks you may need some counseling about what took place at the Conference you attended in Florida last week. It has been reported that you slept with Miss Knepshield. Is that true?"

What does he mean? I slept with Knepshield? "Well, I was in the same room. So was Patty Wilt. Have you talked with her?"

She did help me get undressed when I came in so drunk that I couldn't stand up. I certainly won't tell them anything about that.

81

"Never mind who we've talked with. Did you sleep in the same bed with Miss Knepshield?"

WOW, this is serious. I feel my heart race. I take a deep breath. How could Nancy do this to me? I feel my face getting hot and my hands are sweating. This is sure not a Christian attitude. And Miss Wilson sitting there shakes her head, like she does all the time. I can just imagine Nancy talking to her. They don't have any idea how unchristian they act.

"No, I certainly did not. Why would I? I had my own bed, same as Patti. If you wanted to know who I slept with Nancy; why didn't you ask me?" She can't even look at me. She keeps her head down. "We stayed three to a room to save the college money." I don't believe this is happening. Am I going to get kicked out of college? I have to get out of here, NOW.

"Well, Rose Ann." I hate that name. "We've had reports about Miss Knepshield before and we thought you would help us by telling us the truth." I am telling the truth. "It seems that she has befriended some female students in the past in a way that's not acceptable."

I shift in the chair. I look out the window then back at the Dean. "What do you mean? She's a very good teacher and coach. She's helps all students especially us majors." I start to get up then sit back on my leg. I feel taller. She's been a professor here for more than ten years. What do they think? Why now?

"Has Miss Knepshield ever locked her office door when you have talks? Has she ever made any advances toward you?" He stands and leans toward me. "Did she get into your bed at the conference?"

I explode. I want to pound my fists on his desk. Scare him. Slap my sister. And Dean Wilson; she's hopeless. I'm afraid I'll cry. I don't want to cry now. "You know, you're all crazy. NO, Miss Knepshield has never locked her office door. NO, Miss Knepshield did not get into my bed." I jump up. I look at each one of them as I turn to leave and say, "But today, I will lock her door as I report this meeting to her. You say that this is a Competent

Cultured Christian College. Well, I think it is one Hell of a long way from being Christian. I have hockey practice NOW. I'm leaving."

I walk out and start down the hall. I begin to cry. I want to run away, far away. I hear Nancy call, "Wait, Rosie." I pick up speed and am running when she catches me at the door. She starts to put her arm around me, I jerk away.

"Don't touch me, I hate you. You're sick. You're not my sister anymore." I run to the gym.

I get to the gym just as Knepshield is dismissing her last class. She's headed for her office and I see three girls waiting for her in the outer office. I'll never get to see her before practice. Maybe it will be better that I work some of the anger out on the field, before I talk to her.

I get my gear and go to the field. Elsie's waiting and doesn't look too happy. I'm late. She doesn't even ask where I've been. Does she know? If she does, who else does? Is the rumor all over school about Miss K and me? It isn't true. I hurry to get my goalie pads on and run to the goal. Elsie starts hitting hockey balls at me a mile a minute. I miss several and then get angry with her too. She doesn't say a thing but I can tell something's bugging her. I hit the next few right back at her with lots of force. She finally says, "Rosie, I have to go back to the dorm. I can't stay for practice. Miss K. doesn't want me to be here during practice any more. I'll tell you about it later. See you at dinner. OK?"

"Sure, Elsie, but what's goin on? I just got called in to see Dean Schoolcraft. Do you know what that was about? Did you talk to Nancy, today?" DAMN Nancy anyhow!

"No and No. I'll see you at dinner." Elsie leaves the field and heads toward the dorm. I'll talk to Knepshield about Else practicing with us and being on the team. She's really good and tough. She could score points, but I'll have to find a way to close her mouth. She just says anything to anyone and doesn't care how it sounds or if it might hurt. Maybe I should start talking like she does. They call me

"Squeaky, the goalie" as it is. I'm always screaming "get the ball out of here."

Practice begins as usual. "I want the goalie at this end of the field" comes the cry from the coach. Naturally it's the opposite end from where I've started practicing. She does this every single practice. Doesn't matter where I am, she wants me at the other end. It's hard to run in all this garb. Maybe she just likes to see me run.

Practice goes well, I hit a few harder than usual out of the goal, and I pretend the ball is Schoolcraft's baldhead. When it ends, I walk over to Miss K and say, "I need to see you in your office before I go to the dorm for dinner."

"I'll be right there. Take the keys and open the office so others can get their belongings."

She acts like all is well. I guess she doesn't know what is going on behind her back. Maybe it's happened before and she just can't be bothered. It's about five o'clock and I have to be in the dorm, ready for dinner in half an hour or I won't get to eat. I don't care today; I don't want to eat with Nancy or Dean Wilson.

Knepshield comes in and I follow her to her inner office. She moves behind her desk and I lock the door. "What are you doing? Why lock the door? No one will come in if the door is closed."

"I know, but today I have to be sure. I was called to Dean Schoolcraft's office today." I sit in the chair beside her desk. "When I got there, Nancy and Dean Wilson were already there. It was a terrible meeting. It was about you." I pick up a hockey ball from her desk and roll it in my hand. He actually asked me if we slept together at the conference. I told him we had separate beds and shared a room to save the college money. I didn't do anything when I was drunk, did I?

She smiles and gives a little laugh. "No, Rosie, you didn't and you must not think any of this has anything to do with you." She leans forward on her desk and picks up a small round vase. She rolls it around in her hands. "There's a group of people on this campus who would like to see me

84

lose my job. I don't fit the image they want for Wesleyan women. Your sister has probably been influenced by them and along with Miss Wilson figured out a way to get rid of me by using you. What did you tell them?" She shifts in her chair and moves a few things on the desk.

"I told them that this might be a competent and cultured school but it was a Hell of a way from being Christian. I don't care if they kick me out."

Her eyes never leave mine. I look away. I start to get up and change my mind.

"That's pretty strong. What did they say?"

"I didn't give them time to say anything. I walked out. Nancy followed me and tried to talk to me but I told her she's not my sister anymore. I guess they made me pretty mad." I stand up. I gotta get out of here.

"Well, you run along to the dorm and don't be late. I'll talk to the president before I leave campus today and all will be OK. Don't worry about it and don't talk about it. The less said the better. I'll see you in class in the morning."

I unlock the door, thank her and walk slowly to the dorm. I'm glad I'm going back to camp in Virginia this summer even if Knepshield isn't going to be there. If everything goes as I have planned, I'll be at Slippery Rock next year. I mailed my application two weeks ago. I didn't tell anyone. Not Nancy. Not mother. Not anybody. I skip dinner.

I've been home from camp three days. I wrote to Mother every week and each time told her of my plans to leave Wesleyan and go to Slippery Rock. Now as I lie here trying to get some sleep before I leave tomorrow she's ranting like a mad woman. I have to go to Slippery Rock to find out why I have not heard from them. Miss Knepshield has offered to take me there from her home, which is just about sixty miles from the college. We haven't seen each other all summer. She said in her last letter that she's made major changes since her Mother died but she didn't say what they were. She said she'd tell me when we see each other. That's tomorrow.

Mother is suddenly standing over me screaming, "You will go back to Wesleyan."

I leap out of bed and look into her piercing black eyes. They're like bullets. She stands like a witch ready to pounce on her prey. I stand right next to her. "I'm NOT going back to Wesleyan."

"Yes you will. If I'm paying the bills, I'll damn well tell you where you're going. Who ever heard of this Slippery Rock? You just want to get away from your sister's good influence. I won't pay."

"Pay, you don't pay anything. It's our money. Deh Deh left it for us."

I already have my bus ticket. Slippery Rock is one of the best schools for physical education majors in the country. I'm going to school there. At least I will go there and beg them to accept me. They have to. I want to go. I should take my suitcase and leave now. Never come back. I lie back down and hope she will go away. At least shut up.

"No. I get the money and write checks for you and Nancy. I'll be damned if I write another one for you."

She hasn't sent me a red cent since I started college two years ago. She sends bank checks for tuition; room and board to Nancy and Miss Goody two shoes pays our bills. Mother says it's because Nancy works in the Dean's office and knows how. Bullshit. I hate them both. I roll over so I can't see her. She paces back and forth. Her heels hit the wooden floor like a jackhammer. I can't stand it. I jump up once more and stand in her way. "Mother, go to bed. You can't stop me, I have my ticket and I'm going."

"I'm forbidding you to go. I'll lock you in tomorrow morning. You'll see who is boss in this house."

I almost burst out laughing. I swallow the laugh. Lock me in where? I sit on the bed and hide my head in my hands. While I know she's more bark than bite, I peep every now and then to see what she's doing. She stops and stares at me as if to make me go away by her glare. Granny's probably praying that she'll get tired and go to bed. Nancy doesn't give a damn and is no doubt sound asleep. It must be nice to be able to block everything unpleasant like sister Nancy does.

"I know you think you can stop me. Not this time. I've made a decision. You have nothing to do with it. Why don't you shut up and go to bed. Think of your precious Nancy, she has to go to work tomorrow."

"At least she's respectful. You aren't."

"Respectful? Respectful to you: Why should I be? You don't know what respect is."

She hasn't talked with me about anything for years. Not one word about my father. Not one word about who she goes out with or who sends her the gifts that come now and then. Her life is her life and private to her. And we are not to ask questions. She doesn't even ask about my studies. She couldn't care less. Doesn't know my major or that I played varsity hockey. Just do as she says. Well, this time I will not. It's too late for her to rule. I'm through with her rules and ideas.

"Shut your God Damn mouth. You think you are so high and mighty."

I sit up and say in a very quiet voice, "Mother, I **AM** going to Slippery Rock tomorrow. You can't stop me. So, please, just be quiet and go to bed."

She stops pacing, looks down at me with a smirk on her face. She clenches her fists and starts to sit on the end of my bed but changes her mind. She leans down to say, "There you go with that sweet pleading. You lower your voice and act so pious. Is that what your high and mighty teacher, KNEPSHIELD taught you? Well, it won't get you anywhere with me. So cut the crap. You will not be able to go tomorrow."

I leap to my feet with my arms in the air. I go to the wall and pound my fists. I hear her leave the room. I look at the clock. My God, it's two o'clock in the morning.

I'm wide-awake at five in the morning. Three hours of sleep and I'm ready to go. I get up, tip toe through Mother's room to the bathroom. I really don't care if running my bath water wakes her. I just don't want a repeat of last night. It was the longest time period she's ever ranted. I bath, dress and go to the kitchen to eat some cereal. I think she's still asleep. And so are Nancy and Granny. It is very quiet and peaceful. I hear Granny getting up as I pour milk. She comes in the kitchen shaking her head. "Your Mother sure carried on last night. Are you going away today?"

"I sure am, Granny. She doesn't give a damn what I do. She was just mouthing off last night she was trying to scare me. She can't hurt me anymore." I turn to see Mother standing in the doorway. I say good morning and take my bowl of cereal to the table.

"What time does your bus leave? I'll call a cab."

"Don't bother. I'm walking and I have plenty of time." She turns and goes back to the bedroom I guess. I don't even care. I finish breakfast, wash my dish and tell Granny goodbye. I'll sleep on the bus. It's a long ride.

This bus ride is great. I sit up high and can see everything. I'm shocked at how fast the bus goes on these West Virginia roads. We're in Charleston in less than two hours. I know that's fast because Mother brought Nancy and me to Charleston when I was about ten and it took forever, maybe three hours. Today we'll be in Wheeling in another two hours and that's where Miss Knepshield will meet me. Then she and I will drive to Slippery Rock. We'll get there by one or one thirty in the afternoon. I hope the registrar is in his office. I should have made an appointment. I talked with his secretary last week and she promised to look for my application and get back to me. She didn't and I can't wait. So he better be able to see me. WOW here we are in Wheeling and I see Knepshield waiting for me. She looks great. She's wearing that blue pants suit that I love. She stands tall and looks relaxed. I grab my suitcase and rush off the bus.

As we drive through Pittsburgh, I tell her all about camp and how she missed the best Indian pageant the camp had ever seen. I did it all. I wrote the play, cut the brush by the river so everyone could see the campers. They were in

Indian costumes and paddled canoes down the river for a peace talk and smoked their peace pipes. It was wonderful with torches in each canoe and some along the riverbank. She just nods her head and agrees that she would have loved it. But right now the traffic is demanding her full attention. She still points out landmarks to me like the Cathedral of Learning, the University of Pittsburgh, and the Three rivers stadium where the Pirates baseball team plays. She promises to take me there if I'm accepted.

This campus is as beautiful now as it was when we were here last spring to install a Delta Psi Kappa Chapter. It's an honorary physical education fraternity for women. Knepshield is a national officer. The old buildings are mostly brick with ivy growing all the way to the roof. We find the administration building and I stand there looking at it for a few minutes. It has a round section with a top hat; a square spire with a clock and the rest of the building is rectangular. It's a very old building. I like it. I walk in and look for the Office of Admissions. Before I find it, a woman comes from the President's office and asks if she can help us. She directs us to the admissions office and I'm on my way. Knepshield winks at me and says she will be outside.

The registrar is away. Several people sitting at desks talk to each other about what to do. Finally one of them says, "Come in and I'll see if the Associate Registrar will see you. What's your name?" I tell her again. No one seems to be interested that I have come a long way because they lost my application. They turn back to their work without another word. I shift from one foot to the other, turn to look down the hall and back to the door of the Associate's office.

"Come in Miss Walton. I understand you have had a long trip. Let's see what we can do for you." At last a kind voice. He sounds encouraging. We walk into his office and I sit in front of his desk and he pulls a chair from behind the desk to sit with me. No barrier between us.

He explains that the school is debating whether to admit out-of-state students. They have so many from

Pennsylvania that there may not be space available. My heart sinks. But he continues "But no decision has been made. Tell me why you want to came to Slippery Rock."

I go on and on about the reputation, my impression when I was here last spring and that "I want to be the best physical education teacher I can be and this is where I believe I'll get the best education."

"That's a pretty good reason for us to admit you. I'll get the papers you need to complete and return to us before the end of next week. How's that sound?"

I am dancing inside. I jump up and say, 'Oh, Thank you so much." That was much easier than I thought it would be. He tells me I will be the last out-of-state student accepted this year.

"I'm sorry your application papers were misplaced and you had the long trip but welcome." He hands me the large packet of paper. I shake his hand and go skipping down the hall. I find Knepshield sitting on the steps right outside. I grab her arm and jump up and down. "I'm in! I'm coming here to school. I can't believe they accepted me."

"Why not? You're a good student. They certainly knew you were serious to come all the way here to find out."

"I'll miss everyone at Wesleyan, especially you." I slow down. Look at the campus. See myself running from building to building to be on time for class.

"Yes, and I'll miss you too but we'll see each other. Remember I wrote you about some major changes. Well, I'm not going back to Wesleyan either."

"What? Why?" I stop and turn to face her. I wonder if it's because of the conference stuff.

"Someone has to be home with Daddy and John. I'm the one without family and I got my old job back at the high school. So, I'll be closer to you than if I'd stayed in Buckhannon."

"I can't believe this. Why not take your Father to Buckhannon and let your brother stay at home. He can take care of himself. And he has another sister close by." I'd be

90

mad. Give up a college teaching job to come back to a high school. Not me. Not for my family.

"It's settled. Let's not talk about it. Let's go to Vi and Clair's tonight."

"Are they expecting us?" This news about her move has changed my mood a bit. I walk slowly to the car. I turn and look at her. I stand in her path but she just walks around me.

"My sister's always glad to see me and they both love you."

"They only met me once. How can they love me?"

"We all do."

She smiles and winks at me as we get in the car. My heart skips a beat. I know her sister doesn't have a big house. Where will I sleep? Knepshield has told me about their house being right next to where she grew up. It must be old. But she says they've remodeled. Well, I'll see. Maybe I'll have to sleep with her. She's not my teacher any more. Sleep with her in the same bed? She reaches over and takes my hand. What is she doing? She kisses it. "Congratulations." She says it is the best thing I could do for myself if I really want to major in Physical Education. I guess we aren't going to talk about her leaving Wesleyan; at least not now.

Her sister's very happy to see us. She's excited and eager to hear all about our visit to Slippery Rock. I don't say much. They, mostly Charlotte, talk a mile a minute all about how impressive I was and how all the administrators liked me and how they all knew I'd be accepted. I take a look around this old house. It's been remodeled and is bright and shiny. The kitchen has new appliances and new linoleum with a booth in one corner covered in red vinyl. A very big refrigerator sits almost in the middle of the room. The other porch has a swing and two rocking chairs.

We go out to dinner and I offer to pay for mine but they won't let me. Clair flashes his big roll of money and tells me there's more where that came from. Big deal. So he's rich. But they decide we'll have dessert at home. Soon after, I announce that I'm tired so am going to bed. I climb the stairs slowly to listen to their conversation. Knepshield is telling them about what a good student I am. I'm not. I never study. How much she thinks of me and how terrible my family is to me. That's for sure but she doesn't know the half of it. I don't think that's any of their business but I don't go back downstairs to say so. I could really give them a story. I know she'll say what she thinks anyway.

This is a very comfortable bed. But I can't sleep. I read. Not a good book. When is she coming to bed? Is she waiting for me to be asleep? Maybe she's sleeping downstairs. That's not what she said. I heard Clair go to bed an hour ago. I hear Vi coming up the stairs now. I turn the light out and turn away from the door. I hear the door open. Vi calls back down, "She's asleep." My heart speeds up. Fat chance I'm asleep. Where is she? All is quiet. I turn over turn the light back on and read.

I wake up when she takes the book out of my hands, as she gets in bed beside me. I turn toward her and say goodnight. She slips her hand under my shoulder and says she thinks she deserves a hug for today. Well, so do I. We hug tightly and she kisses me. Oh my God. She mumbles something about shouldn't. My body is warm. She's so soft. She has on pajamas. I forgot mine. I never even thought about it. I ask her why she's wearing them. She says, "I always do but it's OK that you aren't wearing any. Will you think I'm terrible if I touch you?"

What is she talking about? "You talk too much." We kiss.

I'm not sure what to do so I wait for her to make a bigger move. Her hands are like magic. WOW My body has never moved like this to anyone's touch. She keeps mumbling "shouldn't."

What is wrong with her? It's like every nerve goes crazy at once. My body arches and I moan. She tells me to be still. I can't. She puts her hand over my mouth and I kiss it, suck on it. Never let me go. Do it again. Do it again. I like big O's. I want more.

I try to touch her leg and she says, "No, not tonight. I'm sorry I'm not a man."

92

"What? Why? What is wrong with you? I don't want a man." I know that now for sure.

She turns away from me and mutters, "Goodnight." We fall asleep close and cuddly. I guess I'll call her Charlotte.

Slippery Rock is very different from West Virginia Wesleyan. There are more physical education majors than any other major. I'm not in a class as a junior or sophomore but I take classes with both. Most of my credits from Wesleyan count toward my degree except all that Bible and Religion I had to take. It may take me longer to finish the degree because of the added credits. And so far classes are much tougher. I've even had to study. I did very little of that at Wesleyan. But Chemistry of Nutrition is very difficult. I like it so the studying isn't bad.

I made new friends and am thinking about going out for the hockey team they are trying to organize. I won't play goalie here. I've watched some of the women play and they don't wear shin guards or mind hitting each other with a stick. I'll watch a bit longer before I decide. Tonight I'm going to a bar with a new friend: Beverly.

She and I walk into this very dark, smelly bar. I've not been to very many bars and this is my first since coming to Slippery Rock. It has a very distinct odor of beer and smoke. Uck. A few men sit at the bar all with beer mugs in front of them. Only one turns his head as we go to the back room where the pool tables are. This bar is in Grove City, about seven miles from the Rock. Beverly drove and we are meeting her friends who, she says, come here all the time to play pool. I told her I didn't know how to play very well but she said that's OK. She'd teach me to play and drink beer. I hate the taste. As we find the seats by the pool tables she asks what kind of beer I want.

"But I don't like the taste of beer. Get me a coke."

"If you are going to go places with an Italian, you must learn to drink beer and wine. Would you rather have wine?"

"No, it costs too much."

93

"Then I'll fix the beer so you'll like it. OK?"

I look around and wonder if this is how most bars look, dingy and old? Posters hang on the wall of people in different walks of life drinking every kind of beer made. They've been here a long time and are yellowed by age and smoke.

Beverly brings a pitcher of beer, a glass of red wine, and two mugs to the table. I keep looking around like I expect my sister from West Virginia to suddenly walk in. I'm not a drinker. I drank some beer a couple of times with Pat but I didn't like it so I stopped. And besides, all I remember is that I got very sleepy, but we had good sex. I'm not going to do that, get sleepy or have good sex, with Beverly, at least not tonight.

"Here try this."

"U m m. What's this? It doesn't taste like any beer I've ever had."

"My secret, so now drink up while I take my turn at the pool table. I'm going to beat your ass. How about a small bet, fifty cents?"

"I don't know much about pool, but I'll probably take your money, so you're on. Odds and evens, right."

She steps up to the table and breaks the balls like she knows how. She's cute. Her blue eyes are inviting. I must be attracted to blue eyes. She can win at pool and my heart too. I should be so lucky. Maybe I'll change the bet. She sinks the one and three with little effort. She watches my reaction each time a ball drops. She has the cutest smile. I could just pinch those dimples and kiss those lips. She misses the five ball and now I get to show her. I look around again before getting up. I step up to the table and sink the two, four and six without a look her way. I start to brag a bit, when she steps behind me and hugs me and says "That's enough, now you're going to miss. I'll stand this close to make sure."

"Not fair."

She wins the first game and challenges me to a second. I'm feeling the effect of my second doctored beer and don't care about playing but if that's what she wants to do, OK by me. She'll never collect the money; she'll have to take it out in trade. I don't tell her that. I look around to see if my sister or those friends of hers have arrived. I see no one. "Say where're your friends we're going to meet? Do they play as well as you do? "

"I guess they aren't coming."

There's no one else in this section of the little bar. Several men are still around the front bar but they can't see us and I doubt if they even want to since their heads didn't turn when we walked by. Beverly told me that only college students come here during the week, except for a few locals who never bother anyone. It's on Route 8 between Slippery Rock and Grove City and not an eye catcher. She obviously knows the place. The bartender brings another pitcher of beer without any apparent signal. Does she have a standing order with him? Is this where she brings all her friends? I came along to play pool with Mary and Fran. I know them but not well. Mary lives off campus and I think Fran stays with her sometimes.

I win the second game, which means that we definitely have to play the third for a championship. The game begins and Mary and Fran walk in. Mary quickly says, "I get the winner."

"Oh no you don't, she's mine.'

"That right, Rose?"

"If it's pool you are talking about, this is our third game and it's one all. Maybe let the winner choose the next opponent."

"Hey, Bev, you've met your match and I haven't seen her play pool."

Bev wins and she chooses Fran. A quick two games with Bev the winner again.

Fran declares Bev the champion and says, "Now take Rose back to the dorm before you get her into more trouble."

I tell my roommates that I'm going away for the weekend. A friend is coming to visit and we'll stay with some of her friends near Pittsburgh. If anyone calls just tell them I'm out. They want to know who and where and why.

I tell them nothing. It's none of their business. I don't like them anyway, so this will just help me stay away from them even when I'm here. They're very religious and think God will help them through the tests and so they read the Bible instead of the texts for class.

I pretend to be studying as I sit on the steps of the dorm. But I'm watching for Charlotte. I really love her. I missed her in camp last summer and haven't seen her since we came to Slippery Rock in August. I want more love making this trip. She seems hesitant. Maybe it's not real for her. There's sure a lot of talk about being a lesbian here at Slippery Rock. I heard the other day that a senior was told to leave. Made me think of Dean Schoolcraft and Wesleyan. It almost happened to me.

Charlotte is fun and always doing things. Going to see the parks, hiking, and she knows everything about trees and plants and animals. Always showing me something I missed. And I love how she watches birds and knows their songs.

I haven't seen her for almost four months and I'm jumping out of my skin. It feels all prickly when I think about her. I write to her almost every day and she answers about once a week and she calls now and then. But she's very busy and I understand. She moved back home last summer. I feel sorry for her about her family. One sister who lives just eight miles away can't promise to take her father shopping once a week. But maybe Charlotte wanted to leave Wesleyan anyway. She doesn't talk about it.

I'll try to get it all out of her this weekend. She keeps everything inside. I see her car. I act like I'm reading. She stops in the drive right in front of me and opens the car door quickly to get out.

"It's you." I jump up bound down the steps and hug her. She doesn't hug me back. What the devil? I grab my suitcase, throw it in the back seat, and get in. "Let's get out of here."

"Where do you want to go?"

"I don't care." I reach for her hand and she puts it on the steering wheel.

96

"What's wrong with you? Did you come to see me or what? Don't you love me anymore?"

"We shouldn't love each other that way.'

"What way?"

"You know. Now let's just enjoy the weekend. We'll drive north and see the countryside. I know a place not far from here where the ducks walk on the fish's backs."

"Sure you do."

We drive along without a word. I can't keep my hands off her but she keeps moving her hand away when I take hold of it. I slide as far from her as I can and ask if that's what she wants. She says nothing. I don't want to listen to music or radio talk. Damn! Why won't she talk to me? What is wrong? Maybe she's sorry about going home. Her father can't be easy to be with. He has the beginnings of memory loss. And I think he's mean. I look out the window. It's a beautiful countryside. Northwestern Pennsylvania is very rural here and the trees are mostly pine and birch. But I'm not on a zoology trip.

"Shit, Charlotte, why'd you come?"

"I want to see you. I need to get away from Daddy and John. Can't we enjoy a weekend without the other stuff?"

"Listen, you started the other stuff, as you call it, at your sister's. I thought it was love. Am I wrong? Do you just turn it on and off as you feel like it? Well, I can't. So you better start dealing with it."

She stops at a place off the road where many cars are parked. She says, "Come on, let's feed the fish and the ducks. Grab that loaf of bread behind your seat." It's like the conversation is over and on to the next activity. Not that easy for me.

I walk over to a fence where you can see the ducks walking on the fish just like she said. Both fish and ducks are fighting for the bread. I laugh and turn toward the car. I feel like a prisoner who is out but not allowed to be free. We are quiet when we get back into the car.

Very soon she pulls into a motel and tells me to wait in the car. Says she knows the owners. I don't believe it. How?

We're in the middle of nowhere. But she must. A woman is coming with her to the car. She introduces me as her young friend who's at Slippery Rock. She tells me to drive the car to number 6. It's the big red cabin in the back. I walk into the room. It's big and has two double beds. Why the hell do we need two double beds? I don't want to ruin the weekend but I might as well be back in the dorm. My chances for lovemaking would be better. Bev's been hinting and she's cute. I'm not giving up on Charlotte yet. I take the suitcases in and put them on the extra bed.

"I didn't believe you about the ducks. They really walked on those fish's backs to get to the bread. They were adorable. How'd you know?" I brush my teeth and am ready to see what happens with the bed situation. "Boy, I'm tired."

I pull the covers down and crawl in. The other bed is piled up with more than suitcases: my books, her magazines, food and junk. What's she going to do? I've tried not to give her a choice. She slides in beside me and says she'll stay a minute. Fat chance. I grab her and tell her if she goes to the other bed I'll go too. I hold her tight. My hand slides between her legs when she relaxes just enough, so I keep kissing her and get my hand just where I want it. She pulls me closer and gives that last sound before the big collapse. I turn onto my back and smile. She begins to say we should not. "Give it up Charlotte, you're stuck with me."

As she touches me, the throbs are strong and I want to be here forever. I put my hand over her mouth so she can't apologize.

The lounge on the first floor of North Hall at Slippery Rock is always crowded when we have a test the next day. The chairs and couches are moved in different patterns so we can study in groups. I like to study with this group but I'm hungry. I hope we start soon. Tonight we are studying for an anatomy final. Dr. Hess gives weird exams. Tomorrow he will put tiny numbers on many bones, which he will place on the lab tables. He will then let us, four at a time, into the lab, like trained animals, to go to our assigned table, find the numbers, name the bone, describe its place in the body, and tell what it's connected to and something about function. The test will be a timed exam and he will count down the seconds as we look for his tiny numbers. I think it's a crazy way to see if I know the bones, where they fit and what they do. Will I ever need this knowledge to teach a class in PE? I doubt it. But I've learned a lot about testing students.

I sit in a chair in the corner and hope no one comes near me before Beverly arrives. I won't ask her to sit by me, but if there's space available maybe she will. I look around trying to decide who's going to lead this session. Probably Patty or Jane. They're the brightest or maybe just the bosses. I often wonder if taking the initiative now will produce better leaders or if personality is already shaped and leaders are born. And just then Patty begins with a plan and a sheet of questions we should go over. We begin to go around the room discussing each question and possible answers. It's getting late and I'm hungry.

Here comes Beverly. She's really cute, short, with a really pleasant smile and very distinct dimples. She used to spend every weekend with one of the seniors who is student teaching this semester but lately she's been going home. She asked me if I wanted to come with her next weekend. I haven't answered her yet because I really have to study. I'm not doing as well here as I did at Wesleyan. But I'll probably go anyway. She's really adorable. She's coming this way.

"Is this spot taken?" she asks, as she promptly sits down on the floor at my feet. My body reacts and I shift in the chair, pretending to make more room for her.

"No, make yourself comfy. Where have you been? We started studying at seven and it's already nine. You know me I'll. . ."

"Yes, Rosie, we all know you'll want something to eat soon."

I do want something to eat and to go to bed but I can't leave Bev with all these other women who also think she's cute and have already asked me if I know what's going on with her. I see Jane giving her the eye from across the room. Will she move? Can I stop her? I move my foot closer to Bev's behind, just nudge her a bit. It feels warm and she seems to ease over to cover my foot. Am I imagining this or is she acting interested? She did come over here to sit when there are lots of other spots closer to those she usually studies with. She turns her head to look at me and asks, "Are you comin home with me this weekend?"

"No whispering allowed, says Patty, we need to concentrate."

"Oh, don't get so excited, I just arrived," says Bev. "Where are . . . .?"

"On the rib cage, want me to show you where?" I lean over and stroke her right side. "That's the part we are talking about." It just got very warm in here. I wipe the perspiration from my forehead.

"Let's go to my room to study, I can't concentrate here."

"And I won't concentrate in your room; at least not on this anatomy test. I need a good grade on this test so I can stay here next semester. Remember, I didn't study much last semester, I was new and thought I could get by."

"Oh, OK. Let's get serious. I mean about the test and we'll check out our anatomy later."

"Promise", she moves closer so she is now between my feet keeping both of them warm and I wonder just what she has in mind. She must have broken up with Janet. I hope so.

Playing hockey at Slippery Rock is not like playing varsity at Wesleyan but I love the game and so I play. Today is a practice game with the Pittsburgh team. Some of the professors here play for Pittsburgh and they want to have a second team from Slippery Rock. I'd love to be on that team but probably won't make it. I'm trying out for full back.

I run forward and hit the ball back to the center. She dribbles it forward and I realize I'm out of position. I yell for the halfback to trade positions. I'm about five yards behind the right forward when she sends the ball toward the goal. The goalkeeper sends it back and I hit it as hard as I can back toward the goal. It was a reaction more than a planned hit.

I hear loud cheering behind me. Oh my God, I scored. They've never seen a backfield player score. That's what Knepshield taught us to do at Wesleyan.

It's late April and everything is in bloom. Flowers on campus are bright and the trees are full. I love spring. And Charlotte is coming to visit for the weekend. All is well except I must study. The second course in chemistry of nutrition has me baffled and so does the physiology class. But I'm happy she's coming and I will make some quiet time for me to study while she walks or goes shopping.

This summer, Charlotte and I are running a Girl Scout camp for two weeks in a park near her home. Then she and I are running a day camp of our own at the same park. It sounds like fun. And I will spend the summer at her home. She hands me the brochure. I look at every word. I like the colors. Charlotte is listed on the front as the director. I ask why I'm listed on the back with all the high school counselors and not on front with her. "Didn't you say we were co-directors?"

"Yes, but no one in Wellsburg knows you." She goes on about people will send their kids to a known quantity and she's been around for years.

I don't like it but the brochure is printed. And she did do all the work and has been the one to secure the place and she got me a job with the Girl Scout camp. And I will spend the summer with her. I say nothing more and grab my books to study. This motel room has an alcove off the bedroom just right for my study needs.

"You must have spent a lot of nights with a lot of women in Western Pennsylvania. You know all the good places to stay and to eat. Dinner was great."

"No, you're the first."

"Bullshit."

"Honest."

We make love and she still insists that I'm the only one. I'm ten feet tall but I just don't believe her.

I really have to study this year. My grades weren't so great last year and if I want to go to graduate school, I need to buckle down, but not tonight. It's some kind of race in the dorm. I missed it last year and everyone has been talking about it for a week.

"It's a tradition, Rosie. We do it every year. Can't you see that snotty freshman, thinks she'll win the race. She will but she'll really lose."

"I guess I just don't see any point. It's all a put on to embarrass Jo. She's just a freshman and has no way of knowing how this clique of wise-ass seniors will act. You can't expect her to be any other way."

The dorm is built in a square with a courtyard in the middle, so this hall is perfect for a race. We're lined up like spectators at a Roman circus, sending the Christian to the lions. This poor freshman thinks it's a real race; Once around the dorm hall against the best athlete in the senior class. If she wins she'll be held in high esteem the rest of her tenure here at The Rock. I was a new student last year, but a junior, and I'm glad I knew nothing about this race. I might have been stupid enough to try to be a runner, just to show these seniors that they are not the best. Even if I'm a senior, I'm not in their clique. Guess being an out of state student, who came late, makes me, an outsider. And I think that's just OK. But of course I'm joining in the fun.

The race is about to begin. Rachael is the starter and the judge. She begins with, "Do you both understand? You go down this hall turn left, go that hall, turn left, go that hall, and turn left to return to this spot. You must turn this last corner to win. Are you ready?"

The noise level is high. I'm always afraid the dorm Mother, "Gummy," will step into the hall from downstairs at any minute. We're always doing something on this floor so she's never surprised. She's the one who woke me when my roommates and friends moved me, mattress and all, into the hallway one night when I was sleeping. I didn't even wake up when they moved me. She wanted to know why I was sleeping in the hall. Maybe someone went down to talk with her tonight, just to keep her downstairs.

There they go. The senior, Patty, is way ahead all the way down the first hall. I hear the freshmen coaxing Janet on. She's really trying to get ahead. Rounding the third hall, Patty begins to slow down. Jo's beaming as she passes her easily. The freshmen are so excited. Little do they understand? There she goes past us on the last hallway, just about ready to make that fateful last turn. Patty has stopped running and is just walking fast enough to get there just as Jo gets the bucket of water in her face. Splash, splash, here comes the water. And I can hear her scream. She's not a happy camper and is ready to attack anyone who comes near. Funny how all of us disappear into rooms and leave her standing there with her other stunned freshmen friends.

I have checked all the campsites on this side of camp and walk out into a clearing expecting to meet Charlotte to decide who is going to take the seven year olds for a nature walk. She should, but wants me to do it today. I don't see her anywhere. But I hear her. She's calling the birds.

I walk around the camp road so I can see the other side of the building where we gather in the morning. There she stands. Red sweatshirt, baggy pants and one hand on the side of the building. She sucks on her hand and makes a sound like the red winged blackbirds. They swoop at her head and the campers go crazy. That is the nature walk for the day. The only difference is that all forty campers got a lesson, not just the five seven year olds. I look around as I walk up the hill and count my blessings. A camp I help run and make money for next year's books and spending money, and I spend the summer with Charlotte at her home just four miles from the park.

It's lunch time. I get to where everyone is gathered and ask, "Aren't we cooking lunch today?"

Everyone scatters to their campsites. We give them time to get the fires started and Charlotte heads one way and

I head the other. We will meet in the middle to compare notes about who made the best pancakes on number ten cans.

I put the last glass in the cupboard from my snack and their lunch. Charlotte has taken her father to visit her sister in town and I have the afternoon and the house all to myself. I have a very good book and can't wait to finish the last few pages and find another. She has lots of mysteries in her room. I'll just pick one.

I go to the living room. This couch is so comfortable. It's not like the one in my living room at home where I hope I never have to spend much time again. I want to live with Charlotte the rest of my life. The windows were just washed last week and are sparkling. I like the wooden floors. They also shine. Her Mother must have planned it this way a long time ago. I wish I'd known her: everybody talks about how wonderful she was. Charlotte must be like her. She's wonderful too.

I finish my book and am very tired; I didn't get much sleep last night. It was beautiful. I go upstairs to our bedroom and stretch out on the bed. Her scent lingers in the room. It's warm and cozy. I look out the front window, through the treetops and watch the clouds roll by. Half asleep, *I'm in her arms. They surround me in smooth silk. I turn toward her and our lips meet.*

She should have taken her Father and left him. I'd like for her to come back so we are here alone. Someday we'll have our own home; just one more semester at Slippery Rock. Then I can move anywhere and be with her. I could find a teaching job near here.

I fall asleep and wake when I hear the car coming into the driveway. She's back. I go to the top of the stairs and there she stands with a beautiful bouquet of flowers.

I love these nights after a good day at camp and they happen often lately. After dinner we watch a little television with her father and then it's like magic. She says the same thing every time. "Well, Dad, the kid and I had a tough day, so we'll see you in the morning. If you need anything, just yell."

She stands and goes right upstairs. When she gets to the top of the stairs she calls down, "Rosie, I have big plans for you tomorrow. Better come to bed."

And I have big plans for you tonight. I say "Goodnight" to her Dad and turn to go upstairs. He wants a drink of water. I go to the kitchen, get him a class of water, take it to him, wait for the glass and take it back to the kitchen. I pick up a couple of pieces of chocolate candy and go upstairs.

"And what plans have you chosen for your little assistant for tomorrow? She might not want to do them."

"Come to bed and I'll convince you."

This is my last semester. A dream fulfilled. Sometimes I wasn't sure about graduation but it's almost here and I'm job hunting. It is for real. This semester has been the best of all. I played full back on Pittsburgh's second string. Maybe I'll get a job in a school that has a hockey team and I can coach. I have so many options and decisions and I'll have fun no matter what. I want my students to enjoy physical education and if the rules spoil that then we'll just have to change those rules.

Student teaching has shown me two very different examples of teaching. One supervising teacher let students decide how to arrange class and almost every other decision. I had trouble with this because I'm sure I'll be the boss in my class. But the other teacher set strict boundaries and rules for the classes to follow. I will listen to students but I know I'll make decisions and set boundaries.

I'll show all those people in Oak Hill who thought only Nancy would ever make it through college. My stubborn streak and their negative attitudes helped me make it and I never thought it was difficult. If I can do it I think anybody can. I know in my mind that that's not really true. I'll try to teach my students to study, work hard and be determined no matter what messages they receive from family.

I'm home for Christmas break and working in the local Woolworths to have enough money to go for interviews and to get to wherever I go to teach. I'm working as a cashier today and see one of the County school officials shopping. Maybe he'll come through my line and I can ask him about a job.

He sees me and waves. I nod recognition. He is coming to my line. "Hi Rose Ann, I hear that you have graduated. How about coming home to teach?"

"I have to go back to hand in my final reports and then graduation. But yes, I've earned a bachelor-of-science degree. Are you serious about a job?"

"Of course I am. We all know you Walton girls and I know you'll be a very good teacher. You went to a very good physical education school. I'll even offer you a higher salary than other new teachers; how about twenty six hundred?"

"Is that for the rest of the year?"

"No! That's a yearly salary. I doubt you will get better than that in any school."

"Well, one school in Pennsylvania has offered me forty eight hundred. They don't know me at all."

"That's surprising. But you should really think about all the advantages of teaching here at home. I'll call you next week and we'll talk about it."

"Thanks. Merry Christmas."

He might think there are advantages to teaching at home. I don't. I can't imagine living in the same town with my mother and certainly not in the same house. She and I haven't gotten along since I was ten.

The job in Guys Mills, Pennsylvania is going to be just fine. They offered me everything I could imagine when I was there for the interview; new equipment, small classes, student assistants if I want them. It's a very small town and not much there. Two churches, a general store, and a post office. That's OK with me since it's my first teaching position and I'll have lots of preparation to do. I'm teaching physical education for girls in grades seven to twelve and health for all students in seventh and tenth grades. The town is only ten miles from a bigger town but I'll have no means

106

of transportation. Surely some of the other teachers go there to see a movie now and then. I'll make friends.

On my first day in Guys Mills it's cold and snowing. I thank Norma for the ride and get out of the car. As she pulls forward I feel my heart start to beat faster. I walk up the eight steps to the junior-senior high school.

What the hell am I doing here? I'm in the middle of nowhere, ten miles from the closest town, which is no bigger than Oak Hill and I have no car and no bike. I couldn't ride a bike if I had one. I thought when I finished college; I'd go to Florida like I always said I would. But Charlotte can't leave her father or brother. So here I am beginning a teaching career in a school that has 13 girls in its senior class and maybe 20 boys. There are only three hundred in both junior and senior high school. They promised no discipline problems and a salary of four thousand eight hundred dollars.

I pass a couple of students as I enter the building. I hear them say something about the new PE teacher as I go up the steps. If they could hear my heart and know that butterflies are playing ping-pong with the mint I just swallowed, they'd say something else. I go down stairs to my closet sized office and then back upstairs to the Library where I am scheduled to keep the first study hall of the day. I think study halls should be abolished. No one ever studies and, in my experience; the teacher in charge is usually begging kids to be quiet. I will let them know immediately that there is to be no talking and that I expect them to study or at least read during this hour.

Every seat is filled with a talking student. They get quieter as I enter, but not as quiet as I expect them to be. I pick up the class roll and wait. Several students say "Shhhhhhhhh" The room is filled with tables with eight chairs around each one. Not conducive to study, especially for the students who sit looking at each other just across the table. I'd rather have them in desks.

107

I smile at them. This seems to be a cue for others to talk louder. I frown. They stop. Then I hear: "Hey teach, I'm going to the gym."

I wheel around to see a young man, at least six feet tall standing by his chair at the table by the door I just came through. I look as stern as possible. He could wipe me out with one fling of an arm. Who the hell does he think he is? Nice looking, clean cut, nicely dressed. OH, he has a basketball in one hand and is holding the back of his chair with the other. He stands poised to play. I think to myself, I'll take you on for a one on one on the court, but not now.

"In the first place, my name is not 'Hey teach' and you **may not tell me** where you are going. **Sit down!** Keep that basketball still and your **mouth shut**."

My heart is really pounding now. But wait, the room is very still. OK! Way to go, Rosie. Miss Walton, YOU ARE IN CHARGE. TAKE OVER NOW.

I check the roll and give them my "This is what I expect speech." All goes well and they're very quiet. The basketball player has not opened his mouth or moved. And before I know it, the bell rings and I've made it through my first hour of my first teaching job. Yippee. As soon as all the students have left the room, I pull out my map of the building and find that my classroom for my first seventh grade health class is just across the hall. As I enter the room, all talking stops and heads turn front and center. Does word travel that fast? I say "Good Morning" and check the roll and make a seating chart so I can get to know their names. I'm really bad at remembering names.

I sit on the front of the desk and ask, "What do you want to learn in this class?" I wait a couple of minutes and no one says a word. "You know this is your class and I give you permission to tell me what you want to learn during the rest of the year. So please, let's hear your thoughts."

They all shift in their seats and most are looking down at their desks. How can I get them to talk to me? I don't want to make suggestions because I think they'll just agree. I see one boy's hand creep up. I check my seating chart. "Yes, Daniel, what would you like to learn?"

"I don't know but no teacher ever asked me that. Don't you know what to teach us?" The class giggles. I smile.

"Daniel, I can just go through your textbook, decide what I think you should learn and we could have a very dull class if you aren't interested in what I teach. That's why I want you to be a part of our plan for the semester. Of course I'll throw in a few things I think you must learn. Please, tell me your wishes for health class." Again I wait. Then I hear a quiet voice whisper, "What causes colds?"

"Thank you, Amy, that's a good question." I coax some more and they begin to respond.

"How do we get other things that make us sick? Weather. How can I keep from getting sick or hurt? What should we eat?"

I am very pleased. "Thank you very much. If you have any other ideas you can write them on a piece of paper and bring them to class tomorrow." The bell rings and they rush out the door talking. I'd like to listen. I'm sure they are talking about other topics. I bounce down the steps to my office and remember that there is a break for teachers and students. It seems strange, but now all students go to the gym, completely unsupervised, to dance, talk, or whatever, and faculty go to the Home Ec. room and eat whatever the kids made in first two periods. When the principal told me about this, I laughed and said "SURE THEY DO." He assured me that during his ten years as principal there had never been an incident.

I walk out of my office and see other teachers going toward a room just down the hall. This is a very unusual building. The gymnasium is in the center of the building with classrooms against the outside wall separated from the gym by a wide hallway. I can't imagine teaching in a room across the hall from the gym, but that's the way the building is laid out. The second floor has windows around the gym and a wide hallway with classrooms around the outside wall. Does that mean I have to keep gym classes quiet? I won't. I'll go meet the faculty and ask what they do about noise from the gym.

As I walk in the room, Mr. Jones, the principal walks over, puts his arm around my shoulder and says, "I hear you're giving my son a hard time."

I swallow, take a deep breath, and say a quick prayer that my career isn't over so soon. "I don't believe I know your son. But if I gave him a hard time, he probably deserved it." I quickly try to remember having a direct interaction with any student in the last two hours. Oh, the basketball player. But he didn't even argue with me. His dad is as tall as he is. I feel him towering over me.

He leans down. "I knew I liked you when we met. Congratulations, you're probably the first teacher in his 12 years that has ever reprimanded him."

I smile and suggest that maybe ignorance is bliss. As I walk toward the table where I see chocolate cupcakes, Mr. Henry, the basketball coach, says, "Welcome. I guess we'll have to talk about our basketball team. You are coaching the cheerleaders aren't you?"

I met him when I was here last month. He's short and stocky. Not my image of a basketball coach. But I'm not so tall and I play. I was always better than Nancy even if she was taller. He seemed very friendly and Mr. Jones told me that the team might go to the state tournament this year. "I know nothing about cheerleading or about coaching them. I'd be better helping you coach basketball."

He ignores my suggestion of helping him. "You don't need to know anything. You just chaperone them. They're really no trouble and you'll want to see all the games anyway. We have a great team."

"So I've heard. We'll see. I have to get settled into teaching first." I walk over to the food table and take the last cup cake. I meet, Mrs. Shields, the Home Ec. Teacher and thank her for the snack. She's still in her apron with ruffles. Probably been teaching right here for twenty years.

"The kids love making things for teachers." She introduces me to two other teachers. Mr. Perry teaches math and Mr. Lyons teaches History. I hope I remember their names. One with horn rimmed glasses and the other very young with a beard. Math-glasses! History-beard! They all seem friendly and everybody smiled at me even if we didn't meet today.

I listen to this book on tape to shut out the noise of the house, but know I must put it away and get some sleep. Classes start early. At the end of a chapter, I turn it off and ponder. This is the most wonderful teaching position I could ever imagine. It is a wonderful experience for a beginning teacher. Kids, parents, colleagues, administrators are all great. I have fun teaching. But I can't live this way. Room and board with a very dysfunctional family: The McFadden's: father, mother and two adult children. The father is alcoholic and does not work outside the home. He does farm a little and keeps chickens and three pigs in the back yard. Mother is the primary caretaker for her youngest daughter, a thirty two year old, profoundly retarded child. Everything she does is like a two year old, not yet toilet trained. She is in bed all the time. She cries like a baby and calls out sounds that don't make sense. It's difficult for me to understand how a family could live like this for so many years.

The oldest daughter, Norma, is the breadwinner for the family, still lives at home, and works as secretary for the school district. I ride to school with her. I did not meet the rest of the family when I was here for an interview but Norma told me then that it was the only available room in town. After arriving I looked around and found nothing else. My room is upstairs in the house and has cracks that allow the wind to whistle through and the rain and snow to blow in. I go only to school functions and they are pretty boring; except for the basketball games. We might win the state class III championship. I like riding on the bus to away games with the team and the cheerleaders. I'd still rather coach basketball.

I lay the earphones on the floor and turn over to sleep. I hear someone coming up the squeaky steps. Who can it be? I thought everyone else went to bed a long time ago. They usually all beat me to bed. I turn back over just in time to see ole Mr. McFadden walking toward my bed. I grab the covers and tighten them around me.

"What the hell do you want? Get out of my room."

"Now, honey, don't be like 'at. I just wanna tuck ya in."

"I said get the hell out of this room, NOW. I'll push you down the God Damn stairs if you come one step closer." I can smell his breath and he is only half way across the room. He's disgusting. I make a move to get out of bed and he falls to the floor with his head about a foot from my bed. I scream for Norma, whom I know is asleep in the next room. I hear her stir. I scream again, "NORMA, I NEED YOU."

When she sees what has happened, she starts to apologize. She gets him up and all but throws him down the steps. She turns to me and assures me he won't be back.

The alarm clock buzzes in my ear. I am so laden down with blanket weight that it takes a while to get to it. Why am I here? Why did I take this job? The temperature is probably minus ten degrees and the wind is whistling through this room like a train going somewhere in a hurry. I put my feet, wrapped in wooly socks, on the floor and gather my robe around me. Could I go to school without a shower today? I must go downstairs, out the kitchen door to the bathroom, which is really outside, but the passage has a roof over it to keep the snow off the dirt path. After my encounter last night, I don't want to see any of the family, especially the ole man.

"Rose Ann, get downstairs and take your bath. I know it's cold but you must"

"But Granny, the steps have ice on them. I might fall."

I go quickly downstairs. Mrs. McFadden is cooking breakfast and the ole man is just sitting there. I nod to her as I go through the kitchen and run to the bathroom. I know he probably doesn't even remember what he did last night. The bathroom's warm from their earlier visits. I quickly shower, brush my teeth and go back upstairs to dress.

112

Norma walks through my bedroom, says Good Morning and apologizes for last night as she goes. I grunt. I hear her sister, Lucy make sounds as Norma passes her bedroom. I can't imagine living with her all these years and caring for her as though she's a two year old. Thirty-two years in the "terrible twos" stage. She should be in an institution where she can be cared for and maybe trained to eat. She cries like an infant, throws her food at her Mother or whoever is feeding her. I never volunteer. I have been here three months now and I would give half my salary to find an apartment. They don't exist in Guys Mills, Pennsylvania. This will be my last semester no matter how satisfying the teaching is.

Breakfast is great: biscuits, hot gravy, eggs and bacon. I leave off the gravy and take a second helping of bacon. So much for diet. I'll skip lunch. I hear a funny horn outside and turn to see three kids on a tractor. They have come to take Norma and me to school. The snow is so deep that cars can't get through but school is not closed. They say it's the warmest place for the children.

I put on my coat, scarf, and gloves, throw my briefcase over my shoulder and grab onto the tractor. And it's the 24th of April. I cannot live here next year! I will resign today.

I left Guys Mills at the end of that semester and went to a school in Canonsburg, Pennsylvania. It is only about thirty minutes from Charlotte's home. I'll probably spend most weekends there. She only came to Guys Mills once last semester, so I'm not sure of anything with her.

This is a brand new high school built to join two rival school districts. I thought that would be a challenge for students. After teaching for a few weeks, I know that the real challenge comes from joining two faculties when each knew better than the other how to run a school. I'm glad to be from another planet.

We have a faculty meeting every week. It's a time for the principal to let the faculty know how important he is. This is one of the most boring faculty meetings I have ever attended. The principal is explaining how he's here despite his terrible headache as he hits his forehead with his own hand. If he didn't have a headache he does now. What a man. Like a little Napoleon and so many other short men I've known. He has to be the center of attention and in charge. So what's this big issue we're here to discuss? About this terrible girl who got pregnant and now that she has had the child, she wants to come back to school. Oh my, a girl who understands that she must have at least a high school education if she is to provide for her child. I see no discussion. Let her come back to school.

I don't believe it. Miss Sheets, the business education teacher, is on her feet facing the faculty and saying, "We must not allow this girl to return. My students will not do any work. They will want to watch this person who has had a child and listen to her tell them all about it. She will destroy the professional attitude I insist on in my classroom."

I look around. Several teachers are rolling their eyes but Mrs. Wharton and Mrs. Long are nodding their heads in agreement. Why don't other teachers say something? No one ever disagrees with Miss Sheets except behind her back. She's so old and has taught in this district for thirty years. She ought to retire.

I stir in my seat. I'm sure not bored now. I must say something. I don't care that I'm new and not Catholic. There is a big Catholic influence here since only two faculty members are protestant. I can no longer sit and listen to her pious talk. I jump up and wave my arms. I want to be heard. Mr. Deanno reluctantly recognizes me. He has no choice.

"I know I'm a new teacher. Some of you always remind me of that when I bring a new idea. Well, here I go again." I'm shaking all over. It just got very hot in this room. Everyone has turned to look at me. At least some are smiling. "For God's sake, Lori attended all her classes

114

unnoticed until she was eight and a half months pregnant. She had her baby over Christmas vacation and is now ready to come back to school. Her mother will care for her child during the day. I commend her." People begin to whisper and Miss Sheets is again on her feet.

I continue. "All I hear is judgment. That's not our mission. We are here for students. We should seize every teachable moment."

Miss Sheets interrupts. "I've never heard such talk in this school. This girl is not to be commended. She did a terrible thing and must pay for her mistake." Whispering gets louder and I raise my voice.

"Oh, you mean we should not let her darken our door. Keep her from a job and a high school diploma. Make it more difficult for her to provide for her child. I think not. If she's in your class, have her talk about the difficulties, the responsibilities. Let's make this positive for Lori and other students." I sit down. All the other teachers are clapping and standing. WOW. For me! They agree.

The principal asks if we are ready to vote. There is a commotion and the level of conversation is beyond his control. He slams a book on the desk and everyone jumps.

Granny told me Mother had to leave the Baptist church when I was born. That's why Mother, Nancy and I went to the Methodist Church and Granny stayed at the Baptist church. Would they have kicked her out of school if she had been 17 instead of 29?

Lori's coming back to school. HIP HIP HURRAH

I taught in Canonsburg for two years, then, against the advice of the principal and several teachers who thought I should teach in the state for three years to earn a permanent certificate, I left to prepare for a college teaching job. While working as a housemother at Peabody College, I earned my Master's degree in nine months. Being a housemother was more difficult than the classes.

"Hi, Joan, I just brought your painting back. I've really enjoyed our tussle with it. You know I think it's one of your best but after tomorrow's graduation, I can't take it from your room anymore. And you won't have to sneak into my room to get it back. I'm sure going to miss you and the fun we've had this year being House Mothers. I never thought it would be this much fun. But then that's thanks to you."

"Oh, I don't know. It takes two to do the things we did. What's your hurry? Come in. Sit a spell."

"I can't. Have to go meet my mother. She's coming for graduation and she arrives at 3:30 on the Greyhound."

"I didn't know she was coming. You've said nothing about it."

I have seldom talked about mother. I don't like her. I'm sure no one would understand and I don't want to attempt an explanation now. Mother and I should both be proud of this accomplishment and want to share the day. It was a surprise when she called to say she had her ticket and would arrive today. I have no idea what her motivation was and as usual she made the arrangements and then called to tell me what she was going to do. We never had a discussion but she has no consideration for others

How do I get out of here NOW? I shift from one foot to the other. "It's hard to explain. I don't know why she's coming. She just called last week, asked me to send her money and that she'd made reservations to be here for graduation. I tried to talk her out of it but nothing doing. She wants to be here to see her baby graduate. That's a funny one."

"I bet she's proud. She certainly should be. Don't you want her to be here?"

I could really let it out. Tears come to my eyes and I turn so she can't see them. I want her to be proud but I know she's coming to be a troublemaker. To show off that she's here. She doesn't give a shit about me getting another degree. Damn, I hate her. I have to be nice, not let others see my feelings. Straighten up, Rosie. Fly right. Be good. Give her the benefit of the doubt. Maybe she's changed.

116

"Joan, my Mother has never complimented me on anything I've done and I doubt that she will start now. It's a free trip and she can act like Mrs. Astor. I really have to go. See, ya "

I quickly leave the dorm to walk downtown. The campus is so beautiful now. There are flowers in bloom at the corner of each walkway crossing the campus. Lots of iris. I'll get a bulb with my degree. I stop at the end of the campus to look down the center of the mall. It is lush green and freshly mowed. I love the smells. I can see the Social Religious Building at the other end of the campus where workmen are building the stage for tomorrow's ceremony. The mall is at least a quarter of a mile end to end. Students are scurrying across the campus like bees building a nest. I take a minute to visualize tomorrow's colorful march of faculty and students down this mall to the stage. I must admit I never thought I'd be in this march. I have so many negative messages to try to forget. And now I'm going to meet the very person who gave me most of those messages. Will she ever change? Why does she want to be here?

Mother is already sitting in the waiting room when I arrive. I see her across the room and watch as she looks from side to side. Maybe I'll just walk right by her to see if she recognizes me. She's so proper in her suit, holding a small overnight bag in front of her feet, and her purse clutched on her lap. She looks scared and sad at the same time. Oh, well, here goes.

"Hi. Sorry I'm late. I got held up in the dorm. It's tough being a House Mother at graduation time."

"Oh, that's OK." She stands. I take a step closer. She picks up her suitcase and turns away from me eliminating any possible touch of a greeting

"It's not a long walk from here to the dorm or do you want to get a cab?"

"We can walk. My suitcase isn't very heavy. I'm not staying long and you are not coming home with me are you?"

I can't believe it. Not two minutes and she has started. I take her suitcase and step a bit faster. "No, mother. And we've been over all that. Can we try to enjoy tomorrow? It's a big day for me."

"Well, is SHE here yet?"

I should act like I don't understand the question. But I want to be kind. "Who? Do you mean Charlotte? She's coming tomorrow, just in time for the ceremony. I probably won't see her till after."

We walk down the hill and get to the end of campus. We stop to look across the campus and for her to rest a minute. I tell her about the buildings on campus and show her the stage and point out the flowers that have been forced to bloom by the florist just for graduation. She makes no comments about any of it. Just listens and grunts. I don't know why she bothered. We meet Joan as we walk in the back door of our dorm. I introduce her and Joan says how wonderful I am and mother just nods her head. Then Joan says, "I bet you're proud of your daughter, aren't you."

"Well, of course, we all are. She's the first in the family to have an advanced degree. Her grandparents both went to college and I went to Business School. But then, her advanced degree is ONLY IN PE."

Joan stumbles for words. I know better than to look at Joan. I turn to say, "I live on the fourth floor, mother, room 408. Just follow me." I get to my room and kick the door open. In a few minutes she appears huffing and puffing.

The day is perfect. Bright sun. No rain predicted. Faculty and students are beautiful in their robes. It's the first college graduation I have attended. I graduated from Slippery Rock at midterm and there was no real ceremony. We had lunch in the dining room of the dormitory where the Dean handed out blank rolls of paper with ribbons to signify that when the diplomas arrived we'd get one. This is all pomp and celebration. I stand and watch as faculty with their colorful gowns and hoods walk up the center of the mall. It is a beautiful sight to behold. I dream of being at a college graduation in my doctoral robe; marching with the faculty. Some day. But that's another long stint in classes

118

and a lot more writing. I love to write but for college professors: that's tough; they're hard to satisfy. When I teach, I'll be hard on my students too. I'll want them to succeed and most of the time writing is the first thing an employer sees. I see Professor Haddox and think of how she ripped my first resume to bits. But because of her, I now have interviews at two colleges in Florida where I plan to teach next year.

Now I walk with graduate students down the mall right behind the last of the faculty and before the undergraduates. The iris is the state flower and they are everywhere. Iris plants line the walkway and are all across the front of the platform. There are so many full blossoms. Wish Nancy could see me now. That's who I wanted to come to my graduation. But it's not important to her. She told me it must have been easy since I was able to complete everything in nine months.

A few speeches and it's time to walk across the stage to get my hood and degree. I hope I don't fall. I hope Charlotte got here. I didn't see her before the ceremony started but I suggested that Mother save two seats. I don't even know if she would try to do that. I hear my name and start across the stage. First someone hands me an iris bulb, I smile and say "Thank You." He says, "Keep walking." I continue and just as I bend my head to receive my hood, I see Charlotte taking pictures right in front of the stage. I smile, wink at her, and keep going. Look out Florida. Here I come. Maybe Charlotte will go to Florida too, since her father died in March.

Camp is going quickly this summer. We have added more activities and have more campers. Girl Scout camp ended two weeks ago and this is the second week of our day camp. I'm eager to get to Florida in August. I have job interviews at two colleges, several high schools and one junior high. Charlotte and Jo, her niece, are also going and they have written about interviews in some of the same places. It will be a fun trip and I plan to accept one of them. My first teaching experience taught me that much.

Living at Charlotte's house is not as much fun as last summer. Her father died last winter and while he was difficult, I miss him. Charlotte is packing and cleaning out stuff in the house and I'm not much help since I'd throw away lots more than she does. She seems preoccupied, and lovemaking is down to never. We're close but not sexual. She has started using the: "I'm sorry I'm not a man. You deserve a man" routine again. Shit. I don't want a man. I'll just tell her I'll find another woman to love. Making love once every six months and then apologizing for it is not my idea of love. She thinks she loves me but can't let that happen. She would be a homosexual and she says she is not.

I'm going home when camp ends, spend some time with Granny. Charlotte and Jo will pick me up for the trip to Florida. Jo is wonderful. She has two adorable children. We get along really well. I'm glad they will be coming to Florida and living close to us. We talk about what we will do there all the time: fishing, swimming in the warm water and always having a tan.

My anticipation of Florida makes all this camp counseling a bit tedious. Here comes Charlotte now to move me on my way to check out lunches. The kids are cooking eggs in orange-peel halves. Sometimes if the kids aren't careful with their oranges, they lose the egg in coals. I yell, "I'm going to the blue side, you take the red. I'll meet you in the middle."

"Ok. Don't eat too many eggs."

Camp ended smoothly and my visit at home was different. I was determined to make it as pleasant as possible. When mother tried to start an argument with me, I smiled and walked away. Granny and I had long talks about life and her health and my living so far away. I told her she was the only reason I came to visit. This place is just not the same without Deh Deh. We talked about missing him but she wouldn't talk about their relationship. Just said it was OK. The dust in the house doesn't make me angry. I just clean and know I'm helping Granny. She looks so much older. She seems shorter and more stooped. Tears come to my eyes when I think about her not being here and I go hug her.

Charlotte, Jo, and I accepted jobs in two different junior high schools in St Petersburg, Florida. Jo and I are in the same school. We found houses near each other so I will ride to school with her.

She's teaching English and I'm teaching physical education and health. I enjoy the seventh graders but there are seventy of them in one class. It amazes me that other teachers think PE teachers have an easy time. We just play games. I'll trade my field with these seventy seventh graders anytime for your classroom with assigned seats for thirty.

After five months in this school, I look for a college position and within a month, I accepted a position at St. Petersburg Junior College. It is the oldest junior college in the state and has a very good academic reputation. Florida has a system of community (junior) colleges that allows students to complete their first two years and transfer to any University without losing credits or having to repeat classes.

Charlotte and I are looking for a house of our own so we won't have to pay rent. I think it's a very good idea but I don't have much money to invest yet. We ride quietly in the back seat of the realtor's car. She's a very nice person who says she knows exactly what we are looking for, "A Mother/daughter arrangement." I'm sure Charlotte has told her that she's buying the house, will make the down payment and put it in her name. I've said nothing to the realtor.

She shows us one house, which I don't like at all. It has deep maroon fixtures in the main bathroom. It's dark and terrible. Charlotte likes the house but I insist that we keep looking. At least I can say where I will or will not live. I notice a sign in the yard of the house right across the street. I like the white with blue trim better than this brown and tan. I ask the realtor if we can see that house. She makes a phone call and we walk across the street.

121

When I walk in the front door I say, "WOW, look at that mirror. I'd love to decorate it at Christmas." The mirror fills one whole wall half way down with a nice shelf at the bottom. The current people have a couch in front of the mirror, which just fits under that shelf. I'd move that.

"Whoa, Rosie. It's not ours yet"

There are two nice-size bedrooms, a big kitchen, and a big back screened-in porch, and there are orange and grapefruit trees in the back yard. There is an orchid tree in full bloom and the grass looks good. I'll mow it every week. I turn to see where Charlotte is and find her with the realtor, signing a paper. A binder. Great. I walk out the back door and check the fruit on the trees; loads of grapefruit and two orange trees. I'm tempted to pick one but they are very green. I know they aren't ready but they look good and I know they don't have to be orange. I'll wait. Green oranges aren't like green apples.

I go back inside to check the bedrooms. One has twin beds and one a double. Gosh, maybe we'll have to sleep together; especially if her brother comes to live with us. Or the other room can be for company. Charlotte's sister and brother-in-law are coming to visit this winter and that's just a few weeks away. No sense setting up two rooms and then moving when they come. I'll plan my strategy to make that happen but I won't hold my breath. We do have a couch that opens to a bed, which will go in the living room.

I'm sitting in my office having a discussion about classes with three other faculty members. The phone rings and I answer. I recognize my mother's voice immediately. She has never called just to ask how I'm doing. This call is clearly for business. I mouth an "excuse me" to the others and turn away from them.

"Rosie, Nancy and I have decided to sell the home."

"You can't."

"Well, we figured you don't really care about it."

"Well, again you figured wrong."

Do they really think that I will go along with them to kick Granny out of her home? I'm sure they haven't even suggested any of this to her. Deh Deh deeded the property to each of us. He divided it up - two lots each to Mary and Libby, two lots each to Jimmy and Billy, and the house and five lots to Nancy and me with lifetime living rights for Granny. In my opinion that means that Granny can live there until she dies or she decides to go somewhere else. "Now, Rosie, be reasonable. I can't afford. . . ."

I can't believe she has called me at work to ask me this question. I try not to show my disgust here. I knock papers on the floor. Start to pick them up as I stretch the cord as far as it will go. Others begin to leave for the next class and I realize I must move.

"Have Granny call and tell me she wants to sell. Better yet, when I am home next time, I'll ask her."

"I have never known anyone as stubborn as you."

"I really can't talk now, Mother, I have a class. Call me tonight." I hang up and go to my next class. I know I will never agree to sell the house before Granny dies.

I've been teaching at the college only one month and know I made the right decision. A gathering of seventy seventh graders in one class is not teaching, it's policing. Twenty college men and women are a joy on the archery field. I am busier than ever and Charlotte and I are moving this weekend.

Moving always helps get rid of junk. I've packed so many boxes that I'm tempted to throw the rest of it out. If I don't look at it, I won't remember what's not here. I carry the last box of books out to the car and drive to our new house.

"Hi, Charlotte here are more books. Where should I put yours?"

"Just put them in the living room."

Already I can sense the house is too small. So much stuff. I thought we were going to bring everything here then decide together what to do with it. I can see that Charlotte has already begun to put clothes away. Her clothes in the big bedroom, mine in the twin bedroom. She has hung all the clothes and put everything in dressers. I walk out to the backyard. I begin to think about Charlotte's proposal that we might need to add a bedroom and bath on the back of this house. I see exactly where it will fit and we won't need to cut down any trees. I don't have time to solve this problem now.

"Don't forget, Charlotte, we are going fishing this afternoon with Jo and the kids."

"What about all these books that need to be put away?"

"Later, fishing is much more important. Don't you remember that's dinner?"

It is three o'clock and I promised David and Jenny we would pick them up at four. I put on my lucky clothes. The big fish are always attracted to the bright red shorts.

"Does everybody agree to go to the jetty on St. Pete Beach?"

They all say, "Yes." The jetty overlooks the pass between the bay and the Gulf of Mexico. This is my second favorite beach. A section of it is the gay beach but I don't go there very often. I've only been here a year and a few months and I know the climate for gay teachers is not the safest. I remember a discussion I had with some students at Peabody.

We sit in the lobby of our dorm and talk about teaching in Florida. Three of us are definitely going there to find jobs. One woman who taught there for three years before coming to graduate school says, "I just want to warn you about the John's committee. It's a committee formed by the state government to find all the lesbians and fire them from the school systems in Florida."

I squirm and wonder if she knows I'm gay. I keep quiet while others question her. "How can they? The whole state? How do they find out which female teachers are gay? What about gay men?"

I hear the phone ringing in the dorm office and go to answer it. I don't wait for the answers.

I bait Jenny's hook and then David's. Even at six and nine years old, they cast like pros. I want them to catch a fish. I love these kids as if they were my own. And Jo is like a sister who listens and understands.

Charlotte begins to tell them how to hold the pole, how to reel in, how to let the bait hit the bottom, how to . . . .

"Just let them try their way, Charlotte."

"But they're just learning."

"I know. They need time to practice."

Jo smiles at me and looks away from Charlotte. I bait my own hook and hear Charlotte ask for bait just as I drop the bait bucket into the water. I lay my pole down, pull the bucket back up and hand her a shrimp. She asks, "Aren't you going to bait my hook too?"

"I thought you were the expert here."

David hooks a fish. He jumps up and down. I hope it's a keeper. I walk over to him and whisper to keep reeling. I can see it's a drum. It is beautiful silver-white with wide black stripes, has a mouthful of teeth too and tough to clean but great to eat. He gets it up on the jetty and I put my foot on it lightly to hold it still while I remove the hook. This fish cooperates and spits the hook when I apply a little pressure. "Thank you Mr. Fish."

Charlotte catches the next two keepers and Jenny catches a blowfish. I want to keep it but Jo has heard that they are poisonous. I don't think so but when Charlotte agrees with Jo, I throw it back. Both Jenny and I are disappointed that we didn't catch keepers. I take the bait off my hook, which never even got wet. It died on the hook. Poor shrimp. We have enough fish for dinner so it's OK. I step down the rocks onto the beach, take out my trusty filet knife and clean the fish on a big flat rock. I throw everything else to the birds. Gulls and pelicans gather quickly and eye our filets.

I put the fillets in a plastic bag and we head to the car. I didn't even get my line wet but I sure was busy. I smile inside as we carry all the paraphernalia to the car.

Charlotte agrees to cook the fish if Jo and I make salad. I suggest Cole-slaw and all chime in to say, "Yum Yum." We will drop Jo, David, and Jenny at their house, just down the street from ours. They'll clean up and walk over for dinner. When we get to their house Charlotte says, "Give us about thirty minutes."

"Can't we rest a while before we cook?"

"Why?"

"Because I need a drink and a nap. Let's eat about seven. OK?"

Jo agrees. The kids have taken everything out of the car and both say "Thank you" as Charlotte pulls out of their driveway.

I can tell she's not happy about our decision to eat later, so when we get home, I go fix us a drink, her coke and me vodka. I hand her some crackers. "This should tide you over."

"Thanks for cleaning the fish, Rosie. And thanks for doing everything out there."

I shake my head. "Now you want to make nice?" I walk out; vodka in hand.

It never fails. If I make an appointment with the department head, at any time of the day, even ones she picks, I have to wait. It just puts an edge on things. Making me wait just lets me get in touch with why I dislike her style of management. As a department chair, she thinks she owns faculty, that she can tell us how to dress, how to behave, and how to spend our leisure time. She must be about sixty. I keep hoping she will retire.

I sit in the outer office with the secretary. She at least looks busy. The office is in such order that if a paper fell to the floor I think she would leap to pick it up so that nothing would appear out of order. At least ten file cabinets line the back wall. Each locked to secure the information. It reminds me of the stupid key policy for the department. I'm a faculty member and can have a key to each room in the building, but cannot have a key to get into the building. If the custodian has locked up for the evening before I return to teach at night, and it happens often, I must go to security to let the students in the building. I usually just send a small student in through a window that has been left open in the locker room. Some security.

The secretary motions to me that I can go into the office now.

I walk slowly to the door and smile at her, take a seat in the chair in front of her desk. I make no small talk. "I know I told you that I would only teach Health for one semester. Well, I've done that and now I want to teach all the health classes, even if it means I have to quit teaching archery and badminton and volleyball. I love teaching in the classroom. It's a different kind of combat. I want more of it."

"Well, Rose, I don't know. The dean has said a few things about your teaching. That he has had calls from parents about your sexuality unit and about your birth control demonstrations."

I shift in my seat. I cannot believe they think this way about college teaching. "In that case, you and he should come to one of my classes decide for yourselves about my teaching. I can let you know when sex is the topic." She shakes her head and starts to say something but I continue. "I'll bet he has had no more than one or two calls. His decisions about my teaching should not be made on those biased opinions. So while we are discussing health class, what about the new textbook recommendation?"

"I'll show you his memo. He seems to think the book you want has off color pictures in it."

I laugh out loud as I flip through the book I have on my lap. The closest thing to a dirty cartoon must be the picture of a man's body front and back. I could suggest a transparency of his to substitute.

"Where are they? Pictures of the body are not off color."

I rearrange my papers on the chair next to me. I pick up a pencil and start to scribble on the top paper. I look at her and my blood boils. I'd like to throw the book at her. They haven't read any of it, just looked at the pictures. I wrote a ten-page recommendation, illustrating the improvements over the book we currently use and even cited specifics. She probably didn't send the memo. Why should I have to ask permission to use a book? I'll talk to the

127

Academic Dean at the next Faculty Forum meeting. She is a progressive educator who has as much trouble as I do with these old fashioned ideas.

"He says there's a cartoon in the book that parents would not approve for their children to see."

This gets funnier as she goes. I laugh again and she looks really angry. "Jesus Christ, Eleanore, they're college students. We have a real mix of ages in the class. Some of the women have children of their own. He's ridiculous." I get up and move toward the door. She tells me to sit down. I turn back toward the chair and decide to stand for the rest of the conversation. I lean on the chair and put my papers on it. I think of all the things she does to make this an unpleasant place to work: the keys, the uniforms, the constant walking through classes, the checking on attendance sheets, locker room inspections are all her rules. "I really have to go. I have to get something to eat before my night class. I'll see you tomorrow. Maybe we should make an appointment and meet with the dean."

Just as I open the door, I hear Charlotte call from her bedroom. "Rosie, come in before you go back to your room. OK?"

Wonder what she wants now? I am sure it is not lovemaking. We've hardly touched each other and certainly not made love, for at least six months. I've started going places with David, a colleague at the college in the radio-television department. He's as gay as I am and we get along great. He drives a red corvette and we party a lot. We fool around, kissing and fondling, now and then but nothing serious. I left his house early tonight. I'm really tired and I wasn't in the mood to pretend.

It's the same with Charlotte. A kiss now and then; but no real lovemaking. I go to my room and change to a short robe. I'll at least be more comfortable.

"Yes, you wanted to see me?"

"Come on in. Sit down. Aren't you cold with just that little robe?" She turns the cover down and motions for me to lie down. "I'll get you warm."

128

"Are you sure?" It's so damned easy for her. I slip in next to her and melt. She's so warm. Her kisses make me tingle all over. She's so soft, so gentle. She's all over me. My body arches to open wide for her touch. She slides her fingers between my lips like hot syrup. It flows all around up and down, up and down. I move with her and I explode. I lie still, holding tight to savor the throbs and float.

She turns and says, "I wish you had a man to love you. You want it so much. I'm sorry I'm not that man."

I stiffen. Turn away and roll off the bed. I stomp out of her room. I hear her mumble something. I will not go back. This is the end. God damn her. I love her but this is not what I want in a relationship. I thought she wanted the same. I thought this "home" would make a difference.

I pound on my pillow and thank my lucky stars that we added this room and bath shortly after we bought the house. I stomp around the room and hit the wall. I drop into bed and soon turn the wet pillow over.

She's standing at the door opening the louvers and calling to me. I reach the door and she's gone. I turn and hear her call. I go back she's not there. I see her from behind the glass. Why won't she let me in? I call her name and she opens the door. I rush to the door but it slams in my face. I think someone else is there but no it's just she. She calls again and this time I grab the doorknob and it comes off in my hand.

I wake in a sweat.

I'm in the kitchen starting to make my breakfast when she walks in and says, "Last night was beautiful. Why'd you leave?"

I look at her like she's just gone crazy. I raise my voice as I say, "Why did I leave? Where were you? In outer space? Why the fuck do you think I left? You didn't hear me pacing the floor half the night?"

"I have no idea, but there's no reason for that language."

"Boy you're something! When will you learn?" I drop an egg on the floor. "DAMN!" I turn to get a towel and bump into her. She tries to hug me. I twist away.

"Let go of me."

"I'll clean it up. I know you're in a hurry."

I better get out of here. I try to wipe it up. I shove her aside and grab another towel to finish the job.

I stand in front of her. "Charlotte, I love you. I want a love relationship and have ever since Slippery Rock. Thought you did. You stay away for months. Then we act like we are making love and I feel wonderful. Instantly, you spoil it. Always turn it around. Why are you ashamed to love me? Is it because I'm a lesbian?"

She says nothing. Just stands there.

I look her in the eye. "Don't count on me for lovemaking again."

She reaches for me. I go out the door and call over my shoulder,   "Don't wait for me for dinner."

The beaches around St. Petersburg are magnificent. I like Sunset Beach on Treasure Island best but I come to St. Pete Beach to read and watch people. The sand is soft, almost fluffy and makes that squeaky noise as I step, like walking in fresh snow in the North. I love to come here. The Australian Pines wave in the breeze like dancers and the music from their branches is soothing and wonderful. I come here often and sit at the edge of what I have learned is called the Gay beach. I come even if I do teach. Most teachers I know are afraid to come here. I've never seen anyone I really know, just some acquaintances. They don't know me well, and so don't even recognize me. When I see them coming near my spot on the sand, I turn my head and bury it in a book I carry for cover. This living a double life is crazy. Always has been. I have always thought I was different. Is this the difference? I think it's OK to love women. What difference does it make? I hurt no one. But, for now, I hide like every other gay teacher I know.

Oh, there's the big butch. I like to watch her; she's a real show-off. She's getting ready to stake out her territory.

She's laying everything down to have her hands and feet free to smooth the spot for her blanket. It's windy today so she's digging a shallow trench to make her spot lower than the beach so the wind goes across and blows sand over her body and not in her eyes. Her body is very slim, toned and stacked. Maybe she works out with weights to tone and structure her muscles so each of them stands out to be noticed. She's attractive but a bit too butch for me. Ha, look who's talking; I'm certainly not the femme of the year. I'm five-seven and slender. My walk is distinct, not swishy. My hair is short and combed back with a wave to the left. I'm in good shape but no sculptured muscles. I try to wear soft-looking clothes, but no ruffles. I really have not labeled myself butch or femme. I rarely ever think of myself as either. But I am definitely watching a gym dyke in action. She now has her spot all carved out and is ready to place the blanket in perfect direction toward the sun. She is golden tan now with no lines that I can see. Already I see the younger femmes watching and waving to let her know they see her. She nods in their general direction but will not speak to any one until she's ready. I love the show. The umbrella is next and placed just at the correct angle to shade and to identify her territory. It's a bright colored one with a small hammock-like attachment in the middle to hold her Frisbee, paddles and balls. She has all the beach games, ready to give any chosen femme a lesson or time at play. She lies down now carefully avoiding sand so that her blanket is not messy and she's careful to keep her towel dry and rolled just right for a headrest. Satisfied that she is in perfect position for the girls to see as they parade by, she covers her eyes with plastic cups like eyeglasses.

I read for a while knowing that the real show won't begin till she needs a drink of water, and sees how many teetering femmes are ready for their time with gym dyke. She sits up, stretches, and reaches for the water bottle. Seeing a very pretty gal coming toward her, she signals her to come closer and reaches for assistance to get up. The beauty helps her up and they exchange a few words. Next thing I know she has five beautiful women all around her tossing a Frisbee to and fro.

I like to be on the beach but I'm hot, want something to eat, and am jealous, envious, or just plain bored with the same show every week. But I'll come back next week to see it again.

Charlotte and I continue Friday's breakfast/love discussion as I begin to clean the house. I am not happy and she knows it. She sits on the couch reading the paper.

"What the fuck do you know about love?"

"I know I love you. And Rosie, please don't use that language with me."

I ignore the language request. "Oh, sure you do. And I'm the first and only. Bullshit." I continue to dust the living room. Not a speck will stay after this dust cloth touches it. I'm the cleaning machine this morning, the same as every Sunday. Even the windows will be clean. I go to the kitchen and get the paper towels. She tells me I don't have to do all the work. Right. Like last night. I cooked and cleaned up after dinner. What more can I do? I'm a housemaid not a lover. Oops, not supposed to say that word. Not even think it.

"We have a very special relationship," she says. Special. I do as I'm told, pay half the bills, give parties for her school friends and get to invite one or two of my friends if they aren't too butch and, of course, I can invite David. Some reward. Does she really think I'll change and love men? Does she think I want to? From our first love making fifteen years ago she's been ashamed. I spray the top window and let the Windex drip down like the tears that drip down my face. I wipe the top windowpane and go to the next. She sits on the couch telling me just where every streak is. She's like my mother. Always the bad stuff. That's not fair. I don't like my mother and I love Charlotte. She has been so good to me. She helped me through school; some financial but mostly moral support and encouragement.

"Charlotte, why don't you go DO something?"

"I want to be with you."

She picks up the paper and begins to read to me. I could knock the paper and her across the room. She's impossible.

"Shit! While I wash windows?"

"All the time."

"Bullshit."

I shake my head and move to the next row of windows. I like this living room with floor to ceiling awning windows that allow a great breeze. Living in an open house like this one in Florida is a dream come true but with so many strings. I can't move now. I can't afford my own place. I pay rent, not as much as my own place would be. I pay half the bills. If I leave, I know I won't get any of that back. It's her house. I must start saving NOW. Things were much better between us when I was in Tennessee and she was in West Virginia. I saw her once in nine months. It was just eight years ago that we moved here and this is our seventh year in this house that she bought. Why have I stayed so long? It's comfortable and I haven't found anyone else I want to live with. Maybe I should look.

I finish the fourth window and go outside. Now she gets up to point to the streaks on the outside. Damn.

I saw her as she came into the gym. She is about five foot four, one-twenty, curly hair, and very athletic looking. She's an older student, looks familiar, but I can't place her. Why is she taking PE? Older students are not required to take it and why would she take volleyball of all things. Oh well, I'll get to know all of them soon. I can't believe I agreed to teach another night class. But maybe this one will be fun: I notice a few repeats, that is, they've been in my classes before, so at least I know some of them before class begins. I put on my mean face, ha ha, and walk out of my office to the gym floor where the class has gathered on the bleachers.

I welcome them and ask them to tell me their names and a short version of why they're in the class, other than they must have the credit. In other words, I want to know why they took volleyball instead of tennis, badminton or. . . .

133

Her name is Gloria. She says it was the only class open when she registered. She's a nursing student and wanted to have some scheduled activity time. She knew she could do well in volleyball. She used to play in a recreation league but now only plays softball. She seems shy. She's very nice looking, in good condition and is one of very few students who turn my head. I've never really wanted to know students any more than to be friendly during classes and to be open for their questions and concerns. I know that being a lesbian has to be kept as top secret in this Florida school district, even if this is a college. A few years ago there was a statewide investigation to rid the schools of all lesbians. The same school board and trustees still govern this school. This is my third year here and I have not thought about that sad event till now, in this class. She has really turned my head and made the juices flow. Better look out, be cautious and very careful. It's as though the rest of the class is a blur and she stands out.

At the third class she brings me a beautiful seashell. Says she knows I love the beach and wonders if she can join me sometime when I go walking on Sunset Beach. How does she know I walk on Sunset Beach? How does she know anything about me? Is she a spy? She has been very friendly before and after class, but so have I. Have I crossed the line of student-teacher relationship, have I allowed her to cross that line? I have let her help with equipment but so have others. Maybe I'm being paranoid because of my feelings. I'm glad she's in class. I like to talk with her. She's quite the fisherperson. I heard her tell others the other night that she had caught a snook. That's the most sought-after game fish and very hard to catch. As class ends, I hear someone speaking and turn to see her looking at me.

"Say, Miss Walton, want to go for coffee?"

God, I'm tongue-tied. "Uh, what did you say?"

"Want to go for coffee?"

"Now?"

"Yeah, not too late is it?"

"OK, why not. Just let me get things together for tomorrow morning and I'll be with you."

134

I don't believe it. I said yes. And I want to go. Why do I feel so warm all of a sudden? I'm kinda weak-kneed. Stop! Go tell her you'd better not go. Wait and see if she still comes to see you after class ends over in December. She'll think I'm nuts. She has only asked me to go have coffee. Stop jumping to conclusions you want. I straighten my desk, go to the john and get equipment from the equipment room for my first class in the morning. Now I can sleep later tomorrow.

"OK, I'm ready, where shall we go? I. . . uh. . . . I'll follow you so we don't have to come back here for a car."

"Oh, I don't mind, go with me in my little bug."

"No, really, I'll drive my own car."

"Whatever. Meet me at Gigi's. She makes a mean cup of coffee and I really need one, I still have to study tonight."

"Then, let's make it another night. I certainly don't want to keep you from your studies."

"I'm going for coffee anyway to get my head in full gear. You might as well come along. I'd like for you to anyway."

"OK. I'll meet you there."

I drive slowly so she will be there first and have a table. Just as I hoped, it's in the corner. We talk about people she knows, that I've met. They are mostly PE teachers who also play softball on her team. She tells me that she met me on the fishing pier at Ft. De Soto Park years ago and that she only took my class because of me. She wants to get to know me and that's the only way she could do that. I shift in my seat. Look around. Her eyes are intent and she looks at me all the time. I take a sip of hot coffee and burn my mouth. Damn. I can't believe how much she knows about me. I begin to feel uncomfortable with the talk and my feelings. I want to say, come home with me. *Go to bed with me. I feel my arms around her taut body, my hands rubbing her back, then her. . . I know I can't.* I get up to leave, suggesting that I will see her in class, next week. I want no part of starting a relationship. Especially while she's a student, no matter how much older she is. I know lots of student-teacher relationships that have started with good intentions but most have ended with harsh feelings toward the teacher. Too close to home for me.

Did I just run a stop sign? God, what is wrong with me, I'm North of where I turn to go home. It's late and I have to be up and out early in the morning even if I did put equipment together tonight. Will she come by the archery field? Now that I know the yellow VW Bug is hers, I realize I've seen her drive by often. Where does she live? Must be close to the campus. She lives with her mother and another woman. She was very clear tonight that the other woman is just a friend. Yeah, yeah, that's what they all say. Maybe a friend with whom she occasionally sleeps. I better watch out. Better cool it for now.

I walk into the gym knowing it's the last evening of the volleyball class for the semester and just four weeks since I went for coffee with her. Class is really wound up for this tournament. "OK   OK   Settle down. Yes, we're having a tournament. Let's get started; team one will play team three and four will play two. Then winners play winners and losers play losers. If there's time we'll choose an all-star team from losing teams to play the winner. The same substitution rule as usual. Now let's warm up a bit. Five minutes."

I hope her team wins. Does my heart good to see the older students outwit the younger ones in game situations. She's really good looking and my type too. Whatever that means. Face it, Rosie, you like her and want to know her better. But you can't make the advances. So cool it and start the games.

I step aside and watch them begin practice. My eyes naturally turn to watch Gloria play. Yes, I'd go to bed with her but I won't ask. Maybe she'll ask me now that she's not a student after tonight.

"OK, I yell team one and three on the left-hand court and two and four on this one." I check roll, and jot down participation grades as play continues. I hear a strange sound from the court behind me and turn to see students gathered around Gloria. I quickly walk over to investigate. I sure hope she isn't hurt. "Go get some ice from the snack bar. Hurry!" I carefully examine her finger and realize that it's going to be badly bruised but it's not broken. She must have stretched the tendon in the first joint of her fourth finger; it's bent at a ninety-degree angle.

"Oh, really, Miss Walton, it's nothing. I can play. I'll use my right hand and make a fist with the left, so I won't hurt this finger again. Now don't yell at me for hitting with my fist."

"You can't play with one hand and one fist. Now just put that finger in the ice and sit out a while. Your team can go on without you for a while."

"But we can't win." The team begins to protest and wants all play to stop while we treat her finger. Yes, and I'd like to hold her hand for the rest of the evening. I smile, walk to the other court and let them work it out. Soon I hear them playing again and turn to see, as I expected, she playing without a thought about her bent finger.

Class ends and I go to my office. Several students stop by to say how much they enjoyed the class and especially the tournaments. I busy myself with papers on the desk. Straighten grade sheets and look to see if the equipment has been put away. As I see the custodian wave, I know it's been done and he's locked the door. I walk out of my office and chat with him for a few minutes just to kill time. I want to be sure that students are out of the building before I leave. I thank him for helping with the equipment, pick up my jacket and walk slowly out the door. I see her waiting for me at my car.

"Want to come by the house? You can meet my mom and explain how I was injured in your class." She laughs and I know she doesn't mean that.

"Guess I'll take a rain check. I think you ought to see about that finger, if the joint doesn't pop back to normal tomorrow morning. It really isn't serious. But let me know, OK."

I stretch the lines to mark distances on the archery field and just as I go into the storage shed to get the lime, I hear a VW horn. It's only 1:30. How does she know I don't have a class? How's she know I'm here? Is it her car? Of course it is. I turn around to find the keys. She's outside the gate and can't come in. I'll just go out there to talk with her. I hope her finger's OK. I pick up the bag of lime and start out. Then put it back down and start out with nothing in my hands. I grab a couple of arrows just to have something to play with.

"Hi." I lean on the fence so I can see her in the car. She gets out of the car and walks around to stand near me. The fence acts like a barrier. One of us is in and one of us is out of confinement. Which one? I step back away from it. She stands very close to it. She looks at the lock but says nothing.

"Hi. You should've come home with me last night. My mom and some friends were playing poker. You like to play don't you? I told her I'd invite you to play sometime. Would you come?"

I ignore her question. "How's your finger?"

"It's fine." She holds her hand up to show me. I'm not sure which hand it was. "Would you come?"

"Thanks for asking. I don't play cards much. My Grandmother thought they were sinful. Someone would have to teach me the rules and how to play. Would you help me?"

"No. My mom is very serious about her poker playing. She'd give you a card to tell you what you needed to play or win. But she wouldn't allow anyone to help you. You'd love her and you'd have a good time. How about tomorrow after school? It's Friday and you could stay for dinner. OK, it's a date." She starts back around her car, like that's the end of the conversation.

"Uh . . . wait. I'm not so sure. You probably have lots of plans for the weekend. We can do it some other time. After I've met your mom and have learned to play poker. I'll get a book." I shift from foot to foot. She stands very still and her eyes never leave my face. Every time I look at her she is smiling and looking at me. So intense.

138

"Don't be silly. Come, tomorrow about five and just plan to spend the evening. Now don't disappoint my mom. It'll hurt her feelings if you don't come. I've already told her about you."

"What? What have you already told her?" Does her mother know that she's gay? Have they talked about that? Has she told her that I am? Does she know I am or is she guessing like I am about her?

"Oh, it's all been good. Don't worry. And remember I'm not your student anymore." She gets in her car and leans over to show a big smile. What's that mean to her?

I hear my next class gathering behind me and I haven't marked the lines. I just put the string out. "I have to go. I'll see about tomorrow."

I invited Gloria, that's her name, and she agreed to go fishing with Charlotte and me in Charlotte's boat. I don't want to drive the boat because I want to spend time in the front of the boat with Gloria. I pretend I have to fix fishing lines.

"Come on, Charlotte you drive the boat."

"Oh, Rosie you're much better at it than I am, you go ahead."

I continue to drive. I spot some birds eating on little fish up ahead and stop to fish a while and decide I'm not going to take us home. It's her boat and I don't want to drive it all the time. The weather is just right, it's bright, and not a cloud in the sky and the sun is hot. I love it. I just want to lie on the front of the boat and watch Gloria fish. Fish are biting but no luck getting one in. Oh, Gloria has one on her line. I encourage her to take it easy and let em play. Charlotte is shouting commands. "Get the net. Don't lean over so far. Hold the tip up. Get him in." It's like she knows it all. She knows all about cleaning them too, but has never lifted a knife to touch a fish. I will not do this again. I want to be with Gloria but not like this. In fact I'm surprised she agreed to come. I hand Charlotte the net and go back to my spot to keep on fishing.

"Here, Rosie, I can't reach it."

"For God's sake, Charlotte, the boat isn't going to tip over. REACH."

"If you two could stop fighting and help me get this red fish in, we could all have dinner tonight. I'll cook."

"Thanks, Glor. I'll be there. Charlotte doesn't like fish. Right, Charlotte?"

Charlotte gives me a look and reaches for the fish. She gets it in the net this time and it's a beauty. Wish I'd caught it. Next time, maybe. I grab a beer and suggest we go home. Charlotte agrees and sits down in the back of the boat. Gloria stays in the front and I go to sit next to her.

I feel Charlotte watching us. I close my eyes and think about being in Gloria's arms, not on this boat with both of them. I am brought back hurriedly when I hear Charlotte say, "Well, let's go, Rosie. I thought you wanted to get home right away to fix the fish."

"I do but I'm not the captain. You take us home. You have to learn to use a boat if you're going to have one."

She gets up and I think she'll drive. I relax and then realize that she's just turning her chair away from us. She sits back down. Angrily she says, "I'll drive it next time. Take us home now."

I reluctantly get up, move to the controls and blast off. I won't do this again. I'll go with Glor in her little johnboat and six-horse motor. Or I'll fish from a seawall. There are more snook there anyway.

The phone rings at six o'clock, just as I am rolling out of bed to go run. I am not at all surprised to hear Mother say that Granny died in her sleep. I forget the run. Mother tells me to fly to Charleston. I must call for reservations, call school. I'll tell Charlotte later.

"Yes, thank you. Glad I can fly to Charleston. What time will I arrive?" She has called but did not make reservations.

I call mother and ask her to have someone from the funeral home meet me. She should be able to do that. She sounded like Granny's death is a burden.

The plane ride is great. I love to fly. The Florida to Baltimore plane is the usual big jet. But this one to Charleston is a sixteen-seat prop-plane. It is a wonderful view from here. The hills are like paintings of layers of brightly colored ruffles. Fall is always beautiful from above with a sky of light fluffy clouds to guide us. Someday I'll learn to fly. I see the airport out the window. It's like they cut off most of the top of the mountain and paved a runway. A hill still rises behind the terminal like a wall. I hope the pilot knows what he's doing. Watching the land takes my mind away from Granny's death and the ordeal of her funeral. Dealing with the family, especially mother, is not my idea of closure. I have no idea who's meeting me but I guess I'll recognize anyone who might come from Oak Hill.

I step out of the plane, descend the steps, and walk across the tarmac to the door of the terminal. They told me the bags would be brought inside in a few minutes. As I step through the door, I see Curtis Coleman, a tall and very distinguished looking gentleman from the funeral home. I know him from my younger days of playing in the casket room, the chapels, and all around the funeral home while waiting for mother to do the bookkeeping for them. Nancy and I tried on all the caskets and picked our own. Mine was plain and hers was full of silk and pink fluffy lace. I hope mother picked a fluffy one for Granny. The airport is very small. Three counters for airlines and a waiting area with lots of straight back chairs all connected to each other. Not a comfortable place. Curtis comes over to greet me and I let him know that I'll be with him in just a few minutes after I get my luggage and go to the bathroom. He points to the door where he'll wait.

The luggage arrives on a cart, pulled by two men in orange jump suits. Mine is not there. I go to the bathroom hoping that they'll bring a second cart with my luggage. I can't imagine that there was that much luggage.

I come back to find that it's not here. I go to the baggage office and fill out papers, tell them where to bring the luggage. I guess it missed the change of plane in Baltimore. This reminds me of Deh Deh at the Oak Hill train station freight office. He always took the information when people came to get a package sent by rail. I go find Curtis and tell him I'm ready, that my luggage won't arrive till tomorrow and that they'll bring it to me. That's the last time I pack my toothbrush in checked luggage.

Curtis has the big funeral car, not the limo but a big car. He asks if I want to ride in the back seat. I walk around the car and get in the front seat. The ride to Oak Hill is quiet. At first I sit very straight and rigid. But as we begin to talk I feel myself relax and I slouch in the comfort of the big car.

"Do you like teaching in Florida? How is the weather? Very hot, they tell me."

"Sure, it is hot but I'm outside most of the day. There is always a breeze. I love it."

"I'm sorry about your grandmother. I know you girls loved your grandparents. Folks always talk about how you showed respect for them. Your mother sure is proud of you and Nancy."

"Somehow I think that's more about Nancy than about me."

"Well, she does always have a story about Nancy. But we ask her about you. Weren't you in school after you started teaching?"

"Yes, for a graduate degree before I went to Florida."

"Well, congratulations. I did not know that. She should be very proud."

I think two years and she never mentioned my degree. But she came to my graduation. I say nothing and begin to doze but as the road goes around curves, up and down these West Virginia hills, I can't sleep. Curtis continues to ramble on about how he thought my granddad was a wonderful man even if a bit cantankerous at times.

He tells me a story about Deh Deh and a well-known preacher in town, Reverend Shirley Donnelly. How they would meet at the post office and Mr. Walton would tell Donnelly not to play checkers with his church members. Said if they beat you they won't have any confidence in you

142

and if you beat them they won't have any use for you. I remember Deh Deh telling me the same story.

We go by the house and pick up mother. I haven't been here for a while, but it looks the same. Run down and old. The place needs so much. Now that Granny's dead, mother will surely want to sell. When I see her come down the steps, I move to the back seat.

She greets me with a show of relief that she's not alone. "Thanks for coming so quickly, Rose Ann. I'm sure it was not easy to get flights." She seems very subdued, but anxious, to get things done.

"I really did not have much trouble. And you know how I love to fly so I didn't mind the stopover in Baltimore."

"I wish your sister would fly. She'd be here now to help and she knew Granny's wishes."

"Well, we can try to do everything before others arrive. You have done most of the hard stuff. Picking the casket, her clothes. . . ."

She waves her hand at me and goes on and on about how much needs to be done. As we near the door she says quietly that Granny's sisters are arriving this evening and so is Libby. And indicates I can take care of them. As we walk into the funeral home everyone greets her with affection. I hurry past her to find the casket. I hope it's more than a plain pine box.

Nancy and I are waiting for Mother to finish working. She keeps the books for the Funeral Home. I jump in a casket and play dead. Nancy comes up and tells me how beautiful I look and how happy she is that I am dead and will go to heaven. I get out and throw a hand carved box at her. It was sitting on a table opposite the casket. She tosses it back to me. It sounds like a rattle. I see Mother out of the corner of my eye. I signal to Nancy to hold the box. "You two are terrible. That's Pansy Seavy. Put it back and let's go. I'm ashamed of you."

It's different being here in Thomas Funeral Home to see a body of someone I know. I remember when I fixed Deh Deh's hand. But he's not here and there are no ashes to play with. Just Granny's body. I don't want to look at her but I know I'll have to before the wake is over. That's a strange word, I think. Wake. Whose wake? When people come in, they go up to the casket, stand there, look down like they expect the person lying there to sit up and offer cookies and tea or cornbread. Maybe they are trying to wake her.

Granny won't respond. I know she's gone to heaven. She always said good people do when they die. She never said that about Deh Deh, but she knew she'd go. She read the Bible every day and prayed before every meal and at bedtime. She always let everyone else have their way, did all the house-work and cooking without complaint, and never said a bad word about anybody. She tried all her life to get me to do the same. I can't accept that God wants everyone to be passive and put up with abuse like she did.

I walk into the room where she's laid out. That is strange too; laid out. So many flowers already up front with her. She loved flowers too. How do people order flowers this soon after they find out? I go up to the last row of chairs and stop. I won't go closer. I don't want to see her dead. I bow my head and tell her I hope she's at peace and comfortable. "I hope no one yells at you ever again."

Mother comes in and stands next to me. "Do you want me to go up with you?"

"No. I'm not sure I'm going."

"Well, her sisters just arrived. Maybe you can go see them. They are very upset that I told them there will not be room for them at the house."

I turn to look at her. My heart races. "You told them what?"

"You heard me. Go talk to them."

"Then I won't stay at the house either. You take the cake. How can you do that to them at a time like this? There was always room for them when Granny was alive." My stomach turns over and I want to run. Run. Run. What a loving daughter she is . . . so disrespectful . . . so hateful. . .

144

.She should be in the casket. . . Not Granny. . . How will I act when she dies? I bow my head as I walk out and ask God to give me strength. I love these great aunts. I'll get them and me a room at the one hotel in town or find room for us with neighbors. I will not stay with mother.

I go to the next room and find Granny's sisters huddled together like a group of nuns whispering to each other. I hear them saying; "Mary probably asked for the cheapest casket." I flinch. They haven't even seen it. Aunt Blanche says, "Can you believe there's no room for us?" When Aunt Bess sees me, she stands up and opens her arms. They all get up. I go up to them and hug each one. Tears come to my eyes when I touch them.

I apologize for Mother and tell them maybe she's upset. "I'll find a place for you to stay, don't worry." I sit with them and wish I could make it all OK. We shed a few tears together and hold hands and say a prayer. "Are you ready to see Granny, I mean your sister Lilly? Want me to take you to her room? The flowers are beautiful."

They move like they are in slow motion. I step up to Aunt Mary and take her arm in mine. She had polio as a kid and walks with a slight limp. I feel her love as she presses closer to me. Her limp has gotten more pronounced than I remember from when I last saw her. As we walk into the room, mother goes out the far door. They walk up to the casket and stand very quietly. I hear their sobs and hear my Aunt Libby as she comes in the front door of the Funeral Home. She's greeting friends as she comes in but is so much louder than anyone, I can detect her voice.

I go back to the room behind this one, get my purse and go across the street to the Hotel to reserve rooms for Granny's sisters. I pay and ask the hotel clerk not to mention the bill to the women staying. I'll stay with Mary Kessler, a neighbor.

Back at the funeral home all is quiet except for a nose blow or a cry once in a while. This is barbaric. They'll never do this to me. I can hear Granny's sisters and Aunt Libby talking about how beautiful she looks. She doesn't look pretty to me; she looks dead. Her face is pale, with so much makeup that she doesn't look like my Granny. I don't want to look. I want to remember her in her house dress, her flannel nightgown, her old blue felt slippers, her run filled stockings, her wonderful smile, and her rocking in the noisy chair. Put me in a pair of PJs and lay me on my side. Better still, cremate me and throw my ashes to the wind or feed the fish in Florida.

When I walk back into Granny's room, I hear the sisters talking about my mother again. "She's so wicked. We can't even stay in Lilly's home. And Rosie refused to stay. She is going to a neighbor's house. Mary doesn't care. She's going to have a hard time now that Lilly's gone. She'll have to cook for herself. She never has done that."

When I get to them and they see me, they get very quiet. They start to ask questions about Granny's clothes and jewelry. I tell them I know nothing. They should ask Libby or Mary. I want to stay with them but I can't. I want to be alone. To talk with Granny. I walk away. I go back in my quiet room, with no one. I feel so empty inside, like I'm in a tunnel where people's voices are harsh and bounce off the walls. I want quiet. I hold my head, cover my ears, try to keep the words out of reach, hold my breath, close my eyes, and wait for Nancy to arrive.

I finish my archery class and take the equipment to the storage building. I see that cute little yellow Volkswagen coming down the dirt road. Gloria is not my student anymore so we are having a great time together. We see each other at least three days each week. Sometimes, like now, we go to lunch but forget to eat. The VW slows. I know it's Glor and she knows I don't have a class next hour. She pulls over to the gate nearby and rolls the window down.

"Hi, Teach, wanna grab a bite?"

"I shouldn't, but what the hell. Meet me in the parking lot."

I quickly check to see that everything is locked and rush to my office. It takes me awhile to get there and the phone is ringing. I let it ring. I grab my purse and away I go. I jump in the car and Glor takes off. She heads north on

66th street and I know she is heading for my house. Hope Charlotte hasn't come home sick or something. I don't care. Yes I do. I shouldn't care.

Gloria tells me to relax. She knows I'm thinking about Charlotte being home. "We can drive by first and if she's there we can keep going. But I know she isn't there. I checked."

We pull into the driveway and our clothes are half off before we get to the bedroom. We seem to fall in bed together so easily. I hear the oven timer I set as I walked by begin to buzz. I nudge Glor, and say, "We gotta go, darlin, and we must quit meeting this way."

"You mean we must meet more often. Right?"

David and I are hosting a party at his house tonight with thirty for dinner. The last people are about to leave and I'm glad. I slump into the couch and realize I drank too much as usual. David sits close and puts his arm around my shoulders and says, "Good party and they sure ate a lot." He leans over to kiss me and I jump up. He doesn't object.

"I really have to go. Thanks for having the party here." I move toward the door and he walks me to my car. We kiss goodnight and I'm on my way.

I drive home very carefully; sometimes using one eye so I see only one road. I open the door quietly. I don't want to wake Charlotte. I wish I had a key to the back door. Then I could just go into my room without going through the house. I don't turn the lights on and hit a chair as I go through the kitchen. Damn. It teeters on two legs and settles back to the floor. I see the light come on in Charlotte's room. I move quickly to the back of the house and my room. Not fast enough. Shit.

"Rosie, is that you?"

"Who were you expecting?"

I go back to the kitchen. I need a drink. I open the fridge. Nothing. I'm not hungry. I'm still a bit drunk. I get a glass from the shelf and get cold water. I feel better.

"Come tell me about your party."

She sounds so sweet. Just wants to smell my breath. No way. Just go to sleep.

"Nope, I'm goin to bed. See you tomorrow."

I go to my room and begin to undress. Drop all my clothes on the floor. Brush my teeth and hit the bed. I do not want to go in there. What would I tell her? We had a wonderful time. After the party David and I had sex. She thinks I like David and that we might marry. How disgusting. I like him as a friend. We have no chemistry. I tell her he's as gay as I am. But we have great dinner parties at his house and we see all the movies. She thinks because he takes me out that he's not gay. Does she think I'm not? She's crazy. The room spins. I hang my leg over the side of the bed to stop the room. WOW. She better not come in.

I hear her in the kitchen. She comes to my door and starts to step in, turns around and says, "I worry so when you drive that drunk."

"So, I'll move out and then you won't know, MOTHER!"

Gloria and I drive to Sunset Beach so I can show her this great piece of property. We sit in the car looking at the waterway in front of us and just a block away, behind us is the beach and the beautiful Gulf of Mexico. I'd live in a tent on this lot if I could afford it and the town would let me. I tell her that Charlotte and I have talked about building a duplex. I think this lot is perfect but don't say so now.

"You'll never move away from Charlotte. Of course she wants to build a duplex. She'll do anything to stay close to her Rosie."

"I will have my own space in a duplex. And when I move, will you leave your mother and move in with me?"

I watch the dark black clouds gather for the oncoming storm. I don't wait for her answer. She has already said she doesn't want to move to an apartment. I know she wants to live with her mother.

She looks out the window and says, "Let's go home. We can't fish in the rain."

I put the car in reverse and drive off the property. This is my dream place. I drive the one block to the beach and go along the beach road.

I always have a fishing pole and tackle box in my car. I take it with me to sit by the water, solve all the world problems and once in a while I even catch a fish. I seldom keep them unless one happens to be a snook and that only happens at night with great patience and serious attention to fishing. Today, I'm going back to sunset beach to clear my head. I'll use my favorite lure; it's called a deadly dick.

I walk about a half mile on the beach to the pass. This pass goes from the bay to the gulf right past my favorite vacant lot on the south end of the beach. The land between bay and gulf is only one block wide. I stand on the sand watching the gentle flow of light ripples. I cast my line and before I can begin to reel, it's on the beach. So I move to the other side of this jetty and let my line go out into the pass. I find a flat rock and sit watching the gulls and pelicans dive for fish. If a fish bites, I'll let him play.

I always thought that being in Florida meant that work was play and that after work was play too. I dreamed of catching fish for dinner every night. That Charlotte and I would live and love together. Fish together. Cook for each other and someday live on the water. I never thought about what if. It was a solid love. We talked about camping and fishing, planting flowers, fruit trees and having orchids; so much for talk and sex.

I feel a tug on my line. If it's a fish, it's a catfish. I hate to catch them. And I can tell this is one. It's a big one. I feel that identifier pull down and then three little tugs. He's playing a tune with my deadly dick rod and probably just snagged when he checked it out. I reel in and as I lift the fish over the rocks, he's gone. Thanks, Mr. Catfish. Send your neighbors. Not your sisters.

Why have I waited so long to move? Why am I so slow to catch on? She's kind and gentle. Good to me. But she hates being Gay. I better move on. We don't fish together. We don't play much tennis anymore. In fact we don't do anything together. We've made love once or twice in the last year and she ruined that with her talk about being a man. So what AM I going to do? What are my options? I reel in knowing that the second catfish got off the lure long ago. Give them enough slack in the line and they are magical. I cast again and keep it moving a while. I get no bites with my big shrimp. I lie down and catch a few rays.

Why did I come to Florida with her? We have a nice house. I have my own space. But I don't want my own space like that. I'd rather be alone. I can't afford to move right now. I'm having fun dating Gloria and then there's David. I don't love him. Neither did I love George, or Calvin or Fred. They were all fun but not the same. David's as gay as Charlotte. Maybe that's what's bugging her. He's keeping up a front at the college. I do too. Forget it. I pull my line in and walk back down the beach. I sit down on the sand and watch the water. Sandpipers play at the water's edge. They don't even look my way. Just dig into the sand, get a sand flea or small clam and have a snack. And keep on digging.

I linger to watch the sunset. It is magnificent. If I lived on the beach I'd see a wonderful sunset every night. I'm getting hungry. I jump up, go to my car and drive to Woody's. It's a neat outdoor restaurant right on the water at Blind Pass. I order a grouper sandwich with fries and a beer. I sit by the rail at the sea wall. The water in the pass is getting rough. I must find a way to live on the beach. I'll start looking for new home. There has to be a change for me.

Roger and I are having lunch together as we often do. We're colleagues at the college and good friends. He seems a bit edgy today. We've hardly said ten words to each other. Small talk about school but that's Ok with me. I'm very busy. He has been especially quiet. I don't have time for dessert or for trying to comfort him or whatever. I finish my salad and motion for the waiter. He clears the table and asks about dessert: Roger orders. I decline. We both order coffee. I excuse myself and go to the bathroom.

When I return, he smiles and apologizes for his mood. I say it's OK, that I wonder what's going on, but don't have much time now. The idle talk was just right for me today. I wish he and others would just stay home when they are so moody. I look around and wonder how many other tables are filled with uncomfortable people trying to be friendly at lunch. The coffee is good.

"How do you stand working with the women in your department?"

I knew something was buzzing around in his head. I must leave, but I have to know more about what he's really asking. My heart quickens and I take a deep breath.

"What women? What do you mean? We each teach our own classes. We don't really work together that much." Is he talking about gay or just plain dumb? I don't especially like any of them but they were here when I came. I didn't pick them. Is this an issue or is this just gossip? He always has a lot of that to tell. Now who's feeling uncomfortable?

"But you know. . . Uh . . They're lesbians."

I shift in my chair and wish I had not ordered coffee. Wish I had left before this question.

"Are they? I don't know that. How do you know that about them? And how do you know I'm not?" Is this his way of finding out? Or is this what he thinks will make me date him just to keep him from telling others that I am or to keep him from thinking I am. I know this jeopardy. I've had this discussion too many times for this one to change my actions. My sexual expression is none of his fucking business until we are fucking. And that won't happen.

"Yeah, right Rose, give me a break. You aren't anything like they are."

He's right there. I'm not like them. I don't smoke, drink as much, play golf, or bowl. I have other friends and don't hang out with anyone on campus. He's an administrator and maybe they're trying to get rid of all the gay teachers. That's a joke, there are many of us.

"Well, women come in all kinds of packages."

"But your package isn't lesbian. I'd bet on that. And win a lot of money."

151

"Suit yourself.   There probably isn't much of a market for that bet.   I have to get back for a two o'clock class. Thanks for lunch. I'll call you next week: it's my turn to pay." I get up, go around the table, give him a quick kiss on the cheek and walk toward the door.

I wonder what brought all this up today. Is there talk around campus about the others, about me? Who cares? I do my job and a damn good one at that. My classes are more in demand every semester.   I do know some gay students and they talk to me about their gayness. It's always in my office with the door closed. Maybe the word is out that I allow it. I hope so anyway.   Gay or non-gay, I want students to feel welcome in my classes and my office.

As I move through the restaurant I see a former student. She sees me and motions for me to come over. I haven't seen her since she left school two years ago. She's with a woman and child. I always thought Cheryl was gay. It's a coincidence after my conversation with Roger.

I go to her table. She gets up, gives me a hug and a kiss and tells me how happy she is to see me. "Meet Becky, my wife and our darling Meg. We were married, you know, a commitment ceremony, in January.   We're living in Tampa."

I'm surprised at her ease in telling me this and surprised at my own ease in hearing it. I want to ask if her Mother's OK with it, but decide better for another time. "Very nice to meet you, Becky and you are right, Meg is a darling. I must run now. I have a two o'clock class. But come by sometime so we can catch up."

Driving back to the gym, I plan how I will tell the department head, about seeing Cheryl. She's a very good friend of Cheryl's mother. There was a big to-do when Cheryl left school.   She warned faculty in department meetings about being friendly with THOSE girls who get others in trouble. I always ask her to explain what she meant. She glossed over my question by saying, "Don't worry, they are not in your classes." How did she know? I can't wait to see her reaction to Cheryl's marriage.

I teach my last archery class of the day, put away equipment, and head for the gym, knowing that I will see her. Just as I pull into a parking space, she walks out of her office. I jump out of the car, "Hi. I saw a friend of yours at lunch." I walk past her into the gym. I know I have a smirk on my face. I call over my shoulder, "I'll be right back. Don't go away."

I go to my office to find a pile of student-papers and some junk mail on my desk. I go through the mail quickly and pick up papers to take home to grade tonight. I walk out and find her still standing in the doorway between the gym and her office.

"So, who did you see?"

"I had lunch at the Red Lobster and met Cheryl McMann. She's married now. I guess you knew that. And they have the cutest child."

"What? I saw her last fall. She didn't have a child and wasn't pregnant as far as I could tell. I saw her mother just last week. She didn't say. . . . No, I didn't know. Are you sure?"

I turn so I'm facing her. "Well she introduced me to her wife and their daughter." The look on her face is worth it all. I smile clear through. She turns away from me and says, "I don't understand."

I step onto the sidewalk and look back at her. I know she understands. She's as gay as Cheryl. "She considers herself married to a woman who has a child."

"But. . . ."

I walk to my car and open the door. I turn back and say, "You'll figure it out. See you tomorrow." I laugh all the way home.

Tonight I'll tell her. She'll be furious. But I cannot stay here with her. I walk into the living room. I sit down. I get up, go to the kitchen. Get a handful of nuts. I just finished dinner. I don't need these nuts. I go back to my room. I call Glor and tell her I am going to tell Charlotte tonight that I am moving. She tells me to wait.

153

I don't understand. I ask, "What for? Aren't we both moving? I thought we had . . ."

"I know, but I think we should wait a while."

I feel hot. My heart quickens. "I'm not waiting. I don't care. I can't live like this."

Charlotte walks into my room as I say goodbye. "What's up?"

I want to scream. Am I really ready to deal with her wrath? I have to get my plan in better shape.

She shifts from foot to foot. "I thought you wanted to talk." She looks at me and I can tell she wants to sit down. I hear my voice inside screaming: Not now. Get out of my room. I don't want to see you. And don't ever come in without knocking first you pigheaded selfish old woman. You show me no respect. Nothing is mine. The house I pay half on is yours, the furniture I help buy, is yours. I have nothing. Go away. I hang my head and say, "Yes, but it can wait. It's late, and I'm ready for bed." I pick up a book and flop onto the bed.

"Are you sure?"

"Yeah."

As I run this last mile this morning, I am determined to move. This is a great neighborhood but I want to be on the water. I think Charlotte's idea of building a duplex on the water is a good one but I'm not sure a duplex will be big enough. And she'll be there watching my every move. But being on the water is what I want. We could help each other. She's getting older and will need help soon. It will take a lot of time to find property, build and move. I should just move. The apartments I looked at yesterday were OK. Not great. I could afford one of them. But none could compare with a place on the water. I should just move and hope someday I can afford a place of my own on the water. I sprint to the back door.

A shower is a wonderful experience after a good run. I get dressed and come to the kitchen singing. I'm ready to pack my things. I'm ready to move. I hear Charlotte listening to the news in the living room. "Morning,

Charlotte. I looked at two apartments yesterday. I might take the one that's on the beach but a block from the water. It's little but has a good view."

I start to sit with her in the living room but I need coffee first. I turn and go back to the kitchen. She hasn't said anything. I call, "Want more tea?"

"No. Where's this apartment?"

I think about my trip yesterday to St. Pete Beach to see the apartment. I thought it was on the water. They do have a dock across the street, on the bay. I can fish from that dock if I live there. The floors are linoleum and the kitchen has oilcloth covering on the table. Just like Oak Hill. This kitchen is much nicer. But Charlotte comes with this house. I pour my coffee. If we buy property to build a duplex she's there too but I'll have more than any apartment I've seen. I go back to the living room. I pick up the paper and begin to read. I hesitate to answer. I'm not sure I want her to know where the apartment is.

She mutes the television and asks again, "So where's the apartment?"

I feel her looking at me. If I move, will I want her to visit? Of course I will, we've lived together for almost ten years. Can I cut her out of my life now? I'm sure I won't. I throw the paper down and take a drink of coffee. "It's at the north end of St. Pete Beach."

"I'll go with you if you want to look at it again. You haven't signed a lease have you?"

"No. Maybe later we can take a drive." I go back to my room and clean it. Then I clean the bathroom.

Where is this building? I don't recognize it. I hear someone chasing me. Suddenly I see a stairway and run toward it. The footsteps behind me are getting closer. I run faster. As I put my foot on the first step, it becomes an escalator and begins going up. I'm gaining time and space from the footsteps behind me. I turn to see who it is. I can't tell. It's a giant pink blob. I race up the escalator and just as I get to next to the last step it begins to move back down. I keep stepping up as the steps go out from under me. I'm always just one step away from the top. I see the blob on the bottom step. Now, the escalator begins to move upward again. I get off and run down a long hall. A door looms ahead and finally I reach for the handle. I pull the door open but it goes out to a ledge. I can't get away. I turn to see the pink blob getting closer. It is huge and moves quickly. There are people standing just below the ledge. They're shouting, "JUMP. JUMP."

I awake in a cold sweat.

Charlotte and I are driving up and down the beaches, looking for property. We have decided to build a duplex so we will be close but still have our own spaces. I'm not sure it's a good idea but it sounds like I'd get my dream of living on the water and have something to show for all the money. I'd be paying on a mortgage with my name on it.

"I thought you said you had found a piece of land near St Pete Beach. Let's go look at it."

"You won't even consider it. It's on Sunset Beach."

I'm driving as fast as I dare toward Sunset Beach, because that's where I want to live. I'm past the point of caring whether she moves with me. In fact I really believe that both of us would be better off for the rest of our lives if we just said goodbye to each other now. She picks up a map and begins to look at where I have marked lots that I think are appropriate for building a duplex. Why can't I just make a break? I should. She's been so good to me since I met her at Wesleyan. How can I just say to this sad old lady, "Get out of my life?" I feel so responsible for her. It's crazy. I don't really like her. Oh that's not true. Well, I don't like how she treats me. Like a daughter and with all the guilt of taking care of her. She's getting older. Well, I'm not getting younger but I am a lot younger than she is.

"You know that I will have to sell my house to pay for a lot and build a house."

Yeah she'll sell her house on which I'm paying half the mortgage. I know I'll never get half the selling price. What is wrong with me? "I'm not interested in building a house, Charlotte. I want my own space. I'm tired of acting

156

like a child that has to have permission to go out, to stay out overnight, to come home late, to skip dinner, to not get up on Saturday morning. I'm 34 years old. I want to get on with my life. I want to have a love in my life." I look at her. I can tell she is stunned. So am I. I can't believe I'm saying these things.

"You do have a love."

"I mean a real love. That will be someone who loves and respects me and someone who isn't ashamed of loving another woman. Our real love relationship ended before it started because of your self-hate. I can't change that. God knows I've tried."

"You have no respect for what is right."

"Who says it's not right? What's right and what's wrong? I've loved more women than you admit to loving and for me, that's the way it is. It's never been wrong. I don't care what THEY, whoever THEY are, say."

I turn right onto Sunset Beach and notice that she is squirming in the seat. She really doesn't want to see this property because she knows she'll like it. I've been talking about it for months. This strip of land is only a block wide from gulf to bay. A Street coming from the Gulf dead-ends into the lot, which is on the bay. What's not to like? I drive down 78th Avenue and right up on the lot. It's a bit higher than the properties beside it and gives the illusion that you're on higher land.

"Just come look at the sea wall. It's in really good shape. Whoever owns it has taken good care of this wall. Well, what do you think? Isn't it beautiful?" It's pretty narrow but no property on the beach is wide. At least I haven't found any. I bend down and take a sand spur off my sock. We'll dig those when the foundation goes in. "Well, say something."

Just as she opens her mouth to speak, the man from the house on the left comes onto the lot and asks what we want. "We're just looking", I say. "Do you know who owns this lot?"

"Yep."

Oh, that's friendly, I think. I pick up a rock on the lot and toss it aside. I notice his yard is very well kept. He has birdhouses all along the walkway mounted on pipes about ten feet tall with beautiful parakeets everywhere. They're very noisy. He doesn't seem to pay much attention to their squawking. Maybe he can't hear very well. I'm glad they aren't kept in cages.

Charlotte has gone over to talk with him. Guess she doesn't think she should raise her voice. "Does the owner live nearby? I notice the phone number is a beach exchange."

I didn't even notice that. Well, things are looking up. She must like the lot. It's beautiful, on the bay and one block from the Gulf beach. I won't say anything about how I imagine that the water washes straight through when there's a big storm. I'll worry about that when the time comes. But "our" lot is higher than the others so if they don't have water in their houses we won't have any on our yard. I'll ask him but not now.

"Yes, he lives in the last building on this side of the street Mr. Smith at the Smithwick Motel, just down the street." He points in that direction.

"Should I tell him you sent us?"

"Nope."

"Let's go see if he's in, Rosie."

I can't believe my ears. She hasn't even said she likes it. She's never wanted to find out about any of the other lots. I've had to make all the calls. I'm floating in thin air as we walk down the street. I know she knows that I'm serious about having my own space. The motel is the fifth building toward the south end of this finger of land and there's nothing beyond it but vacant land. It's not well kept but it provides access to fishing in the waterway that goes from bay to gulf. I've been here often lately. Some of the fishermen have told me it's the best spot for catching snook.

As I watch people fish all along the shore on the bay side and in the pass, I see myself catching a really big snook. It grabs my bait and jumps into the air. I tighten my hold on my fishing rod and the snook runs with my bait. I reel, he swims away. I reel and he flops in the sand. He's mine.

We find Mr. Smith in the office. He greets us and invites us in. He probably thinks we want to rent a room. But Charlotte gets right to the point. "How much do you want for the lot just up the street?"

"Oh. About nine thousand dollars. Why? Are you interested?"

"Well, we could be. How about $8,500. We're just school teachers and don't have a lot of money."

He doesn't give a damn who we are or what we do. He interested in selling the property. Why does she always have to try to tell all about us when she finds a live one to tell? Maybe she thinks if she tells them enough they will never suspect her dark secret. I wish she would keep her mouth shut about me. Maybe renting for a while wouldn't hurt. The water is very clear. I can see small fish swimming all around the dock. This is a beautiful waterway. I bet people catch lots of fish here. I can always go to the beach or the pass to fish no matter where I live. Oh, please, Charlotte, just say yes. I know I shouldn't want this.

"Give me $8,600 cash and you can spit in the water and call it yours."

"Well, sir, I don't have that much with me but I can give you a deposit to hold it. That OK with you Rosie?"

Is it OK? I'm jumping out of my skin. I'm sorry for all those nasty things I've been thinking lately.

"Yeah, it's OK with me."

I see a student running across the field. She yells, "Miss Walton, You have an emergency call from your aunt in Virginia."

I head for my office. I know it's about Mother. She called last week to ask what I thought about her having radiation treatments for a recurrence of her breast cancer. I told her I wouldn't do that at her age. She had the first cancer nineteen years ago. I don't think that will be what kills her. Her heart is what I worry about. I told her I

159

thought the treatments might affect her heart again like they had years ago. What has changed? I wasn't very patient with her and like most everything between us; it ended with an argument. Is she dead? Will I say "I told you so" or will I feel guilty the rest of my life. Has Libby called Nancy? Probably not, she always calls me first. I get along with Libby.

By the time I get to my office on the second floor I'm out of breath. I sit down, rest a minute and pick up the phone to call Libby. "Hello, Libby, what happened? I know it must be serious if you're calling me in the middle of the day?"

"Well, darling, it's your mom. She's was having one of those treatments. You probably know more about that than I do. She said you didn't want her to have any more."

"Well, not exactly."

"Anyway, she went into heart failure this morning during the treatment. Dr. James called me. She's in a coma, on life support. He thinks you girls should come to see her."

Libby is so gentle. She doesn't want to push me. She always wants me to make the decision when it pertains to mother.

"OK", I said.

"It might be enough to wake her. I told him I'd call you to see what you want to do."

"Of course I'll come. I'll be there as soon as I can make arrangements. Where can you meet me? I've never flown to your place. Have you talked with Nancy? Is she coming? Do you think both of us need to be there? Anyway, I'll come."

"I haven't talked to Nan. I always talk to you first. You know that. You can fly into Newport News or Richmond. It'll take me about two hours to get to Richmond. Newport News is just about 25 minutes. Just let me know. I'll meet you at either airport."

"I'll call Nancy. They were just there last week, weren't they? Maybe I'll come now and depending on what happens, she can come later. Anyway let me see what I can do about flights and I'll let you know. Thanks, Libby, I love ya."

I call Nancy first and we decide it will be better for one of us to go first, see what is going on and then we'll decide what to do from there. And as usual, she's pretty nonchalant about it all. Whatever happens, happens, and we'll deal with it. As usual she thinks everything will be OK. Not me. I think Mother will be a vegetable and I'll have to make the decisions and take care of everything. I don't even like her. I'll try not to make even a little decision without consulting Nancy.

I arrive in Newport News at 10:20 pm the next day and at my insistence, Libby takes me directly to the hospital. She thinks I should wait till morning. She drops me at the front door and says, "Call if you need me or want anything. And I mean anytime."

It's a Catholic hospital and some of the nurses still wear habits and walk silently through the hallways. I meet the first nun just inside the door. "May I help you? Visiting hours are over."

"Yes, I know but I just arrived from Florida and my mother may be dying. I want to see her now. She's in room 408. I'll be very quiet." I walk past her and toward the elevator. I hear her say something but do not turn to answer. I push the elevator button and it opens quickly. I step in and turn to see her coming toward the door. I push 4 and wave. A nurse in all white with a starched cap and gold pins stops me as I step out on floor 4.

"Visiting hours are over."

"Yes, I know. But I just arrived from Florida and I understand my mother, Mary Walton, is very ill. I'll be very quiet and sit with her tonight in room 408."

"The Sisters will not like that, but I won't tell them. Your mother is very sick." She walks with me to the room. I thank her as she closes the door.

Mother looks fine. She's sleeping and breathing easy with the oxygen and seems very peaceful. I speak to her but she makes no motion or sound like she heard me or felt my presence. I sit by the bed a while, just trying to calm myself. I go to the nurses' station and they tell me she's been in the coma since Monday morning and there's been no change. They've done some procedures to make her comfortable and allow the normal body functions to take place without her assistance. Marcie, the nurse who met me at the elevator, makes me feel very comfortable. She says she'll be there till eight in the morning, if I need anything. Come find her.

I'm a mess. First, I don't like her, but she's my mom. Does it mean that I should not want her to stay asleep, or die? Do I care? Can I talk to anyone here about my feelings? Who can I trust? What would Libby do and will she tell me? What if mother does not come out of this coma, tomorrow or the next day? How long do I wait to ask that life support be taken away? Will Nancy agree with me? I know I won't want to be on life support for any reason. If I'm that sick, let me go. But is that what mother would want? Wait and see, talk to Dr. James. He's the one that encouraged her to have the treatments even with her bad heart. Does he know something he didn't tell her? I talked with him once, a couple of years ago when she had an episode with her heart, but I don't remember what he said.

Marcie comes in to ask if I want coffee. "That would be good, may I come with you? She's not very talkative. I could use a cup of strong coffee or a stiff drink."

As we walk through several halls and down one flight of stairs, I listen to Marcie. "I can't tell you anymore than I have about her condition but I can help you with your feelings, if you want to talk."

"Thank you, I may take you up on that."

"I remember your mom from a couple of years ago when she had a heart flare-up. She was sure she'd had a heart attack and we had a very hard time convincing her it was not a damaging attack but rather an irregular beat. Sometimes that happens when people are under stress or have an episode in their life that greatly affects them."

"She certainly didn't tell me that. She just talked about her heart attack."

The coffee is strong and the conversation helpful. I go back to mother's room and take a nap in the straight chair beside her bed.

Since my arrival on Tuesday, my days and nights are all the same. I eat breakfast at about 4AM with the night nurses and go back to sleep on the lounge chair I've moved into her room. Then I wake for the day about 8AM, go to her bathroom and wash my face and hands. Then I read the paper to her. She's not changed expression or made a sound. Her breathing is pretty regular, except for a few times during the night when I wake because her rhythm changes. It's Saturday morning. I'm down to reading the headlines. To say nothing of how tired I am. Time for a change. I don't care what change, good or bad, and I'm not sure which way I think would be better. On Thursday, I talked at length with three doctors who encouraged me to give her 48 more hours before pulling the plug. I call Nancy each day to report how strenuous this waiting is. I always give her the opportunity to say I'll come down, but she hasn't taken the hint. So I decide that today is the day. I'll call her and say that if mother doesn't come out of this coma by Sunday noon, I'm allowing the doctors to end life support. If she wants to see mother before that, she should come on down. I feel good about my decision after talking to the doctors and to Libby.

I call Nancy at noon. She thinks I'm over-reacting, but she and Ronnie, her husband, will come down tonight. They'll arrive close to midnight. "Should we come to her apartment to get you or just go to the hospital?"

I can't believe my ears. I've talked to her each day, told her my routine, and that the only time I'm away from her hospital room is about an hour in the afternoon, to shower and change clothes, and short intervals when I pace the hospital corridors, or to get something to eat in the hospital cafe.

"Nancy, I'll be at the hospital, where I've been since Tuesday night. So just come here. You can stay with her the rest of the night. I'll gladly go sleep in a bed someplace, anyplace by then. I guess I just think someone has to be here in case she comes out of the coma."

163

At exactly the stroke of midnight, Nancy and Ronnie walk in. Mother sits up when she hears Nancy. Thanks her for coming to see her so soon. I'm shocked beyond belief. I can't believe what I see happening. I guess Nancy should have come first.

After a few minutes, Nancy says, "I guess Ronnie and I'll go to the apartment and go to sleep, I'm really tired. Do you want us to take you to Libby's or do you want to come to her apartment and sleep on the couch?"

I am dumbfounded. "No, Nancy, I'll stay here. I've been here since Tuesday, so why not stay through this night. I'll probably go home tomorrow and back to work Monday, if all stays this way."

"Then I'll bring you breakfast." They leave me in a state of shock. How can they react so calmly? Maybe I was over-reacting. But I am in total disbelief about mother and Nancy.

Mother sits up even more and looks at me. She seems surprised that I'm here. I tell her I've been here all week. "Rose Ann! In those clothes? What have the doctors and nurses said about you being here dressed like that? I'll apologize tomorrow."

This is the last straw. I stay through the night, without a word. Nancy arrives at 10:30 AM with cold biscuits to learn that I have an afternoon flight from Richmond to Florida.

Two months later after mother recovered she moved to Pittsburgh to be close to Nancy and her kids. I was very relieved that she did not want to move to Florida. She and I keep in touch by phone. Her occasional visits are not happy times for either of us.

I turn into the driveway, happy to be home from the big statewide teachers' conference. I hate driving and even if the trip from Orlando was uneventful, driving through Tampa is always stressful for me. I look around; the flowers are beautiful. I'll plant more on the waterfront where we're building the duplex. I can't wait to see what's been done since I left six days ago. Soon, I'll be in my own place even if it's right next to Charlotte. I'm acting as the contractor in this building project and I am learning lots. It's a real education. I hire carpenters, plumbers, and "laborers" as they are called. My friend Jim, a builder, is helping and he inspects everything and tells me who to pay and when. Not many of these workers want to take orders from a woman. I gather my stuff and start for the front door. Charlotte is coming out the door like a warrior on a battle mission. I swallow hard and get set for God knows what.

"We need 25,000 dollars by tomorrow and I couldn't find you. You weren't at the number you gave me. Where were you?"

"Well, Hi Charlotte, nice to see you. Good to be home. How are you? Did you have a good weekend? The conference was great. I need a drink of water." I keep walking toward the door. Pass her as I step onto the porch and enter the house. I cannot believe, but I should, that she is yelling out the door so the neighbors can hear her. Thank you God, for my future space. And it will still be too close. Where are my guts? She follows me into the kitchen still yelling.

"Rosie, you don't seem to care. Did you hear?"

"Yes, I heard you. But I'd rather NOT discuss money with the neighbors."

"You think you're so damn smart."

She moves past me to the stove and continues what she was doing before I arrived. My heart is going faster and I feel the redness fill my face. I want to hit her. She has no respect. I quietly go to my room. Drop my suitcase and books and flop on the bed. It's no use. I should just give her the house and walk away. But I want to live on the water and in my own space. I'll double lock the door. I knew there was money in my other account.

I lean back in my lounge chair and close my eyes. The sky is powder blue without a cloud to dream about. Water laps at my feet and tiny fish swim close by. I'll get the seine net after a while and gather a few of them for fishing tomorrow. We have our catch for dinner tonight and now I want to sleep. I don't know where Glor went but she said she'd be back in a few minutes. Pelicans begin to hit the water a few yards in front of me. I don't see how they keep from breaking their necks. But each time they dive, they sit right up and swallow their catch. Makes it look easy.

Is it real? Am I dreaming? No! Damn! I jump when a cold glass touches my arm. I open my eyes and there she is smiling down at me with two drinks in her hand. She tells me that we were out of Vodka and now we have some. "What's for dinner?" She gives me a warm kiss and I'm supposed to start thinking about cooking.

I take my drink and thank her. "Now let's go back to your greeting without the cold glass on my arm."

I'm painting Charlotte's apartment in our new duplex on Sunset Beach, a section of Treasure Island. Both apartments are about finished and I want to wait to move things in after they are both painted and carpeted. Carpet comes tomorrow. It is a beautiful building and I'm so proud of it. I had the stucco put on like wood, which makes the second level, the living level, looks like Cypress. The Treasure Island codes would not let us use wood. The building is cement block filled two stories high with cement. It won't blow away. The cypress color and design causes many people to stop to ask about the wood. If I'm in the yard, people stop and ask if it's wood. I smile and say "No." The living quarters are on the second level with space for parking below. The stairs to the second level are circular, bright red, and in the middle of the building.

I hear people coming up the stairs. I'm not in the mood to give a tour. I can't believe that people from the beach walk in and around like they own the place. I continue painting and just wait for their questions. I never tell the whole truth. It is none of their business.

"Oh! Hello. This is a beautiful building, do you mind if we look around? We live up the street and our neighbors told us to come see it."

166

"No, I'm just painting." I have on cut off shorts, a slim halter, and paint of various colors all over me. They walk past me in the hallway and go right on through the apartment. They are gossiping about us. I hear, "They are two old maid school teachers and they can't imagine that schoolteachers would have enough money. One of them is very old but still teaching. The other is very young and energetic. She fishes a lot from the dock. Guess that's why they built the dock first."

I go to fill the paint pan chuckling to myself. As I pass the bathroom, I catch a glimpse of how terrible I look. Not like a college professor.

"Do you know the ladies building this place?"

"Yes."

"I heard that one was very old and the other very young."

"Really, I ask?

"Are they?"

"Well, one is older than the other but I'm not sure what you mean by very."

"One is about ready to retire."

"I haven't heard that. Excuse me, I need to get there to finish this wall."

"How well do you know them?"

"Sometimes too well."

"Where do they teach?"

I answer, "One teaches at the Junior College, the other at a Junior High School. Now if you will excuse me, I really must finish this so I can start on my own apartment."

"Where is it?"

"Right there." I point to the other side of the duplex. They seem shocked and embarrassed and ask why I didn't tell them that in the first place. They do not wait for an answer.

Health class starts today with student reports. I sit in the back of the room and ponder the dean's comments. I think he's crazy, talking about not spending class time to talk about sex and how to prevent pregnancy in a college-level

167

health class. He told me that Florida law prohibits that discussion in the classroom. That has not deterred me before and it will not now. I invited him to class to listen to the student reports about sexuality. I know they will talk about birth control and I will handle the discussion to be sure they know about abstinence.

Cindy steps to the front of the class and begins her report on methods of birth control. She has everyone's attention and you can hear a pin drop. This class is very respectful of each other especially when one of them is giving a report. Suddenly, class is in an uproar. Maybe I'm not listening close enough. The report was going well and all of a sudden it isn't. "Men will promise anything to get a woman to have intercourse. The worst promise is I'll withdraw."

That's true. What's this reaction? I turn to see.

Kenny jumps up, "Man, that's bullshit. There's no man on this earth who can go full speed ahead, see where he's headed and then put it in reverse. He's moving on. An, Honey, if you don't believe that one, you havin a baby."

Class bursts into more laughter. I must control this but inside I am laughing as hard as they are and I know my smile lets them know that. I let them laugh a minute or two and then say; "Now class, let's let Cindy finish her report. I believe you may have misunderstood her statement."

A chorus of "No way" rings through the room. Kenny is enjoying the support and Cindy is embarrassed and perplexed. She needs a good grade and knows it. She'll pass, but she doesn't know that and thinks she may not.

Good thing the Dean didn't accept my invitation to class today. But he may have his spies here. I look around to see if I can spot a student who looks suspicious. There are three huddled together and not laughing. I know the bell is about to ring.

"Well, class, let's look at the implication of what Cindy and Kenny are saying."

Class gets very quiet. All heads turn toward me. The bell rings. As students rise, I suggest that they keep this under their hats till we have time to discuss it.

168

The next class began with our birth control discussions, freely until all questions were answered and all opinions expressed. I never heard from the Dean.

I arranged for the carpet to be delivered at two o'clock right after my last class. The truck is in the driveway. Great that means moving can begin tomorrow. I have a lot of stuff in my car now and maybe these men laying carpet will carry some of the heavier stuff to my apartment as they go up the steps. Workmen always forget something in the truck and have to go back or they need a smoking break. I won't let them smoke in the apartments.

"Thanks for being here. Have you been waiting long?"

"No, we just got here when you drove up. This is a beautiful building."

"Thanks. And now you will make the floors beautiful." I show them the stairs.

"This turn into the stairs is not going to allow us to bring the big rolls up. Is there another entrance?"

"No, only the spiral stairway in front. That will be difficult, I think." We walk back to the front of the building and suddenly I realize these four strong men can lift the carpet right over the railing on the second level deck. The railing is cypress wood and very secure. "Could you lift the big rolls over the railing? I'll go open the sliding door to the bedrooms on each side."

Since each apartment is being carpeted from front to back with the same color and style, they have one apartment finished in less than two hours. I had them do Charlotte's side first. I call her to tell her she can start moving furniture.

My friends help move my furniture, all three pieces, on Saturday. By the end of the day I was in my own place. I was too tired to cook but invited them to dinner on Sunday. "We'll eat about seven, but come early for a drink."

Glor quickly says, "A drink. You better go shopping today. I didn't see any booze."

Glor and I have been seeing each other off and on for about three years. We've begun to talk about moving in together in my new place on the beach. She's not sure about living that close to Charlotte and I understand. But something's missing tonight as we drive to a dinner party at her supervisor's house. She's not her usual bubbly self. I fidget in the seat. Why did she want to take my car? We never take my car. She has been distant for about a week. Every time I ask, she says everything's great. No sense asking again. The sky is beautiful. Almost sunset and the pinks and violets are mixing with the blues and reds. We are going south; I see the sun slowly drifting toward the water to my right. I talk about the beautiful sunsets on our beach with no response.

We pull into the driveway at Bobbi and Betsy's place. Betsy has cancer and I must admit that I was reluctant to accept the invitation to dinner knowing how very sick she is. Bobbi bounds out the door to greet us. She is bursting with enthusiasm and Glor meets her with more excitement than I've seen her express in weeks. Maybe this is it. I walk around the car and say," Hello." Bobbi shakes my hand and quickly turns to Glor and takes her hand and they walk into the house hand in hand. I follow like an obedient dog.

Glor goes to the kitchen with Bobbi to help make drinks. Like it's difficult to pour vodka over ice and carry two glasses back to the living room. That's why it takes two of them. I look around the living room. It's filled with antique dust collectors. And some pictures. I start to get up and look at the pictures but they come back. I know things are not as they were yesterday.

Bobbi says Betsy's sleeping and probably won't wake for an hour or so. We can enjoy our drinks and then say "hello" if you want. What does she mean, if we want? Is she that sick?

I reach for some nuts and take a sip of my drink. Glor is going on at great rate with Bobbi about work and the patient she had last night who checked himself out before treatment. Bobbi asks appropriate questions and I feel like I'm sitting in a classroom. Why am I here? We have roast beef and baked potato with a very good salad. Glor suggests that we have dessert later.

We return to the living room and Bobbi goes to the kitchen to get after dinner drinks. Gloria sits close to me and whispers, "Rosie, I'm not going home with you."

"Excuse me. You're what?"

"Not going home with you."

"What the hell? Why?"

"Not so loud. Bobbi will . . . ." She sits closer to me and puts her arm around my shoulder. I push it away and stand up. I move toward the door. I want to throw something at her. One of these antique dolls would be perfect.

"I don't give a shit. I can't believe you brought me here. I should have known something was up when you didn't drive."

"I just have to find out how I feel about Bobbi."

"Well, don't knock on my door tomorrow or any time." She follows me toward the door and pleads with me to listen. Listen to her tell me to go to hell. Funny Bobbi hasn't gotten those after dinner drinks yet. Or perhaps she has taken two to the bedroom and then gone to comfort Betsy. Will she tell her about Glor? I doubt it.

"Rosie, please." She wants to know if I'm going to say "thank you" to Bobbi.

What the fuck does she think? I'm not about to say thank you. What for? The last supper? I try not to show her my tears. I don't want her to know. How can she do this? But she left another woman for me. But not like this.

I get to the front door and walk out. She follows but I'm in the car before she can stop me. I back out of the driveway and the tears block my vision. I drive down the street screaming.

DAMN   DAMN   SHIT   SHIT   SHIT

I will never speak to her again.

I roll over to see the clock. Last I looked it was 3 then 4 now 5 AM. All I can think about is Gloria. I haven't seen her for eight days. I told her not to come to my house ever again. But I still love her. I want her to live with me. For all these years we have had no place to really be together. Now, I've built the duplex and I have my own apartment, on the bay, one block from the Gulf and we could make a home together. I want to spend the rest of my life with her. And then BAM! She told me she had feelings for her nurse supervisor at work and must find out if they are real. Well, honey, my feelings are real. And I can't just turn them off like you seem to have done.

I don't have to be in school till 8. But I can't go back to sleep. I get up, put on my running shorts and tee shirt and head for the beach. Running at this hour is so beautiful, even in February. I love to watch the birds, egrets, pelicans, and my favorite sandpipers. The terns flip, fly, turn and come back. They land so easily and are so light on their tiny feet. It's not yet daylight, but it will be soon. I try to think of what I have to do today. Come on Rosie, get hold. It is not the end of the world, just the end of a beautiful love relationship. I don't want it to end. Damn her. But it does match her pattern, with others, before me. Her friends told me to watch out.

I finish my two miles, and sense the neighborhood waking up as I turn the last corner. I love this place, this little spit of land, just a block wide here where our duplex is. I skip down the street admiring it. I built this place and when I shower downstairs I see my handiwork. I tiled the shower with leftover tiles. None of them match but I don't care. It's like a patchwork quilt. And it's big and roomy in the utility room just inside by the pool. I wrap a towel around me, start up the steps to my apartment and drop the towel just inside the screen door and go on up. I'm free but numb. I go through the motions of life. This too will pass. I'll know better next time to take my time before I fall in love. Never mess with students even the ones older than you who aren't in class anymore. I put that thought into my head for keeps. Yeah, I was a very young student Charlotte messed with. I kick at the door. I make coffee, dress, and eat breakfast watching the gulls fly by the dock. They turn and dive for the little greenbacks I need for bait.

172

I pull into the college parking lot and see my friend, Barbara, walking toward the building. I roll the window down and say, "Well, Good morning, what're you doing here so early? I thought physical therapy classes started later in the day. Do you have any funny stories to get me through the day?" I pull into a parking place and get out of the car.

"Sure, and I have a favor to ask."

"I'm not in the mood to do anyone favors, not even you. Just tell me a funny story so I'll laugh all day." I walk over to where she's standing, look around to see that no one else is here and give her a quick kiss on the cheek.

"No, I'm serious, I have a colleague, friend visiting from New York and we need a fourth for dinner tonight. Will you go? You'll really like her. She's a physical therapist and teaches in a Community College on Long Island."

"What? Are you crazy? I've spent the week drinking and crying. You're funny. That's a good joke for the day. Call me in a year and we'll talk. I'm going to the archery field to shoot a few rounds before the students get here."

"I'll give you two hours to make up your mind."

I walk around the building and across the field. That's a funny idea. Me, go out. Tonight? Sure, to a wake. There's not enough Southern Comfort in St. Pete to talk me into that one. I just broke up with Gloria, with whom I thought about spending the rest of my life and within the week Barbara wants me meet another woman. I remember when some people thought I saw two or three women at once but Gloria was special. Maybe I need to try to get back into those fun-filled days of jumping around and never falling in love. I enjoyed that make-believe world of lust.

Oh boy, here comes Barbara again. I'm not going. That is the end of the discussion. I turn toward her and put my hands on my hips. She just won't listen.

"Hey, Rosie, I just talked to my friend Marge and she wants to play tennis at four. You can do that, can't you?" I'm shaking my head and all the time she's explaining how I can look her over and decide if I want to have dinner with

173

the three of them. "I told Bobbie to bring her and meet us on the courts on 22ⁿᵈ. I didn't think you would play on the college courts"

"OK. OK. I'll play tennis. And we might as well have a drink at my house before dinner."

Thank goodness the courts are almost empty. I don't need an audience. Here she comes. She is cute in red short shorts and a white top. Not much of a tan. She has at least two tennis rackets. Barbara didn't tell me she was a pro. Well, we'll see. We exchange greetings and begin hitting the ball. She slices everything she hits. She's quick but her backhand needs some work. Here I go, always being the teacher. I bet she could teach me a few strokes. We agree to play just one set. She wins the first two games before I get a point. So she's good. I win two games and then she finishes the last game with two very good serves just out of my reach. It's time for me to go home, have a drink, and change clothes.

I start for my car and yell, "Meet at my house at seven?"

"OK"

I change clothes three times and end up with my favorite suit. She'll have to notice the bright red top. This Marge is a very good tennis player, funny too. She made me laugh so hard on the court that I had trouble hitting the ball. May be her strategy. She's a stunner too. Tightly packed with curly hair and what a face; beautiful. I take the last sip of my second Manhattan as they open the door.

I'm such a face person. I can't take my eyes off her face. "Oh, would you like a drink?"

She shyly says, "May I have a whisky sour?"

"Sure, have a seat. It's comin' right up." I go to the kitchen, fix her drink and pour myself a cranberry juice. Her lips are little and so beautifully shaped. DAMN, she's a real stunner. I wonder what she thinks of me in this polyester suit. She has on a beautiful pair of brown slacks with a soft white blouse. She's looking the place over and comments about being on the water. I'm not sure of her adjective. She talks very fast. I'll have to listen closely to understand. I don't know what to talk about. But Bobbie will carry the conversation. Not to worry.

Bobbie made reservations at the Bilmar and assures me that service is good and it's a lovely space. I hope the food is good.

Marge orders flounder and I order grouper. We plan to share, her idea. I don't want her flounder but she must taste my grouper. It's the local fish. Barbara and Bobbie order steaks. Half way through dinner, I realize I have quit talking to Barbara and Bobbie. I begin to wonder if this is the Southern Comfort or me talking. Marge is a delight. So comfortable. Asks a lot of questions but so adorable.

I hear Barbara asking about after dinner drinks. Where do I want to go for an after dinner drink? I don't care.

Marge hears her too and says, "What, another drink? You Southerners drink a lot. I pass."

Quick, say something. Don't let it end like this. "We can go back to my place and if you want a drink, you can have one and if you don't, hey, that's OK too. I've probably had enough for one night, myself." I notice Marge nodding her head.

Barbara laughs, "Great idea. I can have your good brandy."

The evening is really about to end, and Marge is going away with them. I have to act fast. How is it possible that for three hours I have not even thought about Gloria? Marge is terrific. I don't want her to leave. She said she likes my house. She loves the sun. She likes to swim. She runs and would love to run on the beach. I can show her shells. We could check out the fish under my dock light tonight.

"Say, Marge, if you stay here tonight, I'll show you the most beautiful beach in Florida in the morning."

Barbara gives me a questioning look and asks, "Do you know what you're saying?"

"Oh, Barbara! I didn't ask her to sleep with me. There are several beds here and I want to show off our beaches."

Marge says, "OK."

Did everyone hear that, she said OK she'd stay with me? She is staying with little ole broken hearted me. Yippee. She's staying. She's staying in my house with me. She's staying with me. She's going to sleep with me. She's going to wake up with me.

Nancy picks me up at the airport. I haven't seen mother since the scene at the hospital. Nancy moved her to an apartment in Pittsburgh near her own house. I can't imagine moving here. Pittsburgh is a steel mill town. They've been cleaning it up for years. I still see it as a soot-filled place. Nancy thinks it's great. That's what matters. I don't have to live here, only visit. The hills are steep and this drive is like a roller coaster. I'll take the flat beauty of Florida anytime.

"I'm going to ask mother just one more time about our father. If she doesn't tell me this time, I won't see her again."

"Why, Rosie? What difference does he make? You've grown up. Now you're successful. I can't believe you want to find him?" She gives me one of her disapproving looks and I shift in my seat. "Do you really think he's still alive? When we get to the house I'll let you read my description of him."

"What do you mean? You wrote a description? And no, I don't think he's still alive but he could be. She is."

"I had to write one when we adopted Jennifer. So she would be beautiful and look like our family." She smiles and pulls into her driveway. She wants to pick up some things for mother both here and at the store. She hands me a paper and says to read it while she gets mother's clothes.

I can't believe she would invent a Father. Jennifer is a beautiful little girl, so she must've done a good job. I barely get through the door and she is shoving a paper at me.

I take the paper from her and walk away. I go outside and sit on their picnic table with my feet on the bench seat. She hates for Jeff to sit this way. Maybe she will reprimand me too. I don't believe what I am reading. How does she know that this is what he looked like? That he

176

worked for the state as an accountant for 20 years? Am I nuts? I never saw him. Did she? Did mother tell her about him? Did this made-up description assure her a beautiful child? I finish reading the description and lay it on the table under a rock. I go for a short walk to clear my head. The sky is beautiful, clear, and blue without a cloud. I kick at a few rocks on the dirt road. When I get back to the house I notice that the paper is gone and the rock is still on the table to hold down napkins. I walk into the kitchen and find Nancy rereading the paper.

"I don't get it, Nancy."

"What don't you get? I told you I had to make up a description of him so we'd get a beautiful little girl who looks like our family." She folds the paper and slides it into a drawer in the kitchen cabinet which must be her special hiding place. If the kids were bigger, she'd have to find a safer drawer.

I shake my head and walk away. I just can't understand how nonchalantly she treats this whole subject. It's been a thorn in my side since I was ten. I think it is high time I know about my father. He's half the gene pool. So now I will see mother and demand the truth. "Let's go Rosie, I'm sure she's waiting for you. She knew what time the plane landed."

Nancy stops at the store. She has owned this little dairy store for six years and really enjoys it. I go in with her to take some penny candy from the checkout counter. Nancy goes to the back of the store and brings back several frozen dinners she has prepared for mother.

"Nancy, I plan to cook tonight. I gave mother the list of ingredients." Cooking will give me a chance to think about how I want to approach her with my questions. I'll try to gauge her mood.

"I know, Rosie, but I don't have room for these here. Just put them in her freezer." We get back in the car and in five minutes are in front of mother's apartment. Nancy has to hurry back to the store so I get out balancing the dishes in one hand and taking my suitcase out of the back seat. It's not big and thank goodness it has wheels. I thank Nancy and go to find the right apartment. Nancy told me where to go but I wasn't listening. There have to be nameplates. And I know it's on the first floor.

Mother is standing in the second doorway, so I don't have to look. We say hello and then hug. One of those "don't touch me" hugs. I look around and compliment her on the apartment. Everything looks spick and span clean. Not like earlier places. Neither of us is good at small talk. We go for a short walk around the complex.

"Are you sure you want to cook. We could call Nancy and ask her to bring something from the store. She has very good things and a good variety."

"No, I love to cook and I make a mean meatloaf." The kitchen is small but convenient. I wonder if she cooks. Probably just has Nancy deliver from the store. Good thing she didn't move near me in Florida. I don't deliver. I won't let myself even think about what that would have been like. Visits are bad enough.

"This is a very good dinner, Rose. This meatloaf tastes just like your Grandmother's. I didn't even know you cooked, but then I'm not with you much."

"Yea, Maw, it's hard to believe. But I really love to cook and now that I'm living alone, I get to try everything and anything." We finish dinner and I do dishes. I put the last of the dishes into her cupboard and go to the living room to sit with her. She seems to be in a good mood so maybe I'll ask my burning question for the last time. That's the reason I came for this visit. It'll be my last if she doesn't talk with me about my dad this time.

I sit across from her in a straight chair. Then I move to a more comfortable one on the other side of her. She sits so straight, not relaxed at all. Is she always on guard? Or just around me? She's always dressed like she's going to work. Nice tailored blouse and skirt with hose held up by that rubber girdle and padded bra. I'm in my cutoffs and a tee shirt. She's knitting something. Her hands move so quickly and in a musical way just like she used to put me to sleep with her typing. I smile and think I should leave things alone. Not make trouble. Those two always accuse me of

178

starting things. But I'm leaving day after tomorrow and I must know. I'm old enough and if for no other reason, health issues are important. How high and mighty will that sound to her? So I'll just say I want to know something about the man she loved.

"Mother, do you miss work or living in Charleston?"

"No. Why would you ask that?"

"No reason. I just wondered. How long have you been retired and how long did you work?"

"Four years I worked more than forty. Why?"

Do I have to have a reason for everything I ask? I do but not these questions. Just the big one I've been asking since I was ten. She puts her knitting down and looks at me. Eye contact is not something we have very often. "WOW that's a long time." She smiles and so do I. My stomach does a flip and I squirm in the chair. I take a deep breath. I say what I have practiced.

"Mother, please tell me about the man in your life when Nancy and I were born. I assume he was our father. You must have cared a great deal for him. What was he like?"

Her eyes change and so does her facial expression. She looks away and then back with a very hardened look and picks up her knitting and throws it to the other end of the couch. I wait. I've seen this face so many times. Even in my dreams.

"Why can't you let bygones be bygones? Why do you think you need to know? It's none of your God Damn business. It's my business. So forget about it. Haven't I given you everything you ever needed?"

I look into her eyes and say softly, "I'd just like to know. After all he's part of me. I have his genes. He had to be special to you. You had two of us and I've always believed it was the same person; right?"

"There you go with that quiet voice. It won't help you. Just shut up. I will NOT tell you. It's none of your God Damn business. It was a long time ago. Forget it. I'm going to bed." She stands up, turns, and stomps out of the room.

179

I turn on the television. Why is this so important to me? I need to know. Why doesn't she want to let it out? Why doesn't she respect me enough to tell me? I will never see her again after this visit. I stretch out on the couch and look at the mindless television. Tears run down the side of my face.

After the quietest breakfast I can remember with my mother, I say, "Don't count on me for dinner tonight. I'm going for a walk now. But I definitely won't have dinner here tonight."

She turns away from the dishes and asks, "Can't I go?"

"No, I really want to spend some time with Nancy." I let the screen door slam. I don't even know if Nancy will go. I'll go to the store and ask her now so I can make other plans if she refuses. I know she's busy but I'll try to convince her that she might not see me very often and we need to talk. I take the shortcut she showed me yesterday. It goes along the road but cuts out two curves.

I see her behind the deli counter as I walk into this great little corner store. I watch as she jokes with customers about the ham salad. I think it could be made with baloney like she did when we were kids. On Sundays she advertises fresh baked bread. Now I'd think that was made here but it's not. She just bakes the frozen loaves here. She comes to the front counter to check people out as I stand like a kid eating the penny candy. Good thing I don't live closer. When the customers leave I suggest we go out to dinner tonight, just the two of us.

"How can you do that to Mother? Really, Rosie, you don't visit that often." She straightens the candy boxes. "You always have to do something to upset her. Then when you leave, she bitches to me." I study her frowning face. I reach for another piece of candy and she continues, "I won't go." She walks over to the bread counter and directs me to call mother and tell her she can go with both of us.

"I will not." I walk around the counter to the better candy side. I look over it all. "If you won't take time to

180

have one meal with me, once a year, then to hell with both of you." I pick up black licorice and pop it in my mouth. I chew hard.

I turn toward the door and say, "It's the same old thing. I think I deserve to know about our father and she thinks it's none of my God Damn business. Well, I won't let her do this to me again. I won't visit her ever again. She's angry and has no respect for me."

"Rosie, you're angry too."

"Sure I am. But she's a bitter old woman who can't even understand that I have no malice for her. I've made out OK." I pick up a small Snicker bar, rip it open and shove it in my mouth. "I wasn't her perfect child. You were. I don't blame her. After all she had two of us in two years. She had to love him. I just want to know something about him."

I take another Snicker. Nancy picks up the papers and throws them in the wastebasket under the counter. I'm glad there are no customers here now. "He died very young, if he really died 38 years ago. What caused that death? Don't you care? Why doesn't it matter to you? What about the genes you have given your children from him?"

She shrugs and keeps on straightening the counter. She stands there shaking her head.

"You have four beautiful children. What did you know about Jennifer's parents before the adoption? Can you see any of our traits in the other three? Don't you wonder about any of it?" I can't stand to be here. I turn and walk out of the store. Nancy comes running after me but she won't catch me this time.

Marge and I have seen each other about once a month for the last year. She does most of the traveling because of my tight schedule and I think she likes to be on the beach. It took some discussion but we agreed early in the relationship that we would make it an open one. She's still living with her former lover who is also seeing someone else. I am not willing to sit here and not explore my options. How do I know that she and I can ever get together as a couple? And I vow that I will never be in a closed relationship again. She told me the other day that her live-in didn't want me to call her for two weeks while they try to put their relationship back together. Who the fuck is "what's her name" to tell me when and who to call. I pick up the phone and call. Marjorie answers. I speak softly, "Hi love. I miss you. I just had to call. Hope it's OK."

"It's OK. I miss you too. And I'm here alone. Thanks for calling."

We talk a few minutes about nothing. Then she tells me she's going away with her former lover for a few days. "She's out now with her new girlfriend so I'm packing. We'll leave in the morning."

I feel my face and body get hot. "When were you going to tell me? Or were you? She doesn't want you to even talk to me and she's out with another woman. I don't understand you."

"Rosie, we promised we wouldn't talk for two weeks. That's next week."

I slam my hand down on the counter. I don't want to deal with this now. I'll say something and be sorry for it later. "Someone's at my door. Gotta go. I love you." I hang up and pour myself a drink. Damn her former lover. Or maybe she's not former. I walk downstairs and out to the dock.

Charlotte and I are walking her dog Pixie around the block when she asks me, "How much sex do you need?"

"Need?"

I kick a pebble down the street. Who the fuck cares? It's none of her business. She can't help but hear since the duplex is connected. Damn. Another mistake I made. She ought to count her blessings, not my women. Jealous old woman. I wanted it to be you. Remember.

"You seem to have a different one every night."

Little does she know. A couple of nights there have been two. It is fun and games for me.

"OH, you're counting."

"Do they all know about the others? Maybe I should tell them or leave notes on their cars. And does your MARJORIE know?"

"Go ahead. Leave notes. Call anyone. They all know. People can't understand honesty. I tell every one of them: Want a tumble in the hay for fun. Let's go." I act like I know what I want. Jesus Christ, I have no idea. I'm like a bumper car and the wheel doesn't turn the car. I hit first this one and then the next. But Marge is a constant.

I see Gloria coming down the street, walking her dog. Charlotte stops to let Pixie do her "business" and waits for Gloria. Let them compare notes on dog dodo. Not with me.

"I gotta go. See you later." I jog back to the duplex. Go to my kitchen, pour myself a drink and walk back down the street to watch the sunset with the drink in hand. DAMN them both. DAMN everybody except Marge.

I stand a good twenty feet from the F 18 jetway. I hear the announcement overhead: US Air is pleased to announce; flight 56 from Islip, New York has landed. Passengers may be met at gate F 18. My heart skips a beat. I haven't seen her for two months. I hold the red balloon and let it float high above my head. I want it to float toward the doorway, but it just goes up. Here they come. Each person looks around like they are expecting someone. Some just look and then walk briskly by. There she is. Beautiful. What a smile. My heart races. I whistle softly, like I do when I want her attention. She knows the whistle and looks around. She can't see me, but I see her. She is looking, scanning the area. She sees the balloon, smiles and follows the ribbon to my hand. A bigger smile. I let the balloon go and she catches the ribbon as it floats past her. We meet, hug, and kiss. I start to pull away and she holds me tighter. I feel all eyes on me. I teach school here. Probably don't have to worry about being gay and teaching in New York, but down here they'd fire me in a red-blooded minute if they suspected that I love a woman. My stomach does a flip and I try to put the thought out of my mind. My Margie is here

183

and I love her. To hell with them. I teach on the college level for God's sake. It doesn't matter though. Some really good teachers lost their jobs and their license to teach just before I came to Florida. I know it hasn't changed. All the lesbians I know who teach are scared to go anywhere in a group. They think when we are in a group a mark appears on our foreheads to let others in the restaurant or wherever identify us as lesbians.

I slip my arm around her waist and we walk toward the main terminal. It is a short visit and here we are back in the airport waiting for the announcement: flight 57 is boarding. We kiss goodbye and I walk away waiting for her next visit. Meanwhile Beverly arrives tomorrow.

I step out my door onto the landing between my apartment and Charlotte's. She is sitting in her living room with her door open. I look down the steps, expecting my new friend, Beverly to arrive any second. She called when she left Miami five hours ago. I turn to go back inside. Charlotte asks, "Which of your women are you looking for today?"

I ignore the question and walk back into my apartment to the other end and scream. "Leave me alone." Why did I ever agree to build this place? But I love it. I should have added more insulation, for God's sake. I did add carpet in the back of my closet that is the wall of her bedroom. I go to the fridge to get grapes, they always sooth my temper. I drop the whole plate on the floor. It doesn't break but grapes roll everywhere. Damn Damn Damn. I hear a knock on the door. Beverly has arrived and is speaking to Charlotte. I yell, "Come in."

I walk over the grapes, toward the living room: Beverly is in, has the door locked and grabs me before I can say, "Hi." She gives me a very big, long kiss and my body weakens. As if she knows what I'm thinking, she tells me not to worry, no one will bother us, the door is locked and the answering machine is on. I start to pick up Beverly's knapsack and she quickly grabs it and reminds me that her women do not carry heavy packages. I laugh as we walk to the bedroom arm in arm. We barely have our clothes off when the phone rings. I reach to answer and Bev stops me.

"It's just Charlotte wanting to see you. You are busy and she'll still be there when we get up darlin. Trust me. And maybe she'll just go out on the front-screened porch and come to your side of the duplex and come in. Now wouldn't that be a shock for the ole girl?"

I laugh again and let the answering machine answer.

A month later, Marge is here for a visit and things are getting pretty serious. We see each other about once a month and it's close to decision-making time for both of us. I tell her that it's great she can be here so often. She can rearrange her classes at her college. I cannot. When we are together we're in bed making love at least three times every day. Today, we're reading on the beach when it begins to rain. We run from the beach, down the street, into the garage and up the stairs to the bedroom. Bathing suits and towels drop in the hall as we jump under the covers.

Her skin is soft like velvet. Smooth as glass and warm as toast. I want to touch every curve, every crevice, every line, everywhere, all at once. Remember each touch. Kiss every angle, every dimple and everywhere all at once, taste the sweetness of each spot. I want to cover every inch, learn every twitch, and cause every ripple. I watch as she sleeps nestled in my arms, her back against my front, our legs entwined like young trees growing together. Her heartbeat is slow, her breathing slower. I stroke her strong thigh and cradle her breast in my hand. She gently moves to allow my hand to get closer. I kiss her back and move to her neck, stretch to reach her ear. She stirs. My body moves to allow her to turn. I smile at her as she looks sleepily at me and grins. I feel the warmth between my legs and reach to touch her going from right breast to right hip across her pubic hair and up to her left breast. I hold it and lean down to kiss the nipple. It rises to my attention. She has turned more toward me and her hands go quickly up and down and all around. My skin is electrified. I snuggle to be in the right position to kiss, stroke and excite. Her body moves to respond and we catch our breath. Our moves are slow, deliberate, smooth and building to a familiar level. We speak softly of love and hold each other closer, harder, stroking gently, getting faster. I feel her throb of passion as she brings her face closer to mine.

"That was a very good report. You covered the topic in a direct manner and your facts showed you had done your homework. Where did you get your information?"

"We have a friend who has lots of books about sexuality. They're more up to date than what we found in the Library on campus. And we talked to some of our gay friends."

"Good. Any questions for Mickey, class?"

"Why are all the women who teach P.E., GAY?"

I feel my face get red and my body gets warm. How do I handle this? Do I have to come out? Do I have to hide? I squirm in this small seat in the back of the room and watch all eyes turn toward me. Do they suspect that I am? Does it matter? To them? To me? Wait till the Dean hears this one. I can hear Eleanor at the next department meeting. Should I go tell her before she hears it? I turn it back to the students.

"Cindy, Jo Ellen, want to answer that one?"

I go down the list of women who teach in this department. We are all gay. I do know three high school teachers who are not gay. Do these students think I will out the faculty? Not my right to do so. I can only come out for me. I'm not ready to do that in this class.

Cindy hesitates and says," I don't know, we didn't find any statistics on that."

"Well, Mick, let's just say I know a couple who aren't and that's enough to dispel your theory. But you can look it up and come back with facts and we'll have another discussion. Any other questions?"

I hold my breath and wait. No comments. No more questions. The bell rings. "Thank you, clock."

"Marjorie, dear, we have to get up. We have company coming."

She turns toward me. Smiles and I melt back into her arms; to hell with the guests. But it's the first time she'll meet any of my friends. I kiss her, roll away, and sit up on the side of the bed. I've never been in bed so much in three days. It's wonderful, but tonight we have guests coming for dinner and I have to finish cooking.

"Come back, I'll finish dinner. And I'll tell them they have to leave by 9."

"Don't you dare!"

"I will."

"Please, they're my friends and I hope will become yours."

"Rosie, I didn't come down here to spend time with friends. I came to make love with you. Come back here."

I finish dressing, shake my head at her and say, "Come on now, they'll be here soon."

"Call and cancel."

"You know I won't do that." She jumps up and is dressed before I get down the hall. She does everything quickly.

I hear people coming up the steps and go toward the door. Marge jumps in front of me. Opens the door and before anyone ways Hello, she says, "Hi, you have to leave by nine."

Everyone laughs and I turn red. I start to say something but she hugs me tight. The ice is broken.

This duplex is not big enough. She treats it just like the house we moved from. It wasn't big enough either. The walls and doors are not thick enough. I refuse to have my doors locked when I'm here. But damn she cannot just walk in without a knock or call or something. If I'm in the bedroom, I'm seventy-five feet from the front door and she cannot surprise me when I turn over. I'll just go tell her to stay out. Would I tell my mother to stay out if she lived next door? Sure. But she's not my mother. Who the hell is she? Why did I allow myself to be in this position? Christ Rosie you've been asking yourself that question for years. When will I grow up? I'm just going to tell her. I walk down the

187

hall and stop in the kitchen. I go to the refrigerator, open it, look in, nothing. Close the door. Go to the pantry and take a handful of nuts. I want a drink. No, not now. Go tell her.

I open my front door and go the four feet to her front door. I knock. No answer. I knock again. I think I hear her. I open the door. "Charlotte, are you here?"

"Yes, come in, you don't have to knock."

"Yes, I do. That's why I'm here."

"What?'

I go down the hall to her bedroom and find her stretched out on the bed. A book on her stomach and, her dog, Pixie curled up beside her. She smiles. I frown. I start to sit down and change my mind. Stand tall.

"Charlotte, we have to talk about our relationship. I thought when we moved it would be clear."

"It is. We still have a very special love relationship."

"Shit, Charlotte you don't know what a love relationship is. We are NOT lovers. We never have been. I've known you more than twenty years. I've lived with you ten. Now we are in a duplex. You don't know what it is to be a lover."

I don't know what else to say. I want her to stay out of my life but I know it's too late for that. We're not lovers. What are we? What do I want? I sound like a twelve year old to me and what must I sound like to her. I think that's what she wants. She can say she's my Mother. So grow up for Christ's sake. I sit and put my head in my hands.

"Well, what now?"

"Well, what? We are supposed to be living in separate places. But you act like it is one house. It isn't. Damn. I want some privacy. Yesterday, you walked in, scared the shit out of me. I wasn't even awake."

I get up. I walk to the door. Open the blinds. Close the blinds. I kick at the dog toy on the floor. I sit back down. I try to calm down. I should just leave. I get up.

"What do you want?"

"What do YOU want?"

"I love you, Rosie. I've given you everything you've wanted."

"Shit, Charlotte. What the fuck does that mean, that you've done all the giving? You know shit about love. You think giving things is love. It is NOT. You think you own me; like I'm obligated to you for what you think you've given me. What about my giving?"

I get up and begin to pace. Go to the bathroom, get a tissue, crumble it. Throw it at a wastebasket. Look at her. Look away. I'll leave. Can't! I must finish this talk. Talk, that's a joke. Why did I start this? Leave. Stay. She acts so God Damn pious. "Oh, what's the use? I just wanted your love. I gave you mine. You are so ashamed of who you are. DYKE DYKE LESBIAN LESBIAN."

"Now, that's enough. Go cool off and come back when you can speak with respect."

"Respect? You and my mother ought to look up that word."

I pick up a book from her shelf about love and want to throw it at her. I drop it on the floor. My heart races and I start to leave the room and can't. I have to get this out of my system. Such a selfish son of a bitch! What will the neighbors think? I don't give a good rat's ass about what the neighbors think. I am not ashamed. Now I know who I am. Why am I here?

"Rosie, I've been very good to you. I do love you but not like that. Is this the appreciation?"

She gets up and straightens the cover on the bed. She sits back down. I want to knock her down.

"What the fuck does that mean. LIKE THAT? Like what?"

I feel the tears coming. I don't want to let her see how she hurts. I blow my nose. I should get the hell out of here. I can't. I must. Pixie has gone under the bed. Her dog understands more than she does.

She asks me once more to leave the room. Hangs her head and tells me how sad she is that I don't understand her. That she has given me everything a daughter could want.

189

I explode. My heart races and I feel my face redden. "God damn, Charlotte, I am not your daughter."

I stalk out of the room and back to my apartment. I throw myself on my bed exactly like an angry kid and pound the pillow with both fists.

It's hard to believe that just three months ago I told mother that she would never see me again and now I'm here in Virginia with Nancy to make funeral arrangements.

As Nancy and I ride to the funeral home with Libby she tells us that she answered all the questions for the death certificate but didn't want to pick the casket. I don't blame her but it would have been Ok with me if she had. A plain pine box would be just fine. I wouldn't have it open for the wake either but Nancy insists. I have decided to let her make all the arrangements.

We pull up to the door. Libby says she will wait in the lobby after she parks. Nancy and I go in, introduce ourselves and are directed to see Mr. Harris. The lady at the desk lets us know that Mr. Harris was in mother's Sunday school class and loved her very much. I think BIG DEAL. I never understood how she could teach a Sunday school class and then swear all afternoon at her family. Nancy says, "Thank you."

Mr. Harris is a short, skinny man in his late twenties or early thirties. He starts to hug me and I put out my hand. He shakes it and says how much he loved our Mom. We sit in front of his desk for a few minutes as he talks about what we need to do. Like going over the death certificate and picking the casket and giving him clothes we want her to be dressed in for the viewing. I sit nervously in this uncomfortable straight chair. As soon as he moves I stand. I'm ready to get this done. Nancy gives me one of her "What's wrong with you?" looks. I don't like this man. He is mousy. We follow him to the room of caskets.

I lay very still in this smooth pine box. I hear Mother calling me. I'm hiding in the casket I like best. But as she opens the door I know she's looking for me because she's finished with her work in the office and wants to go home. I moan. She turns and sees me. She screams, "Get out of there." I laugh and climb out.

I walk over to a very plain casket and motion to Nancy that I like it. She says it's too stark.

"It's going in the ground, who cares?"

"Come on Rosie, be reasonable."

Mr. Harris hands Nancy a price list with letters on it for each casket in the room. I look over her shoulder and smile. "You pick, Nancy. But don't spend all my money."

"Was your Mother married?"

"What?"

"For the certificate. Was she married?"

Nancy says, "Yes." And I say, "No."

As I turn to look at his sheepish grin, I explode. Nancy's running from the room already sobbing. "You son of a bitch. Why the hell would you ask that question? What the fuck is the difference? Leave it blank." I throw the price list Nancy handed me into the casket beside me. I'd like to put him in and close it. "I'll have your job if I hear one mention of this to anyone in the community or from your high and mighty Christian friends. The nerve of you."

I walk out to find Nancy in Libby's arms still crying. Libby wants to know what happened. I tell her "Nothing" and go to find the owner.

I step into the room where mother's body is in an open casket in the front. This is so barbaric. I hope no one ever has a chance to see my dead body all dolled up in satin. And I don't want to see hers. I told Nancy not to leave me here to greet these little ole ladies from the church who expect a family member to go to the casket with them. Three of them have just walked past me into the room. Two go right up front together and the third one hangs back and looks around. She spots me holding up the back wall close to the door.

"Are you one of Mary's daughters?"

"Yes. Thank you for coming."

191

"Mary was a wonderful person and a good Sunday School teacher. I bet you will miss her."

"Well, Uh . . ." I look for Nancy. She is nowhere to be found. No one else, not Ronnie, or Libby or Clarence is in this room. The other two women are at the casket.

"Would you take me to see her?"

"I'll ask my sister." She puts her arm through mine and turns toward the aisle. I have no choice. Nancy will be sorry she did this. We walk in silence and I step back at the first row of seats. I do not want to do this. I hope she will get the message and go on by herself. But she holds on tight. We go the next four steps and I focus on the flowers from *FAMILY*.

"Doesn't she look lovely?"

"No, I think she looks pretty dead." How does a dead person look lovely? I guess that's what she thinks she should say.

She drops her hand to my wrist and smiles. I glance at mother's face. It does look softer than usual. No frown. But not a smile either. The yellow roses are beautiful. I look around for Nancy.

"My, you're very dark skinned", says this little ole church lady. She is so prim and proper. What the fuck do I think she means. Compared to her lily-white hands, I am very dark.

"Maybe my father was a black man." I turn and walk to the door and keep going till I'm outside. I see Libby coming from her car. I'd better not tell her what I just did and for sure I won't tell Nancy. Anyway not till tomorrow after the funeral.

Nancy and I sit on the floor in mother's apartment going through jewelry. I'm looking for a wedding band. "Don't you think mother would have a wedding band hidden somewhere in this collection of pins, earrings, and junk jewelry?"

"Rosie, why are you still looking for a connection with a man? She's dead, she can't tell you anything now. Let it go."

"I'll never understand why you don't care about who your father was or is. He may not be dead like she said. Wouldn't you like your children to know their other grandfather?" I find a diamond ring. It fits my little finger. Maybe he gave this to mother. I'll just keep it and not say a word. It's a pretty setting with a little diamond.

"Truth is I really don't care. I'm more upset that they hardly know you. I love you Rosie. You're the only sister I have. So stop worrying about who he was and deal with us. Your family is here and wants to see you more often." She picks up a silver pin. An abstract flower. She pins it on her blouse and smiles. A pin and a ring claimed without a word.

"Right, Nancy. Who are you kidding? You don't approve of my life and wouldn't want your kids to know that I'm a dyke. And I'm not hiding it any longer. I'm happy with who I am."

"Let's promise that we will at least talk with each other once a month. We don't have to talk about your lifestyle. We'll just keep each other up to date with our lives. OK?"

"OK."

Marge offered to go with me for the funeral and apartment cleaning but I said thanks but no thanks. I am glad she came back yesterday. I need her. We are just finishing breakfast at eleven this morning. "If you finish the dishes, I'll get everything ready for the beach."

"Be sure to take my book. It's on the floor by our bed." I'll have to hurry with the dishes; she'll be ready and waiting for me downstairs. She is so quick doing everything. I guess that's the influence of the pace in the Northeast.

Marge is in the water before I can adjust my chair. She comes back and puts her chair very close to mine. She has something serious on her mind. I can tell. "Rosie, my love, I think it's decision making time. I want to be with you, live with you, sleep with you every night."

We've had this conversation so many times in so many ways. "I want the same. But how can it happen? You have a job you love and so do I. I live in the sunny South and you live in the cold North. And more important is my graduate work. Nova University is not granting degrees to those of us who have started. I have to finish. I'll have one more semester of classes. Then the dissertation." I look at the Gulf. The water is beautiful. So calm, it rolls in and out without a thought of change. The wind can do that. Can love make me leave this beach? It's very hot right now.

"Have you heard of airplanes?"

"What do they have to do with my degree?

"If you move to New York, you can fly to St. Pete for your classes. You can write your dissertation anywhere."

She's so direct and straightforward. I can't make that decision so easily. "What about a job or are you going to support me. Everyone here thinks you're rich. I'll cook and clean." I've almost covered my feet with warm sand.

"I'm not that rich and you wouldn't want that anyway. But you can probably find a job at the University at Stony Brook. In fact I have two friends who are the Deans in the School of Allied Health. They are also lovers. I'll get you an interview."

"Marjorie, I teach health and physical education, remember?"

"Then why are you getting this degree in higher education/curriculum-development? Don't you want a job using your new skills? You're a very good writer and the Dean is always looking for a grant writer."

"Let's take a walk. Sounds like you've already decided who is moving. Have you already talked to them?" She better say no. She's counting her chickens before they hatch. I don't think I can go to New York or to a University. "How about you coming here? We have a physical therapy assistant program. The director is a good friend."

We both get up and go toward the water. It's cold for me but she runs right in and motions for me to join her. "No way. I'm not a tourist."

She comes out of the water splashing me. I want to grab her and hold her close to me. But even if this is the "gay beach", I don't. As we walk, I say again, "How about you coming here?"

"I'll investigate the possibility. Get me an interview. I'm coming back in two weeks. I'll get you an interview on the day after Thanksgiving. You're still coming up, aren't you?"

I can't believe she will try to get a job here. Would she really come? I think the physical therapy assistant program runs all year. She won't like that. No summer vacation. And I'm sure the salary is not what hers is now. And she thinks it's too hot here most of the time. "Yes. I already have my tickets."

"So, we'll both interview and then decide which is best for both of us. OK? Let's go back to the house. I'm starving."

"That sounds good to me. Maybe we should take a short nap after lunch."

I kiss her goodbye. She goes down the runway to the plane. I wait a few minutes to be sure the plane is leaving. I see it pull away and go quickly to my car. Suddenly I hear car horns. I look around and realize they are blowing at me. I guess I shouldn't stop to ponder moving to New York in traffic at the airport even if it's at a stop sign. I wave my hand and move quickly into the lane going south.

Traffic is backed up on the bridge, even though there are five lanes. The view of the water is beautiful. I move to the right where cars are slower. I'm alone and can let my mind wander through all these questions. Will I move? Maybe. Maybe not. Our relationship is perfect. We've gotten to know each other during the two years we've been commuting. Do we need to be together all the time? I'd have to stop seeing other women. We must be together. I don't love any of the others. I really love her like I've never loved anyone. So why see the others? I can talk to her about anything. She's so grounded. Knows what she wants and says so. Why can't I do that? I'm always afraid of hurting someone's feelings. I let others decide for me. She's trying to change that. If I decide what I want, everybody will be happier. I'm trying. Gee, I almost missed my exit. How'd I get here so quickly?

A few minutes later I make the right turn onto my beautiful beach. I love this beach. It is so special, especially when the sun is going down. If I hurry, I have just enough time to get home, fix a drink, and walk back to the beach to watch the sunset. The sun goes fast to a certain point then slows like it doesn't want to get wet as it goes through the water. Maybe tonight I'll see the green flash. As I run up the steps, Charlotte yells, "Come in." Damn. She's in her living room just behind her door and four feet from my door on the landing at the top of the stairs. I don't have time. I don't want to see her now but I dutifully open her door. Smile and wait.

"Did Marge get off okay?

"Sure, we had lots of time at the airport before her plane left. In fact, I parked and went to the gate with her. We're both getting tired of all this traveling. She doesn't even like to fly." I stand in the doorway ready to escape.

"It's nice that she can afford to fly so often. Come in. Sit a while. I miss you when she is here."

She always says that. At least she doesn't walk in on us without knocking like she does when others are here. I think she's afraid of what she thinks Marge might do or say. I hesitate. "I can't. Want to see the sunset and think about what to do. We want to live together. Be together. You know that. I've said it so many times. Now we've decided that both of us will interview and then decide which one of us will move. I'll have . . . ." She raises her voice and interrupts.

"What do you mean which one? How could you leave this place we've just built?"

"Now don't get excited. I didn't say I'm moving. I just mean that we're exploring our options. I'm going to the beach to see the sunset. Want to come."

"NO." I step across the landing to my door and hear her yelling something. I don't go back.

I have been trying to find time to get to see Roonie and George Bibb since I came home from Mother's funeral. When I was four or five, I used to hide in Roonie's garden in Oak Hill. Now they live in St. Petersburg not far from where I lived before the beach house was built. They were good friends. I want to tell them about mother's death.

I know they live on thirtieth-avenue but I don't come often enough to know the number. I look for the two giant trees in the front yard. One on each side of the walkway. I pull into the driveway, take a deep breath and walk to the door. I love them and am always glad to see them. George tells the funniest stories about West Virginia.

Roonie opens the door. "Hi, I'm sorry to disturb you. Are you eating? I can come back. I've been meaning to come over."

"Come on in, Rosie, you know we're always glad to see you. Have a bite to eat."

"No, please. I'll come back." They're always the same. Warm, loving and full of caring. Good for my ego. I go in and walk toward the table and see my favorite cornbread. Reminds me of Granny's. "I'll just sit with you. I have something to tell you. Oh, Roonie, I can't pass up your cornbread. I'll get a plate." She starts to get up. "No, sit. I'll get it."

I walk to the kitchen and return with a plate, knife and napkin.

"So, what's the big news?" George asks.

"Mother died last week. I've just come back from the funeral and apartment cleaning. I thought you'd want to know." I'm surprised by my shaky voice. I didn't like her. Relieved that she's gone. Oh well.

Roonie jumps up from the table and goes toward the bedrooms. I look after her and then to George. "What's she doing? Where's she going?" He shakes his head and says he's sorry about Mary.

She comes back as quickly as she left. "Here, Rosie, go look up these people. They can tell you about your Father. I know you've always wanted to know and your Mother can't do anything to me now."

My heart races. I reach for the paper and see three names written on it. Why is she handing me this now? We've talked about him so many times when mother wasn't around.

It's none of your Goddamn business. I don't want to hear you ask that question ever again. Why do you always remember the bad? It's none of your Goddamn Business. It's none of your Goddamn Business. It's none of your Goddamn business.

"I don't know what to say. Do you know these people? Did you know them in Charleston? Do you think my father's still alive?"

"I don't believe so, but these people can tell you. In fact, I'm not sure they're all still alive."

They express their sympathy that Mary has died and I exchange a few facts about how she died and the funeral and the family. But my mind is not on my mother. I can't wait to get out of here and call these numbers. The cornbread is good but I must go.

On the way home, I find myself past where I should have turned to go to the beach. I go the long way to the other bridge and see Charlotte in the driveway as I drive down 78th avenue.

I jump out of the car and say, "Charlotte, you'll never guess what just happened to me. I went by to see the Bibbs. Roonie gave me three names of people she thinks can tell me about my father. Maybe I'll go to West Virginia this summer."

I walk toward her waving the paper. She takes it and reads the names. I can't wait to see these people or at least one of them. I've wanted to know about my father since I was 10. Now I'm almost 40 and maybe, just maybe, I'm going to get some true answers.

"Why would you want to go see these people? Maybe they won't be as anxious to talk to you as you think you are to talk to them."

I take the paper from her without a word and go to my apartment. Who asked you anyway? I change clothes and begin a letter to Marge. She'll be glad. She'll go with me. She'll encourage me. I love her so and she doesn't judge me or try to tell what to do or think. She always wants to know what I think.

There's not even a sign as Marge turns onto the campus. I see three strange looking buildings. This University at Stony Brook is not like any other college campus I've ever seen. Marge explains that these are the health science buildings and the hospital. The rest of the campus is across a main road. She points out the hospital and calls the others the health science towers. The hospital is very tall and all black glass. At first glance they all look like giant salt and peppershakers with a sugar bowl on the side. But they are not "ivory-tower" looking buildings. I'll never find the school of allied health. Good thing Marge is driving and knows where it is. At least I won't be late.

"Don't be nervous, Rosie. Bob and Edmund are very good friends. I've told them all about you. The deans will find a job for you."

"They're your friends. What if I can't do what they want me to do? This is a well-respected university. I looked it up. They aren't going to have me teach archery or badminton. Remember that's what I've done for almost twenty years."

"Oh, relax. You can do anything."

"Sure I can. Love is blind." She is always telling me how bright I am. She's the first person in my life who gives me positive encouragement. I still have doubts but I have accomplished everything I ever set out to do. I'll soon finish my doctorate in higher education at NOVA University. I finished all but the last class in one year while I was teaching full time. Now I'm thinking of changing jobs and moving. I must ask if I can finish my last class and my dissertation while I work here. That's a big part of this decision.

We park on the top floor of the parking garage and walk right into the shortest building. Marge tells me to turn right at the first hallway. Is the school this close to parking? One side of this hallway is all glass. People are sitting at desks with no walls between them. They are scattered all around this huge room. How can they work with this hallway distraction? When we reach the next hall, Marge guides me across to an open office door.

A woman sits at a desk just inside the door. I say, "I'm Rose Walton. I have an interview with Dean McTernan and Dean Hawkins. Am I in the right place?" Of course you are. Marge brought you.

There are two offices along the back wall and one on each end wall. Suddenly six people say, "Hi Marge. How are you?" They come to kiss her like she is a long lost relative. I guess they do like her. The two men must be the deans. They kiss her too. One is wearing a beautiful suit with a colorful tie. The other has a sport jacket with a dull tie.

Marge is very close to both men. She lived with Bob Hawkins for a few months when she was breaking up with her partner two years ago.

One says, "Come in Rose, let's have a chat. Marge has already told us how wonderful you are. But I still have a few questions."

I'll bet he does. I follow him to the office on the left side of the room. It's a beautiful office, big and comfortable. A sitting area on the left and a big desk in front of a wall of windows on the right. There is a lot of glass in this school. The couch is a soft maroon with beautiful tan chairs. And the other man joins us after he tells Marge to wait and we'll all go to lunch. They motion for me to sit on the couch and they sit in the chairs facing me. Here comes the third degree. They introduce themselves and now I know which one is Edmund, the dean, and which one is Bob, the associate dean. The dean has better taste in ties.

They work well together. Very easy back and forth with questions. Edmund asks about how I like New York and about my moving in January. Bob asks the academic questions about my skills and background. After the first few, I relax. My stomach is just growling, not doing flips and my hands are dry.

Bob says, I understand you are in a doctoral program at NOVA University. When will you complete the degree?"

"Yes, I am and expect to finish in another year. I have one seminar and my dissertation to complete. I'll meet with advisors once a month and then write. The seminar is held in St. Petersburg at the Junior College."

"Does that mean if you come here you would need to go to Florida once a month?"

"Yes. At least for one semester."

"What is your topic? Has it been accepted?"

"No I have not submitted a proposal but I have an outline. The seminar is designed to prepare us to complete the dissertation. My degree is in higher education with an emphasis in curriculum development. I must investigate a curriculum problem. "

Edmund breaks in and says, "Well that sounds like a fit." He looks to Bob for approval. Bob nods. "We can offer you a position in the Physician Assistant Education Program to develop curriculum. Will you consider that? Maybe you can couple your writing for the degree with your writing here. How does that sound?"

"It sounds scary. It's what I want to do but I'm not familiar with physician assistants."

Bob ignores my comment and says, "We'll have a written proposal with title and salary before you go back to Florida next week. When will you be ready to sign?"

It sounds like a done deal. Now I really have to make a decision. "Before the Christmas holiday, I hope. If yes, I'd like to be in New York by the New Year."

Edmund says, "I'd like for you to meet the director of the program but he's away." Before I can ask anything about the department Bob stands and moves toward the door.

"Let's go to lunch. Marge is probably starving." Introductions are made in the outer office. I'll never remember these names. I nod my head to each and edge my way to the door and Marge. She squeezes my hand.

If we could see each other this often then neither of us would have to move. This time last week I was in New York having an interview at the University at Stony Brook. Now Marge is in Florida having an interview at my community college. She arrived last night and is leaving tomorrow. Too short but it is quality time together. About a year ago we quit ruining our last day together with sadness about leaving. We pretend we are always together but travel often.

"Marge, are you sure you don't want me to drive you? I'll quickly leave so no one sees me drop you off."

"No. I'm a big girl and I want to go alone. But thanks for the offer."

She's been gone less than two hours. I hear her coming up the steps. It must have been a very short interview or not an interview. I open the door and spread my arms wide. "Well, did they offer you the department and promise to pay you double your current salary?"

"No. How about twice the time on campus for twelve months and half the salary."

"I'm not surprised. Down here the sunshine supplements salaries. I've already begun to tell some friends that I'm moving to New York. Of course they don't believe me."

She hugs me very tightly. "Are you sure?"

"I've never loved anyone like I love you and never been loved like you love me. I am ready to give it a try. I'm scared but I want to do something different. I need a good challenge."

The sun comes through the sliding door like ten spotlights to say Good Morning. I'm not ready to be awake. I snuggle closer to my love and bury my face in the pillow. Marge's body is warm and fits mine like a glove. We move together to be more comfortable. We sound like the mourning doves as we get situated to sleep just five more minutes. Five becomes ten and we turn to say more than just good morning. As she slips her hand around my breast, I turn to face her and it's the first kiss of the morning before brushing. She responds and I move to be in a better position. Our musky odors blend as we ebb and flow in our first morning lovemaking of the day. I didn't make it up in time to run but who cares when I know I've won the race.

What a party. Only eight of us but we are having fun. I cooked chicken and they brought veggies and salad. I'm about to serve my fresh key lime pie with chocolate crust. Maybe I should have made two. The phone rings and I grab it from the kitchen wall. I know it's my sister. She has called twice this week to ask why I'm moving to New York.

"Hello"

"Rosie, I know you hate cold weather. Why New York? Why not back to Pennsylvania? Close to us."

"Hi, Nancy. Thanks for calling but I can't talk now. I have dinner guests in the living room and am about to serve dessert. I'll call you tomorrow."

B.J. comes into the kitchen and wants to know if she can help. I shake my head and mouth to her that this is my sister. She goes back and announces that my sister is on the phone.

I'm getting things out of the refrigerator, holding the phone with my shoulder. Maybe I'll just drop it. Maybe it will disconnect. I know that she doesn't want to hear the truth but she's pushing. I drop a fork and as I bend to pick it up I fall to the floor. Guess I had more Southern Comfort than I thought. I hold my hand over the receiver and tell my guests that I'm OK.

"All I want to know is why you're moving to New York. I know you say a new job, a new adventure, opportunity, and all that but I want to know the real reason. I know you love your job and your new home. Why would you move from Florida?"

I get up, hold the phone on my shoulder and start to cut the key lime pie. "I told you I can't talk now. Goodbye, Nancy. I'm going to hang up."

"Rosie, you can tell me. What's with you? I'm your sister."

She probably knows in her head but wants to hear it from me. Why is she pushing? This is the third time I've danced around telling her that I'm in love with a beautiful woman. I can hear her now when I finally blurt it out. "Well, Nancy, I'm in love with a beautiful woman. And I'm going to New York to live with her and start a new life." There I said it and I'm glad. My heart skips a beat and I feel my face get warm.

"Damn you Rosie, why did you tell me that? You know how I feel about that and I don't want to hear about that part of your life."

GOODBYE." I mechanically finish cutting the pie and invite my friends to come get dessert. I go to the bathroom to hide my tears.

Today is the day. I start my new life. I'm going to New York to start a new job, a new relationship, and a new home. I have not slept well and am wide-awake at four am. I lie here thinking about my decisions during the past two years that make these changes seem inevitable. Are they the right decisions? Do I really want to leave Florida where I've loved teaching in the sunshine for 15 years? But I've only taken a leave; the job is still here if things don't work out there.

As I roll over and feel Marge near me, I know I have to give it a chance. This is the most wonderful thing that has happened to me in my life. For two years we've seen each other about once a month and have become very close friends and lovers. The telephone bills have been astronomical. But this is definitely passion that's taking me away from my Sunny South. I hate cold weather. I hate snow and so HOW can I be making the right move. Going to the frozen north. To the east end of Long Island. I have to assure everyone it's not New York City but close enough for me. Scary. Scary. But I love her.

It's been a whirlwind for two years. I've been so busy with graduate school. My doctorate is so important to me. I've enjoyed this experience better than all my other years of education. I'll fly back for research meetings and talk with my major reader by phone. I've made those arrangements and everyone at the University and at my new job says it's a good plan. They are all encouraging.

Marge moves closer and I feel the electricity. "Yes darling, it's a bright and beautiful morning. We need to get up and finish packing. I'm going out for a run first." She reaches for me. I kiss her lightly and pull away. "No not now, I have too much to do and think about. How about tomorrow night in NEW YORK or on the train in the dark?" I get up, dress and bend down to give her a quick kiss and go out the door.

Two miles will be a cinch. The sun is bright and the earth is warm. Not a cloud in the sky. Hardly anyone on my beach. That's how I like it. Up early enough to see the uncluttered beauty without a lot of strangers. That's a seasonal thing and this is the season: February 20, 1977. No one on the streets either. This is my beach and my time. Others just think it belongs to them, but I know it's mine. And what glorious sunsets I've watched these last five years living on Sunset Beach. Over and over I ask: Do I really want to leave it now? To go to New York. To take a new job in a very different field. Maybe I'll fail. Oh, no I won't. I'll be a star. Of course I can write curriculum materials for Physicians Assistants! I didn't know what they were or what they did two months ago. But I can read and if I have a content expert, hey, a piece of cake. But I'm going there from the archery field. I'll be teaching professionals. I've been teaching students here. Oh my God, I think I'm jumping off a cliff.

Packing is easy. I'll just take a few clothes and buy new ones. I gave all my winter things away years ago. I have no idea what they wear in NEW YORK. I'm not small enough to wear Marge's clothes but she'll help me find some. I know she will. Slow down. I have to get there first.

Marge has two friends, Lois and Donna, who have been visiting Lois's mother near here and they're going back to New York today. They drive part way and then go the rest of the way by train. Even the car goes by train. Marge has made arrangements for us to go with them. They've been friends for a long time. I met them once when I was visiting on Long Island.

I'm looking forward to the train ride. I haven't been on a train for years. I hopped a freight train when I was eight or nine to go see Deh Deh. But those trains were very different. We'll ride all night in coach and be in Washington DC tomorrow and then drive to NEW YORK. I know it's crowded and people talk very fast. Even Marge talks so fast that I can't always understand her. My friends look at me and say, "What'd she say."

Will New Yorkers make fun of my slow talk? Like when I went to Slippery Rock to school, they teased me about my Southern hillbilly-twang. I practiced long hours in front of a mirror, so I don't talk like that anymore. But I do talk slower than anyone I've met from NEW YORK. Oh well, I'm going to give it a chance. I must be running pretty fast, I'm almost home. Hope Marge has had her swim. I'm starving. But if she isn't back, I'll shower and dress, then get everything ready for breakfast as soon as she gets back.

I start to make breakfast. I'll use the most of the eggs and give Charlotte what's left over and the cheese and tomatoes. Bet they don't have this kind of tomatoes in NEW YORK in February. I'll pack a few. Surprise Marge with a snack on the train. She loves little surprises and little things. So easy to please. And I love to touch her. Such velvet skin. Oops, getting off course here. Best I go invite Charlotte to eat with us. I'll try to get her to understand that her life isn't over and that I'll be back to visit. She's an old woman and bitter: not the kind soul she used to be. Just two more hours till Lois and Donna will be here and I'll be gone. So be kind Rosie.

Charlotte walks in as I'm pouring myself a glass of juice. "I hope this is really what you want." I bristle. I slam the refrigerator door and turn to glare at her. I remind myself I'm leaving and smile instead. "You'd probably be a Dean at the College if you'd stay. But, you know best. So, I hope it's what you want." She begins to straighten the books and papers I've laid out to take in the car. She looks at each one and then puts it down. "Just remember you can come back. I'll take care of the place, you don't have to worry and when I can't we'll just have to sell it. You'll have a new place by then so you won't care."

The eggs slosh out of the bowl. I reach for a paper towel and another egg and wipe up the spill. I turn to look at her and notice tears welling up in her eyes. I bow my head. Softly I say, "Charlotte how can I answer that? Can't we just be kind to each other these last couple hours today and not go back over all those feelings that neither of us are honest about. Would you like to have breakfast with us? I'll fix your tea. We're having scrambled eggs with cheese, tomatoes and some left over broccoli."

"Oh, I might as well. Thanks."

I suggest she bring her own cinnamon bread and tell her it'll be ready in about twenty minutes. She turns to go back to her apartment and bumps into Marge coming in our door from her shower down stairs. I'm glad she kept the towel around herself. They exchange pleasant greetings and I repeat that breakfast will be ready in twenty minutes.

Lois and Donna arrive at the stroke of ten. Marge quickly put things in the car. "I'll be right there." I take one last walk through to see that everything's in place. The best home I've ever known. It's beautiful and what I've always dreamed of having. I'll be back. I don't think I'll have this kind of space in New York and surely not on the water. But I'll be with my love and that's better. Hope the job works out. As I lock the door, I tell myself to keep a stiff upper lip and say goodbye, get in the car, and just be quiet for a while.

We board the train and sit in our assigned seats. It's in coach and we sit facing Lois and Donna. Look around, out the window. I can't think of words. I can't talk. I don't know what to say. Can't even talk with Marge. I need to move. This is for real. I'm leaving Florida.

As soon as the train is moving, I get up to go for a walk. They all ask in unison, "Where're you going?"

"I don't know. Just to look around and see the train. I can't go far."

Marge asks if I want her to go with me and I say, no. I have to be alone and think. I walk two cars forward and find a car with seats arranged like booths in a diner. It's not the dining car but a space for playing card games or just sitting at a table. There are a few people sitting talking and one is playing solitaire. I could bring my book and come and sit here. I explore a few more cars and find no other space for hiding. I go back and sit down. The three of them are talking about Long Island and where Marge and I'll be living. It's across the street from a marina. That means water. Sounds pretty. It's not close to where Lois and Donna live on the north shore of Long Island. It's farther East. Will I ever learn where things are? They sound far from each other. Lois says where we are going to live is country. We are going through farmland now. Wonder if there are farms there? What do they call country? Isn't it close to an ocean?

"There's a car up ahead with room for playing cards and tables for writing or whatever. I want to be alone for a while so I'll be two cars ahead if you need me." Marge gives me a funny look as I get up to go. I feel sick. I better find a bathroom too.

As I move on the train, traveling to a new home, a new relationship, a new position at the University, I pinch myself and ask two questions. What are you doing? And is this really real? I have never felt as happy, never wanted to do anything as much, never dreamed I could feel about a person as I do, and never thought I'd have the guts to leave. I sleep for a while and am awakened by the three of them nudging me to go to the dining car. Dinner is pretty good. I'm surprised.

This coach, where we will spend the night, is first very hot and then very cold. The heating system on this Amtrak is wacky. That's what most of my friends in Florida think about me and this move. After 14 years as an associate professor at the Community College, I'm taking a leave, to move to New York. I hate cold weather. And believe me it is cold out the window.

"Good Morning, darling. How did you sleep?" I watched her as she slept. She is so radiant. She smiled in her sleep. She has the most beautiful hair in the world. Will I always feel like this? If I do it will make working very difficult. We'll be in bed from morning to night and then through the night. But we'll have to find a way for nourishment cause she loves to eat. And of course she'll have to have time for her exercising. She's so fit. I have to work to catch up. She gets up to go brush her teeth. I will follow.

"I slept fine. How bout you?"

"Fine. I'll catch you. Go ahead." I'm always a step or two behind her. I walk in the ladies room and can't believe my eyes. There she stands, bare to the waist. All these strangers standing around waiting for space. She just goes about washing like it's the natural thing to do. No one seems to mind, except me.

We pulled into a parking space beside the beach at Fort Desoto Park the day after we met. Oh my God, she's changing her clothes right here in the car. "Marge, the rest rooms are right over there. They have showers and all."

"Why, am I embarrassing you? Sorry, I want to take a dip. Can I swim here?"

"I guess so. I thought we'd go walk on the beach first. But if you want to swim."

Boy, she sure is straightforward. Just does what she wants.

She finishes washing, picks up her things, turns, sees me standing there, hands me the toothbrushes and cosmetic bag and says, "I'll see if Lois and Donna are up. I'm ready to eat. How about you? Hurry." I nod and she leaves. I meet them back at our seats. They are ready to eat and remind me that we leave the train soon and will drive to Long Island with Lois and Donna.

As we get closer to New York everything looks crowded. Buildings are close together and they look dirty. The sides of the roads are filled with trash. And the odors are not pleasant. I say nothing but I don't like this place. Maybe it will be different on Long Island. So many cars and they are all going fast and the drivers look intent and angry. I'll know soon when we arrive at Lois and Donna's. Why am I here?

We've been driving in Marge's car for almost two hours since we left Lois and Donna. How long is this Long Island and where is Westhampton Beach? I guess she'll tell me when we arrive. We ride for long periods without a word and then we burst into conversation and talk a mile a minute for a while. So much more to learn about each other. It's hard for me to believe it's been two years since we met. It seems like only yesterday, but I've known her all my life.

There's a trace of snow along the side of the road but the roads are clear. We are on the Long Island Expressway and there's a lot of traffic. We just passed an exit for Stony Brook. And suddenly there are almost no other cars going our way and only a few going in the opposite direction. The exits look like they lead to nowhere. Not much sign of businesses or anything as we go by. Exit 68. Wonder where it goes. Three cars ahead of us went that way. Marge says we get off at 70. Here we go. There is a gas station and a traffic light at a diner. There is a little trailer where someone is selling hot dogs just before the diner. How could they make money with a big diner right beside them? "What's the story behind that little trailer and the big diner?"

"The story goes that the couple who own the diner divorced and she put her little hot dog stand right on the property line just to show him."

It has a big sign over it: GRACE'S. "I think I'd go to the diner."

"Grace has a lot of regular customers who stop for coffee and lunch so she's doing fine."

We go to the end of this highway and on to another called Sunrise Highway, route 27. We get off at exit 63, Westhampton Beach. I guess I'll have to learn all these roads next week when I start work at the University. Oh, boy, I adjust my seat. I keep looking for signs of life. This is a small town. Everything looks closed. It's only 4 pm, but it's beginning to get dark. Marge told me we're right across the street from the water. I see a marina but no water. How can there be a marina without water? Oh, it's frozen. Salt water, frozen? WOW. That's cold. Oh well, she'll keep me warm. I look at her and get a warm feeling, especially between my legs. We drive down a long driveway to our house, past another house and a tennis court and stop right by the steps. This is a big house. She told me that we are renting the upstairs and just for the winter. The owners spend summers here and their things are stored in the three bedrooms downstairs. She leans over, kisses me and says, "This is it, darling." We climb the stairs and go in. Right in the middle of the floor in this big open space of living, kitchen, and dining rooms is a brand new 10-speed bike. It's silver.

"Happy Birthday" She takes me in her arms.

I walk into the Dean's office. Four people turn to look. The dean motions for me to come in. We shake hands and he says, "I have a meeting but you can just go down that hallway to the last door on your left." He points to the hallway. "That's Ed Brown's office. He's expecting you. He'll give you your first day's introduction to the program and probably some work. We're really happy you are here, Rose. Welcome."

"Thank you. I'm happy to be here too. I'll see you later, Dean McTernan, and thank you."

I walk along a wall of glass past several offices. I can see that the rest of the room is laid out in spaces that resemble offices without walls. I can't imagine getting any work done like this but I guess everyone copes. I was told months ago at the interview that partitions would soon be erected to divide the space. I guess soon is not yet. I see Mr. Brown as I approach his office. He meets me at the door and shakes my hand. He introduces me to his assistant, Lucille, and goes into the next room. She says, "Welcome. We're meeting in the conference room. Come join us. We're in the middle of grant renewal so we are writing full speed ahead. You can help with that, I'm told."

What has she been told and by whom. I stiffen a bit and hope she isn't always this business-like. "I'll certainly try." She seems uncomfortable. I hesitate and step back so she goes ahead of me.

We walk into the conference room where the department faculty is gathered around a table with papers spread everywhere. How do they know what they're looking at, I wonder. They barely look up when Mr. Brown introduces me. Just a few grunts around the table. Lucille seems to be in charge. She quickly begins to assign parts of the grant to each person. She turns to me and says, "I understand you're an excellent writer. Here, might as well get started." She hands me a large stack of paper. "You can write the review of departmental activity for the last 5 years. These are the notes for those years. It'll give you a chance to get to know who we are and what we do."

"Thanks. I'll give it a shot." Is it my paranoia or is she upset that I'm here. I wasn't introduced to her when I was interviewed in November. I believe she was away. I think I better watch my P's and Q's around her till I get to know the lay of the land.

I don't believe I've been virtually alone for four hours. No one has interrupted to say anything. I'm getting to know who Physician Assistants are and something about this department. It's a good assignment. I've summarized most of what I've read and find it's difficult to get things into three pages. I wonder if there'll be page limits on all curriculum materials. And I realize that Lucille is also the chief of curriculum. Is she going to be my content expert or am I to be her flunky? Here she comes, holding out her hand as if to say, "Well, let's see how good you are?"

I hand her the three pages and wait for a response.

She begins reading as she walks toward her office. I follow and think I see a little grin. She turns and says, "This is a very good beginning. Thanks."

Today is Saturday, I want to do something. "Come on, Marge, let's go see Westhampton in the snow."

"It's freezing."

"Oh! Come on. I'm the one who is supposed to be cold. I'm the Southerner."

I can't believe I'm trying to get her to go outside. I hate snow. But it is so beautiful and so is she. We've only been here a month and it's now very cold and snowy. But everything is great.

"Rosie it's only 28 degrees. You'll freeze, darling. Let's go to bed and make mad passionate love."

"We did that this morning. Remember. Now I want to go see this great little town. I'll go myself. I'll drive my new car. I call her Rita Mae, you know."

"When did you name it and how do you know it's a she?"

"Cause she's a real winner. Maybe today all the gears will work in the snow. The other day I had to wait for her stubborn streak to go away to move in reverse. The buttons don't always click in. Come on, I'll let you drive her."

"Oh, OK, but don't you complain when you get cold. And we'll take my car." We both dress in many layers. I see my breath as we go out the door. It is very cold. She takes off down the driveway like there's no snow. We're headed for the water if she can't stop. The bay looks like a lake waiting for the ice skaters. She turns the corner out of the driveway. There's ice hanging from every boat. "Look at those ice pops. Almost like single Popsicles. Too bad they aren't in color. Stop! I'll get you one."

"You're crazy."

"About you."

213

We laugh and I take her hand. We sing: "A you're adorable, B You're so beautiful." We drive over a little bridge and around a corner. I'm not sure where we are but we are going east. It's just glorious. The houses are like mansions. The yards are perfect and all the trees look like a winter wonderland. It begins to snow and Marge wants to go home. I agree. Now it's time to snuggle and get warm. She turns around at a driveway where new construction has just begun. I'm glad I'm not a builder. The foundation is finished and walls have been started.

I hear a funny noise and Marge frowns. I ask, "What was that?"

"I think we have a flat tire and we don't have a spare."

"You have to be kidding."

"The one I had was a donut so I took it to Zima's Tire store to get a full sized one and he had to order it. It'll be there Monday morning."

We sit by the side of the road and laugh. She didn't want to take my two hundred dollar car I bought to use till I get a new one and here we are in her fancy car with a flat. We decide we have to leave the car, walk home, about a mile, and call AAA.

I run ahead and knock snow off the closest branch to drench her as she follows. She chases and the fun begins. We're covered with snow as we finally shake and hug in front of the garage door.

We moved out of the house for the summer. We spent a little time in Florida, visited friends and then went to West Virginia. I wanted to show Marge where I was born and I had to look for my father or his family, if he is really dead.

"Thanks for driving, Marge. I'm a bit nervous. Turn right. This is the street where his office is and there's a phone. Park right here." Charleston, West Virginia is a lazy looking town. No one moves very quickly.

"You know, Marge, I bet mother brought us here for weekends when we were little just so she could see our dad.

214

Nancy and I went to a movie while she went to the main office of the State Road Commission. She said she had to go there and we believed her."

"You had no reason not to believe her then. Maybe she was telling you the truth and he was already dead. Don't be negative now."

"I'm scared. What if he won't see me? And worse, what if he will?" I step into a phone booth on the corner of Kanawha and Capitol Street. I dial the number slowly. 8 - 7 - 8 - 4 - 9 - 4 -5. Ring, ring ring "Hello, this is Sam."

"Hello, my name is Rose Walton. May I come to see you? A friend gave me your name and said you might be able to help me with some history I'm trying to track down."

"What? What are you talking about? This is Sam A.... I'm an optician."

"Yes, I know. My friend suggested you might help me find some older A...s. Please may I come talk with you? Your office is just a block away, I believe. If another time would be more convenient?"

"No, no, come now. I don't know who you are or what you're talking about but I'll see you. I'm not too busy. I'm on the third floor of the Rattner building. Room 304."

Marge has been standing leaning on the phone booth door; all ears. I smile widely and say, "Let's go." I hear and feel my heart pound. I step quickly. I'm very warm. I find the building just as I expected, a block from where we stopped. It's a dirty building, but they all are. The industry around Charleston makes everything look dull from all the soot. "What should I say?"

"Just tell him you'd like to know about **C.M.A**."

I say the name over and over in my mind. I've said this name so often. Is he still alive? He'd be very old, I think. If he was older than mother, and she died two years ago at 69: he'd be at least 80 or 85. Maybe older. I look for the elevator as we enter the building. We walk up the steps hand in hand, giving each other support. Maybe rent is cheaper without an elevator. But I always wanted them to be very wealthy. "Well, here goes."

I knock gently on the door and open it at the same time. A gray haired man, in a light gray suit with a red and gray tie walks toward us. "Hello, I'm Rose Walton and this is my friend, Marge. I'm the one who just called."

"Oh, come in. Have a seat. I'm Sam A.... Now what is it you think I can help you with?" We sit on a small wicker couch. Only big enough for two people. He sits in a chair facing us.

"I believe you can tell me about **C.M.A.**" I sit on the edge of the couch he has pointed to and Marge sits close beside me. I'm glad she's here. My heart is racing and I feel really warm. I lean forward.

"You want to know about the old man or the young man? Actually neither one of them is very young."

Does he mean they are still alive? "The old man, I think. I was told he died about 40 years ago."

"He has been dead a long time, but I don't think it's been that long. He was OK. My dad. Why do you want to know about him?"

I knew I'd have to answer that question but I wasn't sure I'd ever be ready to do that. I clear my throat. Try to push the excitement down and get calm. I shift on the couch and sit closer to Marge. I swallow hard and say, "Uh, his name is on my birth certificate."

"You mean you think my father is your father?" It's like we are all suspended. The world stops. "Well, I'll be damned, the old man played around. He was gone a lot of the time when I was a kid, but he was a pretty good Dad. So you're my half-sister. How about that? And I'm your half-brother. How old are you?"

My heart seems to slow down. Not the answer I expected but I'm not sure I knew what I expected. He talks on for a while. I hear some of it but I'm busy surveying the office and thinking about all those years that I asked my mother the same questions to be told it was none of my Goddamn business and here is a son who casually says, "I'll be damned, the ole man played around." As he talks on, the rage inside seems to evaporate and a calm comes over me like I've never felt before. I feel like I'm sinking into the couch.

A customer comes in and Sam suggests that Marge and I go back to his back office and wait for him. He shows us the way. As we walk this short distance down a hall, Marge spots a picture of a young girl in her teens. I can't believe my eyes, I feel faint as I look at it. I could put a picture I have of myself beside this photo and anyone would believe they were looking at identical twins. Same hairstyle, same eyes, same little nose. Is it my picture?

We are out of earshot and I ask Marge what she thinks so far.

"Rosie, I was so frightened when you told him why. And then his answer! I never expected him to answer so casually."

"I can't believe I didn't bring a tape recorder. All these years and no tape recorder. What was I thinking about?"

"Gee, Rosie, I can't imagine what might have been going through your mind. Something like: maybe he'll kill me; maybe he'll call the police; maybe he'll drop me out a window. Give yourself a break will you? I think you are the bravest woman I know for even coming here."

As Sam approaches the office, Marge walks to the door, points to the picture. "Who is that?"

"Oh, that's my granddaughter. Why?"

"I've seen a picture of Rosie when she was about the same age and if you saw both pictures you might think you were looking at identical twins. It's kind of spooky."

I couldn't hear his comment. I'll just have to take notes. I know I won't remember half of what he has already said, much less what he may say.

He begins to take papers from a file above his desk. I thought the front reception area was messy. This office looks like mine often does. Maybe it's the day before he decides like I do; this mess must be cleaned, today. Maybe it's a gene.

He talks about the pictures and shows us a picture of my great grandfather standing at a fireplace with a picture of

Sir Andrew A... of Lochnaw, Scotland. How about that? I'm part Scottish. And my Great Grandfather is very nice looking. Hey, this family isn't so bad. He has a genealogical report of the A... Family. Some Scottish and some French. He hands me a copy and I look at the coat of arms. He explains it all. Then he takes my copy back and begins to write on it. He hands it back to me and I read across the front page: "To Sister Rose from your brother Sam A...." He continues to talk about the family for almost three hours.

One of his daughters comes in and he introduces me as her Aunt. She wants to know if we're coming to meet her family. I am overwhelmed. I can hardly speak. I have no desire to be part of this family. I just want to hear someone who knows about my father say he was an OK guy. And I hear that now. We say our goodbyes. I am lighter and have a bounce in my step as we go back down the steps. I take a deep breath and a long exhale. It is unbelievable. "Come on Marge, let's go to Oak Hill."

"How long will it take us to get to your hometown?"

"Probably, an hour and a half. The road is very curvy."

As we drive away, I sit very still for a long while. Marge doesn't say a word. I break the silence with talk about Oak Hill and the people I expect us to see. I begin to show Marge landmarks as we get closer. As we approach, I show her the curve at Chimney corner, the graveyard, the East End stores and the post office. We pass the post office and make the next right, go down Chestnut Street and turn onto Park Street. I show her the house where I grew up.

"Stop here. This is where Mary Kessler lives, if she's still here." I jump out of the car and run up the steps. I open the screen and knock on the door. It's not closed and as I knock it opens slightly. I see Mary walking toward me and behind her is Hazel Walker. She lived across the street but moved away a long time ago. I hardly believe my eyes and begin to cry as she reaches to open the door.

"Well, I'll be damned. It's Rose Ann. Hazel, come here. I didn't think we'd ever see you again. Get in here. Let me look at you. Where've you been all these years?"

I step into the room and throw my arms around her. We stand there clinched and crying like two lost souls. Hazel gets to us about that time and I feel her take both of us in her arms. It feels so good; it's been so long. I haven't been in Oak Hill since the early 60's when Granny died and now it's 1978. I suddenly remember that Marge is standing on the porch. She doesn't know what is happening and probably thinks we're all crazy hillbillies just acting out. I pull away from both of them and step toward the door.

"Marge, this is Mary Kessler and this is Hazel Walker." I turn toward them and say, "This is my partner, Marge Sherwin." She steps toward the door and both Mary and Hazel nod and in unison say, "Hello. Come in."

I take her hand as she steps into the room. "You have to excuse us. It's been a long time and it brings back a lot of memories. Mary lived here when I was a kid and Hazel lived across the street."

Mary turns to me and continues her questions. "What are you doing now? Where are you living? Still teaching? In Florida? How's Nancy? How many kids does she have? Are you married?"

I should have expected the questions from Mary. She always had too many questions.

"What do you and your grandfather talk about all the time? You sit for hours. He's so mean. Seems you're the only bright spot in his life. Does he swear at you too?"

I'm older now. I don't have to answer her questions. Why did I ever? I can dodge her questions without being rude. "Hey, not so fast, I'll tell all after I hear how your children are and how Dorothy is, Hazel. Where are you living? Of course, I want to know how both of you are?"

"We were just having lunch. Have you eaten? Come sit with us in the kitchen."

"OK. But we can't stay long. We're on our way to the Smokies."

"Well, Hazel, at least we know it's the same ole Rosie, always in a hurry except when she was hidin from Mary or Nancy. I never blamed you, Rose Ann for hiding from your mother. She was the meanest woman I've ever known."

Hazel quickly says, "Now Mary, you know what old man Walton said. If you can't say something good, keep your goddamn mouth shut."

I laugh. He told me that lots of times and I can't remember anytime he said unkind things about anybody.

We swap stories for a while and Marge nudges me. I know we must go.

"I'm so glad we got to see you two. I love you both. But we must go."

We hug and say our so longs.

This two-week vacation was wonderful but I'm glad to be home. The Long Island expressway is still a very very long road.

"Boy, Marge I'm glad this is our last day of driving and we are almost home."

"Didn't you have a good time? We sure saw some beautiful sights and I enjoyed meeting your neighbors in Oak Hill."

"I had a great time and I liked seeing Mary and Hazel. Were you surprised when Mary said my mother was a mean woman?"

"Yes, but you have been saying that since I met you."

"I know. Maybe I should stop saying that. I loved the hiking. You made such wonderful snacks and I could use one now."

"Well, precious treasure, here's exit 70 and that means in 15 minutes we can eat."

Just as we walk in the house, the phone rings. Marge answers and hands me the phone. Who could be calling me? Who knows we are home? I drop a bag and say, "Hello."

"I want to speak to Rose Ann Walton."

"That's me. Who are you?"

"I understand that you think my father was your father. That you think his name is on your birth certificate."

Thanks for being so polite. Who can this be? "Who are you? Who gave you my phone number?" Whoever she is she's not nice. Her tone is demanding. It's been a month since Marge and I went to Charleston and met my half-brother. Is this his sister?

"My name is M. A. A. I'm 72 and I've been very sick. My brother told me that you came to see him and made this claim. This news is not good for my heart."

And this call isn't good for my head or my heart. "Listen, why don't you just remember the good times with your father? Remember you had one! Just forget about me." I feel the rage creeping up. I want to throw the phone at her. My hands are moist and my ear is burning.

"My father would never have done anything like you suggest without telling me."

Sure lady your father would have told you he was having an affair and she was going to have a child. Then the next year he would have told you the same. Even in West Virginia, I don't think men bragged to their daughters about their affairs. "I doubt that but that's all the more reason for you to remember his closeness. Enjoy that memory. And if he didn't tell you, well maybe he didn't know."

I can't believe her brother told her after making such a point of insisting that I not contact her. Guess he thought it might be fun. Or maybe he thought I really would look her up. He did give me her name and address. Poor woman. My God, she's the same age my mother would have been. I'll just hang up. I fidget with the things on the table beside me. Marge must wonder who this is. Knowing her she's probably already guessed.

"I want you to send me your birth certificate to verify his signature. And I understand that there's another one of you."

I shift from one foot to the other. Who the fuck does she think she is?

None of your Goddamn business.

"I bet that your own birth certificate doesn't have his signature. No, I will not send you a copy of mine. Forget that you ever heard about my sister or me. You had a father. Remember that. Keep the good memories. I wish I had known my father."

None of your Goddamn business

I move the telephone from my ear. If my mother were alive, I'd tell her to call Mary Walton. That would be some conversation. I can hear Mary now. It's none of your God damn business who I am.

"Well, I don't believe it and I expect you to send. . ."

"Listen lady, I'm sending you nothing. I'm hanging up and I don't expect to hear from you again. Good-bye." I hang up and drop into a chair. This lady is my half-sister.

It's none of your Goddamn business. It's none of your Goddamn business. It's none of your Goddamn business.

Marge is giving everything to her accountant for this year's taxes. I'm in the car waiting for her in front of his house. It's a beautiful neighborhood called Remsenburg. Here she comes. That was quick.

As she opens the car door, she says; "Let's just drive down this street and see if there are any houses for sale."

"Can we afford a house in Remsenburg?" I have no money now. I took a pay cut when I came to New York last year. But we're just looking not buying. Why not?

"I don't know but let's look."

"Ok." It's very cold. Still have about six inches of snow. But if Marge wants to look, I'll look. I love being with her and this year is going very fast. We've been talking about looking for several months but just haven't taken time. Our lease in Westhampton is up in May. Remsenburg is a very quiet community with wonderful houses and nothing commercial except the post office. It's only about five miles

West from where we live now. I've driven through many times just to look.

"Marge, look! There's a tennis court or at least it looks like one. And it's on the property with a mansion. It is a beautiful place. Let's find a house close. I've never lived near a brick mansion. I'm a long way from Arbuckle Creek. Turn here."

"No, let's go to the end of the street."

"But there's a For Sale sign down that street."

"Really?"

As she drives on down the street, I realize we are on a dead end street that ends in the bay. I'd like to live this close to the water. I could fish. We get out of the car. I wonder if I'll be here two years from now. She turns around and says, "Over there is Dune Road." She points across the bay. "That's Westhampton Beach."

Back in the car, we get to the street where I wanted to go and she turns just as I'm about to say, "Turn." We get out and walk through the snow to look in the windows. We can't see in the front so we go around the house. It's all glass sliding doors that open onto two decks. This is OK. Room for a small pool and not a lot of yard.

"This looks great. I'll call this week or when you go to Florida, I'll come by here to see if I can find the builder. I'd like to get in to see it before I call a realtor."

"Good idea. If you like it and you think we can afford it, buy it." I can't believe I said that. I don't even know I'll be here next year. I like this area. Nothing but wetlands across the street and a mansion behind it. "Check it out!"

We kiss each other as we walk to the car.

I'm so happy to be in the warmth of Florida's sunshine. I pull into a spot for visitors at the Central Administration building. I speak to a few people as I go to Norm's office. They just seem to smile. Maybe I'm already forgotten. I'm fifteen minutes early. I have my topic and an outline of all the chapters. If he approves these I'll be ready to write the dissertation and have my degree in January.

"Good morning, Dr. Stephens."

"What's the Dr. stuff? Trying to get used to hearing it? Good morning, Rose. You look very relaxed. Does that mean you have everything ready for my red pen?"

He always threatens but his bark is worse that his bite. He is very helpful. "Yes, Norm, but I don't think you'll have to mark it up much. I really worked on this and rewrote and rewrote. So I'm ready." He takes my folder and sits at a table near me. As he reads, I detect a smile. That's good. I pick up a magazine and turn the pages. I can't read. I look at the pictures.

"Rose, your topic is very timely and I think your outline of chapters is workable. Call Dr. Ross to get his approval and start writing."

"Thank you. Do you think I can finish this semester?"

"Sure if Dr. Ross and your reader at Stony Brook approve everything and you commit to writing NOW. You've done the research and your literature review is finished. Go for it."

I skip across the parking lot and head for the beach. Watch out fish here I come.

I get to the house in about twenty minutes and rush upstairs to change clothes. I grab a beer and the telephone and head for my dock. Sitting here watching the fishermen go by in their big boats, and feeling a slight tug on my line, I wonder why I ever left this place. The phone rings and it has to be Marge. Now I know why.

"Hello."

"Hi love. We bought the house. I went by on my way to school and the builder was there. He told me the price and we made a deal. So hurry back, we have lots to do."

I really didn't think she'd buy it so quickly. She sure knows what she wants. I'd have to think about it for at least a week. By then someone else would have made the purchase. "Not so fast. Is the inside of the house what we want? How did you decide so quickly? I know you didn't have to be in school till afternoon but it's only four o'clock now."

"The house is perfect. You'll love it. And remember you told me if I liked it to buy it. How was your meeting?"

"My head is spinning. He approved everything and told me to start writing. I'll call Dr. Ross tomorrow. If he agrees I'll have to buckle down to finish this semester."

"Great. Edmund called and left a message about a new position he wants you to take: something about you directing a graduate program. So hurry home."

"I'll be there soon. Just two more days. Should I call Edmund?" How can I possibly do anything with the graduate program? I'm not sure I know enough about all the allied health professions. But I have learned a lot this year. He is very persuasive and he has been talking about changes in that department.

"No, I'll call him. He has to know you're away. I'll meet you at baggage claim. Hurry. I miss you and don't forget we are moving next week."

"I love you. Should I bring the fish tugging on my line? "

"Sure, if it's a big snook." She hangs up and I know I've lost my bait. I put the phone in my tackle box and get another shrimp. I should eat these. They're really big.

I walk into my office and see two stacks of paper on my desk. One appears to be letters and notes on single sheets of paper. The other is a pile of multiple sheets put together by paper clips or staples. They are arranged so that each set of sheets is separated by a yellow sheet of paper. I hang my coat and sit down to begin the sorting. I quickly realize that the pile closest to me is a collection of student papers from my class. I move them aside for reading material tonight. I hear the Dean, saying "Good Morning" to everyone. He stops at my door.

I look up and say, "Good Morning, Edmund." He smiles and I know he's about to share another idea with me. That usually means more work.

"I'm glad you're here. Did you have a good trip? Are you Dr. Walton, yet?"

"Not quite. But very soon, I hope. Maybe two more trips."

"Good, cause I have a new job for you. I want you to direct the graduate program. And before you say "NO", listen to my proposal. You are the best person in the school for the job." He must be in a hurry. No small talk today and right to the point. I can't believe what I'm hearing. He continues. "You are an educator. You have no preconceived ideas about any of the health professionals who enter the program. You will help each student plan a graduate program to accomplish future goals. You see the big picture and I like that."

"But, there is a director. Is he leaving?"

"No, but you will encourage him to seek another job when you're his boss."

"Is that fair?"

He shakes his head and sits down and outlines his proposal with good reasons for the changes. I agree with him and of course I'll say yes. It's a steep learning curve in a short time but he says he will help. He's very supportive and I appreciate his belief in me.

"You make me sound like I can do anything. How can I say NO? I'll give it a try." He gets up, thanks me and is gone. I cannot believe what just happened. My career sure is changing. Just one year after arriving to write curriculum materials, I'm going to direct a graduate program. What a challenge and no one is saying, "You can't do that."

I can't believe we have collected so much stuff. I have packed boxes of books and kitchen stuff and tablecloths and just plain junk. I should throw half of it away. I can't. "Hurry with that box, Rosie, the car is about loaded"

"Don't rush me."

226

Marge's friend, Walter is bringing his truck this afternoon to help us move big stuff. We really don't have much. We rented this place furnished and only added a few things we couldn't live without, bicycles, chairs and a desk.

"Thanks, Walter. When we get settled you'll come to dinner. Rosie will cook."

"What do you mean, you're the better cook."

She puts her arm around me and whispers in my ear, "no I'm not." We wave goodbye and go in to put things away. We work for about an hour and Marge decides we should go for a walk to see our new neighborhood.

"No, Marge, I want to see it all. Let's bike."

"OK. Are you sure you have that much energy?"

"I can keep up with you any day. Let's go."

Marge comes jumping in the house waving a round package. It looks like a tube for a picture. I know she has been to the post office. Maybe somebody sent us a picture. She bounds up the steps and starts calling, "Rosie, Rosie come quick. You got it."

"Got what? Why are you so excited?"

"Come open this."

I walk slowly to our office where she has taken all the mail. She hands me the tube-like package. I look at it and start to smile from the tip of my toes to the top of my head. I open one end and shake the rolled sheet out. "It's my degree. WOW It's beautiful. It's big." I read: Rose Ann Walton-Doctor of Education-NOVA University-1978. And it's signed. It's official.

Marge hugs me very tightly and says, "We'll celebrate tonight. Where do you want to go to dinner?"

I am so proud. I'm smiling inside and out. "No one ever thought I could or would do it. They almost had me convinced. I should send a story to the *Fayette Tribune* in Oak Hill to let them all know that the idiot child made good." Funny how that childhood stuff keeps coming to the surface.

"I'm very proud of you and always knew you could do it, Dr. Walton. Now where do you want to go to dinner?"

I take her in my arms. She has always been supportive and never minded the long hours of writing time I needed. "Thanks. You have been the best cheerleader anyone could hope for. Let's go to *The Patio*."

I want to tell the deans about my ideas for the graduate program and I'm getting hungry. Maybe now is a good time to talk with both of them. I'll tell them it's my turn to pay for lunch. That'll get us away from the health science center. I don't like the cafeteria. I round the corner going to their office and here comes Ed and Bob is right behind him. "Let's go to lunch, I'll pay."

"We were on our way to ask you to go with us. We have a proposal for you. But if you're going to pay we can go to a fancy place, right Bob?"

Now what? They always have some new idea for me. I'm like a bouncing ball. I'd like to stay in one place for a while. I've only been director of the graduate program for nine months. Maybe we'll have an exchange of proposals.

"I don't think that's what she has in mind. But where do you want to go?"

"Let's go to the deli where we can sit outside. We need to talk about this proposition."

What's the difference between a proposal and a proposition? Sounds like I may have to do something either way. We go to the parking lot to Bob's car. He always drives. What could they possibly want me to do now? I'm doing as much as I can. I don't want any more responsibility now. Leave me alone. But of course I'll listen and try a little bargaining. I want them to make some changes.

We get our lunches and move to a table outside. It's warm with a nice breeze to keep the yellow jackets away. I sit quietly waiting for one of them to spring this new idea. Edmund complains about the onion in his tuna fish sandwich. "They should tell you or have a sign. Everyone doesn't like onions."

Bob shakes his head and asks; "Why don't you ask before you order?"

"I shouldn't have to ask."

"OK you two stop complaining and tell me what you want me to do."

"Well, Dr. Walton, it's a natural for you. You've done the background work for the position."

"What position?" I know of only one vacancy in the school. It's a department chair position. They'll never ask me to do that. I finish my last bite and start to carry my trash to the garbage can but Bob takes it with the rest and walks away.

"Rosie, I want to appoint you chair of your department. You're an educator and a good administrator and we need you. What do you say?

"No way, Edmund, you have to do a search. I'm not an allied health practitioner. Others in the school will never allow you to appoint me."

"I searched and found you. You're in the department and can move up. No search necessary."

"I need some time to consider this change. What about the graduate program? What about salary? I'm going on vacation next week. I'll think about it. I still think you should do a search. I'm sure many faculty . . . ." Bob comes back shaking his car keys. He's the rules man in the school. I'm ready to go. I think I'm in shock. I never expected them to consider me. I postpone my ideas for the graduate program changes. On the way back to the office, I agree to be the department chair for the rest of the year; just three months.

I turn as I hear a knock on my door. "Good Morning, Edmund. Thank you for this new challenge. I really like being in charge. Thanks for the confidence. I still think you should have done a search."

"Well, Rosie, didn't I tell you about our search? We found the best. So you're it."

I smile and thank him again. "So now that you have me loaded with responsibility, what's on your mind today?" I know he has another project in mind. I overheard two colleagues talking about it yesterday. I cannot do another thing for a while. I need to learn all the ins and outs of scheduling the electives and I need to make teaching assignments for next semester. I'll just say NO.

"Well, I've been thinking about your proposal."

"What proposal?" He thinks if it was my idea I'll do it. I can't remember making a proposal.

"You suggested we begin education about this new disease, Gay Related Immune Deficiency (GRID). I agree and I think we can do at least one or two programs through the Health Promotion Disease Prevention Project (HPDP)."

I shift in my chair and wish I'd learn to keep my mouth shut. It always gets me in trouble. But I also know we must begin to educate health practitioners about GRID. Everyone is scared, even our students doing clinical assignments. And we have to find a way to do some kind of on-going information for the public. The public is also frightened. But I'll wait and get Bob to help push that project.

"Then shouldn't you be talking to Elaine? She's head of HPDP. Not me."

"Well, maybe. But I thought you'd have ideas about a program for training those who would go back to their clinics or departments and teach others. You're the teacher trainer aren't you?"

He has me hooked and he knows it. But I have to start saying NO. I can't do it all. "So are you writing the background and justification?"

"Yes, in fact I have the first draft for you to read. Remember it doesn't have to be a proposal for a grant. We just have to submit a justification and plan for a program not in our original grant."

"I don't believe you. Do you stay up nights writing?"

He hands me several papers and says he'll be back this afternoon. As he backs out the door he says, "Maybe you can outline the plan of how we'll do it."

"Sure, give me three hours."

I'm overwhelmed with the response to this program. Elaine and I planned a full five-hour session. After introductions, I will begin with our objectives so everyone will know that we expect them to go back to their clinic or hospital to teach others about this disease. Dr. Green from University hospital will give an overview including the background and current status of cases on Long Island. He will talk about diagnosis and treatment. After a short break a panel of two mothers and one patient will tell their stories. I know how powerful this panel will be because I've talked with each of them.

Edmund told me last week that we'd be lucky to have twenty-five health care providers attend. I have counted over one hundred and they are still coming in. I'm glad I did not listen to him. We ordered snacks for 150 for mid-afternoon and it looks like we may not have enough. I'm sure the cafeteria will have more. I'll alert my secretary.

Now the lecture hall is full. That means there are about two hundred people. I step up to the podium to welcome everyone and quickly turn the program over to Elaine, director of the Health Promotion/Disease Prevention Project. She introduces key people in the room and hands the microphone back to me. I quickly talk about our expectations and introduce Dr. Green.

He reviews some of the history. "These epidemic opportunistic infections we are seeing have been called GRID – Gay-related immune Deficiency   The history and overview of this terrible epidemic goes well without many questions. The discussion of identification of those at risk was very lively. I almost laugh out loud when one physician says, "I've never treated a gay patient and would not know how to identify one to ask the appropriate questions."

Dr. Green quickly says, "You've probably treated more than you think. But now you'll ask EVERYONE questions about sexual activity; like what they do and with whom. And you'll ask how often they have sexual activity and how many partners. Let's take a break. This afternoon's panel will answer most of your questions. And we'll allow more questions then."

231

The panel is outstanding. One mother tells about three doctors refusing to treat her son. Our patient has everyone in tears telling about his hospital stay, "the nurses looked like space cadets and my food was delivered to the floor outside my door. The cleaners never came in my room. They'd look in and shake their head." Then a mother with her newborn daughter says, "Everyone in my doctor's office criticized me for having a child. One nurse said I didn't deserve to have a child. And she said it to my face."

Reaction from the health care providers is overwhelming. Every question to the panel was prefaced with "Thank you for sharing your story."

My voice cracks as I thank the panel. I apologize for the lateness of the hour and thank the participants. Many come to me asking, "When's the next session?"

It's hard for me to drive on the Long Island Expressway and read directions but this morning I'm driving to the county health department offices and need these directions. The AIDS Institute, a newly formed agency in the state health department, is holding two meetings today. I am attending both, this morning as a health professional and this afternoon as a member of the gay and lesbian community. Mel Rosen, director of the Institute, called last week to ask me to convene a combined meeting of representatives from both groups tomorrow. Because I co-chair a large gay and lesbian organization on the East End of Long Island he asked for a list of gay men and "a few lesbians" to include. He said, "I know that gay men and women have difficulty working together sometimes but you will know who can from your organization." I know the difficulty has nothing to do with our gayness.

As I drive into the parking lot, I see two Stony Brook social workers. I wave and they stop. "Thanks for waiting. Do you know where the meeting is?"

"Yes and we're glad to see you. Thank you for that wonderful program last month. We need another one just for social workers. Can you arrange one?"

"Yes, I think so. I'm counting on the Institute to start a grant program to allow us to do more education for everyone. When I spoke with the Institute director about this meeting, he hinted that money would be forthcoming." We walk in the door and I am amazed at the number of people. I recognize some but not many. I get coffee and a doughnut and find a seat near the front of the room.

Dr. Andrews, commissioner of health for Suffolk County calls the meeting to order and introduces other people in the health department. After recognizing members of Nassau County health department she introduces several politicians. I hope we can keep politics out of this work. It is so important and we don't need territorial fights. But I know politics enters into everything. I had better listen. Dr. Andrews turns the meeting over to Mel Rosen, director of the AIDS Institute.

"Thank you, Dr. Andrews and thank all of you for coming to this meeting. I hope we are beginning a journey together to stop the spread of this new disease and to give the best care we can to all who are already infected." Sounds good. He goes on to describe Long Island as a standard metropolitan statistical area, "Where we expect the epidemic to flourish because of the close proximity to New York City."

He briefly describes how the morning session will, "gather your thoughts about health and social-service needs. We want you to feel free to identify problems you have already experienced." He talks about this afternoon's meeting with representatives of the gay and lesbian communities and suggests that both groups will have the responsibility of planning a response for the region. A murmur cloaks the room. Several people walk to the back of the room to get more coffee.

I can feel the tension. Everybody wants something to happen but they are not ready to accept responsibility. He has not described a plan this morning but did have one in mind when he talked with me earlier.

Mel attempts to ease the mood. "We are here to help you develop a plan and the Institute will help pay to implement your work. We have asked Dr. Rose Walton, an administrator at the University and a leader in the gay and lesbian community, to attend both meetings today and to convene tomorrow's meeting of the combined groups." He turns and motions for me to stand. I feel all eyes turn my way. I smile and sit down. Now everyone in the room knows I'm a lesbian. I sit taller.

As we move chairs to form small groups, Mel asks me not to join a group but to walk around, listen to the discussions, and if needed help move the process along. Each group is to create a list of needs and expectations. Most groups add a list of fears.

I suddenly realize I'm not going to get lunch between meetings so I go to a vending machine I saw on the way in and get a Snicker. Snickers are always helpful no matter what time it is.

I know most everyone who comes to the afternoon meeting and feel comfortable as they greet me at the door. I realize I'm in the right place at the right time and that I am about to add more responsibility to my work. It's going to be very meaningful work even if this is all about an awful disease. Thank you, Marge for changing my life. I can't wait to tell her about these meetings tonight. And thanks, Ed and Bob for giving me a job at the University.

The room is full. I quickly count fifteen health professionals. There are ten gay men and six lesbians, all of whom are members of the East End Gay Organization (EEGO). The organization works to defend human rights with an emphasis on gay and lesbian issues but everyone's rights are included. Social activities are planned for our community on the east end of Long Island. Some of the men are sick and getting care in New York City. Many members live in the City and have summerhouses out here. Weekends are especially busy in the summer. I know that Marge and I will be involved and I'm glad to see members of EEGO here.

Of course some of the health professionals may be lesbian or gay and I just don't know that yet. In the days of tighter closets I only counted those I'd slept with as lesbian.

I step up to the lectern and instantly it is very quiet. "Good morning. Thank you for coming to this meeting. I know that some of you had a long drive, which meant you were up very early. We'll try our best to make it worth your efforts." I introduce Roger and Mel, the two representatives from the AIDS Institute.

"Thank you, Dr. Walton. Roger and I are observers today. We did our talking yesterday. We are pleased that so many of you are here to begin Long Island's response to this major crisis."

My heart is pounding and my mind racing. Will I be able to initiate a response? And will my school and the University allow me to do what I believe must be done. The resources are here. Hospital researchers, an open attitude, support, space, grants, and health profession educators. University hospital is the only public hospital in Suffolk County. Please. We must make it happen.

"Thanks Mel. But I hope you'll feel free to participate." I turn to the group. "Let's move our chairs to form a circle so we can more easily talk with each other. It will also make passing the doughnuts easier. My secretary tells me the doughnuts are on the way and coffee is in the back of the room."

As they move the tables and chairs, I continue to talk about the epidemic and Long Island. I tell them that I do not believe the disease will stay in big cities or in the gay male population. It will surface on Long Island in gay and straight communities. I'm not sure why I believe that but we must be ready for a different kind of epidemic in terms of spread. Many more women will be affected on Long Island.

"This is a better arrangement. Please introduce yourself and tell us why you are here." Usually there is a hesitation. No one wants to be first. But this group is ready for action.

I know almost everyone in the room but I quickly write names of those I don't know and mark their position on my notes. I want to be able to call people by name even if I have to look at my chart. About half have spoken when my secretary comes in with doughnuts. Most of the group turns to see what is happening. I stand and say, "Excuse me. Let's stop here to take a short break to satisfy our need for sugar and caffeine." They move quickly and come back to the circle without starting conversations. I'm surprised and pleased. This group means business. Great. As introductions are finished, I hear someone say, "Now who are you, besides Rose?"

I realize some don't know who I am. So I say, "I'm Rose Walton. I chair a department in the School of Allied Health Professions and direct a graduate program for health professionals. The department members can write grants to secure monies for special projects. I teach at least one course each semester. Some of you attended our first HIV/AIDS education program last month. I'm lucky, I think, that the deans support my willingness and desire to get involved in the education about HIV/AIDS."

"Today's challenge is a demanding one. We've been charged with identifying and prioritizing the needs on Long Island. Marie, will you write on the flip chart as people call out ideas?"

This conference room is perfect for this meeting. We can't hear anything going on outside and it's just the right size. We don't need a microphone. The responses begin and are much faster than Marie can write. "I don't want to stop you but let's give Marie time to write."

> information
> hotline
> clinics
> education about the disease so we can treat
> doctors willing to treat
> how is it transmitted?
> what are the symptoms?
> how can I keep from getting infected?
> am I more at risk at work because I work in the hospital or clinic?

special places to bring the patients
how will I know if a patient is gay?
who do we ask about sex?
what's different about gay sex?
how do I ask about sex?
who can I ask?
transportation for patients
what about lesbians?

It is very clear that the number one need is for information about HIV/AIDS. How it is transmitted seems as important as diagnosis. Dissemination of information will be a challenge because of the stigma and discrimination that has already reared its ugly head. And because of the geography of Long Island, 118 miles long and 12 to 20 miles wide, we will have many problems that cities do not have to worry about. Communication and transportation will be top on the list.

"Thank you for being honest and open today. It has been a very productive meeting. Your questions, I hope, will be turned into services that answer all these needs." I turn to Mel and Roger. "Would you, Mel or Roger, like to comment? You've been very quiet today."

Both thank everyone and tell us they are impressed with the positive response and hope we all stay involved. "We hear the need and will send our requests for proposals to Dr. Walton and this group." I jump up and down. As everyone is leaving, I ask Mel if they have time to meet the Deans. They both say, "Yes."

I am almost skipping down the hall. Ed and Bob better act pleased and eager to get started. Edmund is the best grant writer I've ever met. I learned so much from him when we did the Health Promotion grant. We can do this. I'll help write.

"Do you think the administration will let you have a hot line in the school, Rose?"

As we go through the door to Edmund's office, I smile and say, "They better."

This is the first grant that is my responsibility. The request for proposal, from the AIDS Institute, arrived two days ago and the deadline for submission is just two weeks away. That's quick turnaround. I plan to go to Florida for Christmas day after tomorrow. I guess I'll burn some midnight oil for this one.

. I think we have a good chance of getting this money to establish an information and referral hotline and to hire staff to do community education. We will use many volunteers to answer the hotline and they must be trained. The budget is going to have to be creative to match the plan for action I have written. The state has set a limit for each proposal. We do not know how many they will fund. I think they will be chosen geographically to cover the state. As far as I know we are the only submission on Long Island. But they might lump the Island with the City. Edmund has taught me not to try to second-guess the grantor. So instead of guessing what they will do, I'd better finish my plan for what we will do.

I sense someone reading over my shoulder. I turn to see who it is. "How'd you get in here without me hearing you, Edmund?"

"That looks like a good outline. How about the plan? Scroll down so I can read it."

I scroll down a page and offer him my chair. But he would rather stand and have me correct the mistakes or change what he doesn't think possible. "Rose, we will never have enough calls to justify phone service to allow free calls from the entire island."

I turn my chair to face him and motion for him to take the other chair. "We can't expect people from Western Nassau County and Eastern Suffolk to pay for a call to the hotline for information. They are going to be frightened folks who think they are infected. And I checked with the phone company. It's not that expensive."

"Did you check with the vice president's office to see if he will allow it?"

I squirm and pick up a pencil. "No." I watch his reaction and hesitantly say, "But I have a bigger problem right now. Glad you stopped by."

"What, you want more office space for this project?"

"Yes, but No." We both smile and I go on, "The proposal must be postmarked on or before December 27th. I'm planning to go to Florida on the 22nd."

"Will it be finished before you leave?"

"I hope so. You have to proofread it and Bob is doing the budget. Can that all happen before I leave?"

"I think so. For a minute I thought you were going to cancel our Christmas." He laughs as he turns to go, saying, "I better have the proposal this afternoon and you better talk to Bob about the budget."

"I will. Thanks."

"I want all of you to know that Dr. Walton has received the first of what we hope will be an ongoing flow of monies from the AIDS Institute in New York State to continue an educational program for HIV and AIDS. The first grant is to establish an information and referral hotline for Nassau and Suffolk Counties. Dr. Walton, will you tell the faculty what you have planned?"

"Thank you, Edmund. All of you know about the success of our first educational program when we expected 30 and 200 arrived. I hope we have just begun with grants for education. This grant to establish a hotline will be done mostly by volunteers once we have the phone lines. People will be able to call from any place on the Island without paying for a regional call. I will give you the number as soon as it's ready so you can pass the information to your neighbors and friends and so you can redirect any calls that come to your office. Any questions?"

"How will volunteers be able to answer the questions?"

"Good question. We'll hire a project coordinator to develop a referral list and to help train the volunteers. Then we'll have training sessions from New York City folks already doing this work. Other questions?"

No one says a word. Some begin to whisper and others squirm in their seats. So I say, "The need for education and services is greater than any of us can imagine. Health care workers at our first program were frightened. You know the epidemic has spread to seventeen states and five European Countries. It's no longer a gay men's disease. Women as well as men are infected. But I know that lunch is more important than this project right now. So let's go eat and if you're interested or have any other questions just drop by my office."

Edmund nods his head, makes a few more announcements and the meeting ends. I will never understand professional jealousy. I've always been happy to hear about other departments receiving grants because I know it helps the whole school. I must be patient. Everyone is afraid of this disease.

I park on the top level of the parking garage beside the Health Sciences Center where I work. Maybe I should have parked in the hospital garage so no one in the school would know about my appointment in the neurology clinic. I walk to my office and drop my books and papers. I don't want to see or talk to anyone. My secretary walks in and begins to ask questions. I cut her off. "I have an appointment upstairs and want to buy flowers from the hospital auxiliary. I'll be back in about an hour. I hope."

"Where's your appointment? Can I call if I need you?"

"No, just act like I haven't been here this morning." I quickly walk out and toward the escalator. I see people carrying flats of beautiful flowers. I must hurry. Forget the appointment buy flowers. I rush up the escalators to level five. There are flowers everywhere as I enter the hospital lobby. Beautiful. I have a great choice. I want them all to make our yard a giant spot of color this summer. It's May first and time to plant. I'll put red and white Impatiens in the flower boxes around the pool and that means about 200 plants. Then I want a variety of marigolds for the new rock lined garden in front. That's another hundred. I ask, after I

240

make my choices, if I can leave the six flats under the tables for about an hour. I don't say why. Why should I tell them I can't take them now because I have to go see the chief of neurology to find out why my leg collapsed?

I walk down the hallway to the Clinical Practice offices, sign in and sit in the waiting area. People are running and walking like they're in a hurry. I pretend to read a magazine. If anyone who knows me in this Health Science Center comes by they won't recognize me. I bury my head in the magazine. Maybe my head will soon really be buried. Maybe it's a brain tumor, maybe cancer of the spine, maybe nothing. Just a weak leg. Happened suddenly. My leg just wouldn't hold me up. I only fell twice. Then it was fine. I'll leave. Don't need to know. I'll tell Marge and everyone else that it was nothing. That we have to wait for it to happen again and test when it happens. I just fell. I didn't get hurt. My leg just collapsed when I was running. Maybe I just tripped. There was nothing in the road. I didn't see anything when I fell. Could have been my other foot.

"Dr. Walton."

"Uh, yes." Should I say I don't need to see Dr. Morris? He's probably busy. Doesn't need to see a crazy, scared, lady who has nothing wrong with her. I walk toward the nurse.

"You may come in now. Dr. Morris will see you."

I walk more slowly. The nurse is dressed in all white, neatly pressed, has a folder in her hand and is smiling. I could just bolt out the other door. It's very hot in here. Why don't they have a window open? She explains that since it's just a consultation for a colleague, I don't have to fill out all the forms because he checked my records in family medicine. "Have a seat. He'll be in soon."

The room is stark. All white. A desk with nothing on it. A chair behind it and this chair facing the desk. She closes the door and I can hear her place the clipboard in the rack by the door. I am now a number in room 5. I wait. I hate to wait. I'm here because I know his secretary and she tells me he's gentle, kind, and considerate, with a deep understanding of people with neurological problems.

241

Although, I know I don't have one. Where is he? This is important. I have a job to do. I have an AIDS grant due in two days. I get up to leave and almost hit the door as he opens it. We shake hands and he instructs me to follow him to a different room. I do. I say nothing. He's glad I came to see him. I shouldn't worry. It's probably something simple to diagnose and to treat. We enter an even starker room with an examining table and a chair. He instructs me to sit on the table. He stands right in front of me. Very close.

He has me do several movements with my hands. My forefinger to my nose and back to his hand. With my eyes open, then closed. I bring both hands to my nose and back out, stretched to the sides. He asks me if my eyes have ever bothered me. "No, uh well once when I couldn't see out of one and it hurt to move it. That was years ago. Maybe twenty years ago."

"Yes, and did they call it optic neuritis."

"I don't remember. Maybe." Does he remember if anything hurt him twenty years ago?

He takes my shoes off and runs a key up the bottom of each foot. "Hummmmmm, he says. Let's go back in to my office."

Already? But what about the examination? Five minutes and that's it. Can't be much. I get off the table, sit in the chair, put my shoes back on and follow him. We go back to the same little room - his office. How boring, and he's head of the Department of Neurology in the School of Medicine. I have a better office than this, and I'm just the head of a department in the School of Allied Health Professions and I'm not a medical doctor. Maybe that's why he makes the big bucks. So why go back in this office? He could have told me in the examining room. He sits behind the desk, waits for me to be seated, leans forward and says, "You have a disease we call Multiple Sclerosis."

"WHAT?" Did he say what I think he said? How could he know that quickly? Doesn't he have to run tests? Take blood? Watch me run? Examine my whole body?

"Don't worry, some people have it and never even know it. Others live to tell their grandchildren about it and, yes, some people die in six months."

Who does this asshole think he is? I came for a professional opinion. If he thinks this is cute, he can have his Multiple Sclerosis. I'm getting out of here. I'm really hot. I can't breathe. I have to tell him to go to hell. "If this is your idea of kind, gentle, and considerate care; I don't want to see YOU or any of your staff. Goodbye." I run out, not sure which way to turn but I'm out. I get to the top of the escalator going down. My secretary is coming up the escalator. She is the last person I want to see right now. I lower my head as we pass. She didn't see me.

I go as quickly as possible to level two, run into my office and close the door. I begin to clear everything off my desk. File this and file that; throw away notes and messages, turn the computer off and sit down. Tears are running down my face and I can't seem to stop them. I'll just go home. Plant my flowers. Oh, yes, my flowers. I have to get them. Then I'll leave this place. I knew I shouldn't have seen that doctor. I hate him. I won't ever recommend him or any of his staff. Wait till I talk to his secretary again. I should call her now and tell her not to recommend him to me or to anyone again. Who should I tell that I am leaving? I pick up the phone and put it down. I have to call Marjorie. How can I tell her this terrible news? In her physical therapy practice, she treats Mrs. Dorn, who is a quadriplegic and has multiple sclerosis. She can ONLY move her head from side to side. She's in bed all the time. How soon will I ONLY move my head? I'm going home.

I roll over and see the clock. Five o'clock. My mind is racing about what needs to be done before this conference ends today. The training has gone so smoothly and I know these representatives from the State University campuses will take our message of prevention and safer sex to their students. They have been so intent on learning the information as well as the techniques of presentation. These three days have been hard work for my colleagues and me but it's also been fun. I will commend them before we leave. They deserve the praise and I'm proud of them. They are among the best educators I know and I'm very glad I hired them. I sit up on the side of the bed and begin my list. Remember to: praise staff, then praise participants and challenge them

This motel has been a great place for the group. It is centrally located and easy to fly or drive to from anywhere in the State. Maybe that's why it's the capitol. So I must check the dates for next year and secure the space. I add to my list.

secure motel in Albany
review food offerings
schedule breaks

During breakfast I go over my notes for the last session.

"Good morning. It's our last morning together and this one is yours to start your plan for AIDS education on your campus. You have a curriculum and you have experienced examples of the teaching for most of the curriculum. Now it's time for you to decide what you can do on your campus for students, faculty and staff." I signal Joe and Dee to hand out the action-plan sheets. "The form you are receiving is an action plan, YOUR action plan. You will identify an activity you want to try on your campus, identify the obstacles you expect, and identify your plan to overcome or get around those obstacles. Any questions?"

They are all smiling and begin writing feverously. These three days of intense training has paid off. They get it. They can reach thousands of students with the prevention message, hopefully before it's too late.

A hand goes up in the back. "Yes."

"How do I know what the deans on my campus will allow?"

"You don't. And perhaps as you identify the activities you want to try on your campus, the deans may be obstacles and you will have to find a way around their concerns. That's why we want you to identify your proposed activity, the obstacles, and the action you will take to put your plan into action. Set a deadline for yourself for each activity you plan." She nods and continues writing. I see others nod their heads. Many of the participants have luggage with them this morning and I know they are eager to get started on their trek home. So am I.

I know they all believe that I think they can do anything. We sure have tried to convince them that anything is possible. Now it is up to them. They've been very enthusiastic and that spirit has increased each day. The forty teachers and counselors attending this session represent about two-thirds of the campuses in the State University system. I am pleased with the turnout and hope the AIDS Institute will be as pleased. We will continue to receive grant monies if we produce. The hotline and information center continues to be very successful and this program will generate discussion of prevention with thousands of college students, faculty, and staff.

At the many national conferences I now attend for educators doing AIDS work, I ask about what is happening in other places. I know of very few efforts to teach students about the epidemic on any level and of no other statewide program in the country. New York State is a leader in this effort. We should be doing the same thing for junior and senior high school students. We know they are sexually active and therefore at risk for being infected. They need the safer sex message but parents and school administrators do not want us to mention sex to them. It reminds me of teaching about birth control in health classes and not being allowed to demonstrate how to use the condom, or show any of the other devices like the sponge or pill or IUDs. Maybe I'll propose a program for public schools and see if the Institute will fund it. I have already spoken at many high schools.

"Dr. Walton, do you want a copy of our plan?"

"I'd love to have one. But if you have to leave to catch a plane or your ride home, you may mail a copy to our office at Stony Brook. You have that address in your curriculum packet. And thanks for mentioning it. My

245

associate will bug you if we don't get them in a timely fashion, before the end of the month?" It's the seventeenth now. I add it to my list.

As they leave the room, all say, "thank you" and some hand me a copy of their plan. Three representatives ask if I will come to their campus to speak. I tell each one the same thing. "Call my office and if I can fit it into my schedule, I'll be there. I have about three speaking engagements every week. So be sure to call well ahead of your schedule."

"Marge, remember how I didn't want to go back to the second meeting of the East End Gay Organization when I came to New York? And you insisted. Thank you. Now, 3 years later, I'm a co-chair going to our first HIV/AIDS fundraiser." It's such an important group. I thought it would be just social and the women wouldn't talk to us. Now I know it does good things for the community and the people on the east end. We have raised money and given clothes and food for the migrant workers. Delivered turkeys last Thanksgiving and Christmas. "The benefit today will be the beginning of many to come for this disease and the people affected. Can't you go faster?"

"Relax. They won't start before you get there. Who's making introductions?"

I get out of the car and move quickly toward the tent. As I walk up the driveway, ten people all at once come to ask me where I've been. "Traffic was terrible. WOW this house is beautiful. I can't believe he gave it to us for the day. Is he here?"

Bernice looks at me like I'm nuts and says, "Are you crazy? This well-known writer and famous gourmet cook is not attending an EEGO fundraiser even if it's his house. He left in a limo about an hour ago."

"Were you here? The music is wonderful. You did a great job getting everything in place. Thanks."

Marge walks up and puts her arm around me. "Rosie this is wonderful. We'll raise a lot of money for the Gay Men's Health Crisis. Let's go look at the items on the

246

silent auction tables." We move arm in arm toward the first table. There must be at least a hundred items. Bids are high for paintings, books, clothing, antiques, and gift certificates for very good restaurants and Broadway shows. Marge starts to add her bid to one of the restaurants and I remind her, "We're having a live auction of art donated by artists from the city and the East End of Long Island. Better not spend all our money here."

This is the first fundraiser on Long Island for HIV/AIDS. All across the country it is the gay and lesbian communities that are providing services and monies for care and research. It is hard for me to understand how our government can stand by and watch this epidemic begin and explode without doing anything just because the first known cases happen to be in the gay male population. I think about it all the time and write letters in my head to the president and every congressman. We are raising money today for the Gay Men's Health Crisis, an organization in New York City founded by gay men to help provide social services for those affected. We need this kind of organization on Long Island for all people at risk including gay men. Already we have physicians and dentists refusing to treat patients they suspect are infected. Next year EEGO will raise money for Long Island.

"What are you thinking about? You haven't looked at one item on these tables. Don't you want to bid or at least tell me what to bid for?"

"I'm sorry, Marge, I was planning how to save the world. Sorry."

Stan comes over and gives me a kiss. "Isn't this wonderful? Will you do the introductions? You know all the political people. OK?"

"No I think we should divide them as we usually do. You're a co-chair too. I'll thank the politicos and you introduce the auctioneer. OK? Has he arrived? Eastbound traffic was terrible."

"OK. No, he hasn't but he called, so let's enjoy the moment. We need to relax for just a minute. "

247

"That's for sure." We walk toward the bar and have a stuffed mushroom on the way. Everything is perfect. I'm tingling all over. But I have to get ready to open the auction. I made notes but probably won't use them. I move to a quiet place behind the auction tent to collect my thoughts. I turn the notes over and start my list.

1. Thank the committee
2. Recognize politicos
3. GMHC-Gay Men's Health Crisis directors
    a. doing what the government hasn't done
    b. conducted training for new hotline at Stony Brook
4. The disease
    c. spreading quickly
    d. gay men are still most affected   may soon be different on Long Island
    e. drug users and women
    f. spread through blood and semen
    g. more than 400 cases in US - half in NY
    h.

5. WE MUST
    a. dig deep   make a difference   first fundraiser on Long Island   Many to follow   Up to us

I pace back and forth watching the crowd. As they begin to move toward the tent, I go to the microphone. There is a hush and then applause. I grow taller. "Welcome to the first HIV/AIDS fundraiser on Long Island. I want to thank the committee and introduce a few people who are here today." I introduce my list and then turn to the audience. "You are the most important people here today." I say a few things about the epidemic then get to the business of the day. "It's your money, today, that will help the Gay Men's Health Crisis respond to many Long Islanders. It's an absolute necessity that we do our part to help this critical effort. We'll be called on again and again to fill the void left by our lagging government whose leaders can't even begin to say the necessary words. So dig deep, folks. Buy the art you like and help those in need in our community."

I introduce Stan and step back. Marge puts her arm around my waist and whispers, "Good job. You speak so well. I love you."

"And I love you." I squeeze her hand. "It's really hot today."

"No it isn't. It's just you."

"Maybe you?" I smile and put my arm on her shoulder. "Listen to those bids." I am in awe. Five hundred, one thousand - sold for three thousand. It's a big success. We are raising lots of money in a short time. Next year this money will go to Stony Brook. The epidemic won't stay in the City. I turn to Marge and say; "We'll have to do a fundraiser like this for Stony Brook next year."

"Why? You're the only one doing anything and the State's giving you money for the hotline and education. Our members who need a doctor go to the City."

"Sick people can't go to the City. And our members aren't the only ones who need care. The state health department is not giving me enough to meet the increasing demand." I move away and listen to the last bidding.

I can hardly believe it! We've raised more than one hundred thousand dollars. My heart pounds. There must have been three or four hundred people here. I sit in disbelief with the money and checks staring me in the face. We do and the government won't? We should be marching in the streets every day. I slam my fist on the table.

I walk into the project office and pick up the log of calls for this week. I have a bet with Ed and Bob. They say we won't have more than ten or twenty calls a week and I say it will be more than fifty. I scan the first page and go to the next. Already by the second day we have had thirty-seven calls. OK, I'm right. I knew it. The volunteers tell me that things are going great. They have put stickers with our phone numbers on trees at the rest stops on the Long Island Expressway. Some other volunteers took posters to put in store windows. I thank them for their efforts and race to the Dean's office to report our numbers.

I see Edmund walking down the hallway. It's unusual to find him in the hallway without three or four other people. I'm glad we're alone. "Edmund, I need your advice. But first telephone numbers are higher than either of us expected. Day two, 37 requests for help. I guess I win that bet. But now I need advice. You're the grant guru. I just received another grant announcement. This one's from the National Institute for Mental Health."

"Do you want to respond? Is it an education grant? Of course we want you to reply."

He's always positive and supportive. The rest of the school is not. They see me, not the projects, taking new offices and getting new computers. "Yes to both of your questions but that's not my question. They're only going to fund a limited number of proposals. We can submit our own or we can join New York University School of Nursing. We would cover Long Island and they would cover the City. You know at least one project will be funded in the City. So what do I do?"

"Well, Rose, we know you can write a strong proposal. Nassau and Suffolk counties were just designated as a standard metropolitan statistical area, right? We must be considered an important area with the number of cases we have and with that description. And you're right that someone in the City will be funded. Has NYU contacted you?"

"Yes, but only to ask if we were submitting a proposal. If not, they will include Long Island in their proposal. I haven't answered. But I can't imagine they would get enough money to do both areas."

"Maybe they will get the money if the proposal is strong enough. Then they'll ask you to do the work on the Island."

"No. Not without giving us some of the money. Our staff is stretched to the limit now. In fact we are turning down some requests."

"I guess I'd explore submitting a proposal with NYU but the decision is yours. I'll support you either way. You know that. How much money have you gotten this year?"

"I have no idea. Somewhere around four hundred thousand but that has to last longer than this year. Thanks for the confidence without a decision. I hoped you'd just tell me what to do." I turn to walk away and he adds, "But you really knew I wouldn't."

I walk back to my office saying, "Yes, join NYU" on the right foot and "No on the left foot. Should I call? Do I wait for her call? Maybe she wants us to join her proposal. I pick up the phone to call and immediately put it down. I have to know what we want to do before I call. That's right: What We Want. I go to the project office to talk with the staff with note in hand.

I rearranged my office yesterday so that I have my back to the door. I hope it will help in slowing the interruptions. Everyone stops to say a few words. I want to be polite but right now I don't have time for their small talk. I could close the door but that's rude. I'm in the middle of two grants. I love writing them. It's like a game of chance. The request for proposal arrives and my staff and I, sometimes with Ed's help try to figure out what they will fund. Then we write our proposal using their words so they think we are thinking the same plan. Others who play this game might not agree.

One of these proposals goes to the state and one to a new grantor: the National Institute for Mental Health. It's another federal grant and we are submitting our proposal with New York University. The other grant is to educate physicians in New York about testing and counseling patients who may be at risk. I think that's most patients except lesbians and other women who don't have sex with men.

251

I'm writing the budget justification and gazing out the window. I must convince the grantors that I really need every penny in this budget. It's just a bit over their proposed amount. I sense someone behind me. I glance at the mirror I put on top of my monitor and see two men standing at my door. I don't recognize either of them. I turn in my chair and say, "May I help you?" Both are nice looking and dressed in dark slacks, white shirts and really beautiful ties. One is taller than the other. The taller one looks maybe 40 and the other looks 12 but I'm sure he's older. They are probably physicians. But why on earth are they here? They must be new and lost on the wrong floor, wrong school. Maybe they are looking for Edmund.

"Are you Dr. Rose Walton?"

"Yes. Come in." I motion for them to sit at a round table I have on the other side of my office. As I move my chair toward the table I ask, "Who are you?" I wonder if they are from the AIDS Institute. Here to check the progress of the grants. Maybe they want to know if I'm submitting a grant to do education statewide about testing and counseling for physicians. I'm working on it. Or, who knows what?

"I'm Roy and this is Tom. We are in the department of Infectious diseases working with HIV/AIDS. I'll be in charge of clinical care in the dedicated unit in the hospital when it opens. Tom will also be in clinical care and we are both doing some research. We need your help."

You want my help? He used my title but not theirs. Maybe they are physicians who believe in cooperation with others doing AIDS work. Combine education with research with and clinical care. Wouldn't that be nice?

"I'm flattered. But why do you want my help? I'm sure my staff will be looking to you for answers but what can we do for you or with you? And I'm curious, who sent you to me?"

Dr. Rushing, quickly says, "And we will try our best to answer your questions. We want to work with your staff."

My head is spinning. I've heard there's to be a dedicated unit in the hospital and that new physicians have been hired. But to have them want to work with our

252

education staff is like a dream. Clinical care, Research and Education, all connected. Wait till Edmund hears this. But I have to finish this grant today. I shift in my chair. Pick up a paperclip and begin to bend it back and forth.

Roy says, "I'm told by friends in Rochester that I won't be able to do anything at Stony Brook or on Long Island without Rose Walton. They tell me you started the response to HIV/AIDS on Long Island and that I must get to know you. Work with you. You're the leader in the gay and lesbian community, right? They think you're wonderful."

Oh boy. I'm always cautious when someone says that. Who knows me and how? I can't remember having an affair with anybody from Rochester. "Well, again I'm flattered. But who knows me in Rochester? I don't think I know anyone. But maybe I should get to know them if they think I'm wonderful."

"Well they have a great deal of respect for you and your work. You established the first information and referral hotline for people on Long Island. The folks at the AIDS Institute verified that and also said you were a very good grant writer. That they have funded other education projects and that you have monies from NIMH and HRSA. You're chair of the gay organization on the East End that does the big fund-raising?"

"They sure have told you a lot. May I ask them about you? And yes, I am heavily involved in the response and education on Long Island but the credit goes to a lot of people, especially the deans of this school. I didn't do any of it alone. And we don't yet have HRSA money." I fidget in my chair and I'm sure my face is beet red.

"Well, my friends in the gay community in Rochester give you the credit. And some of the physicians there and here say you are terrific." He tells me of his plan to establish a care center with education and research as essential components. I think I'm hearing my own dream with elements I cannot put together. I like these men immediately.

And now he looks very serious. "Can we count on you for help?"

"I'm certainly not going anywhere. I'll do what I can and my staff will be willing to help. That help goes both ways; Right?" Maybe I shouldn't have said that but I want to be sure.

He nods his head and we talk a few minutes about Long Island and the University. Dr. Rushing says he's glad to meet me, and looks forward to working with both of us. He has been very quiet. Before the conversation ends, we are on first name basis-Roy and Tom. My stomach is doing flip-flops. I tell them they must meet the Deans of this school. I'll arrange the meeting soon. They leave me in a daze.

I sit looking out the window thinking about how people make such a difference. I still wonder who in Rochester knows about my work here. It's wonderful to hear a physician talk comfortably about the gay community. If he gets an HIV clinic and a dedicated unit in the hospital established, I guarantee that next year's fundraiser on the East End will send money to us at Stony Brook. I'm in the right place and it's the right time. I rush to make an appointment to see both Ed and Bob and tell them the news. I must call Marge to tell her I'll be late for dinner. I'll call after I deliver the news to the deans. I pinch myself and laugh about being an archery teacher. It seems a lifetime ago.

I skip out of the Health Science Center to my car. The sun is setting and the sky is brilliant. The big grant is finished and when it's funded, I will be the director of the Stony Brook's AIDS Education and Resource Center. Finally a name to tell the public who we are. We've mostly called ourselves the AIDS project. The center will be one of the nation's seventeen AIDS Education and Training Centers through partnership with the School of Nursing at New York University. The first cooperative grant from the National Institutes for Mental Health worked well and I think this one from the Health Resources and Service Administration will too.

I go over the summary of projects so far. The Long Island information and referral hotline, funded in 1984; a

254

curriculum development project with a train-the-trainer program for college campuses that allowed participants from 64 campuses to reach thousands of students with the prevention and safer sex message, funded in 1985; and a program to train physicians and other health care workers about testing and counseling at seven sites in NY, funded in 1985. We have conducted many educational programs with AIIDS Institute monies. In 1986 we joined with New York University to do training for health professionals with an emphasis on psychosocial issues. That grant from the National Institute for Mental Health is the first federal money and it will continue for at least three more years. We have accomplished much and health care workers on Long Island are better prepared to care for HIV patients and their families. But I see so much more to do. We must try harder to reach more health care workers and to encourage them to go back to their work places and teach others. We will give them tools for educating their colleagues. I believe we can change attitudes and stop the discrimination. There is so much prejudice toward gay men and it spills over to lesbians because people don't understand transmission. Lesbians have the lowest rate of infection of any group. I want to scream when we get lumped together. And in our education sessions, I scream inside and then quietly repeat the modes of transmission. I must be positive. We can change behaviors and I see it happen every day. I can't wait to tell Marge about the center. Even if she complains about my long hours, she is very supportive.

As I walk through the door I smell dinner. Didn't know I was so hungry. "Boy, it sure smells good in here." We stand hugging and she whispers in my ear, "Tad called. He met the deadline for Fed Ex. The proposal is on its way."

"I knew he'd do it. He's the best associate director anyone could have. And I'm sure this grant will be funded. It's money for at least three years and a bigger staff. It adds so much to our efforts."

"Oh, now you have an associate director?"

"Yeah, with this new grant, we; Ed, Bob and I, decided to establish a Center. You are now hugging the

255

Director of the AIDS Education and Resource Center in the School of Allied Health Professions at the University at Stony Brook and of course a department chairperson. We'll be able to include more health professionals in our programs with increased medical information and still focus on the psychosocial issues. The NIMH grant has three more years of funding. I'll also hire more staff."

"And how big is your salary increase? That sounds like two full time jobs."

I pull away and say, "Let's eat. I'm starving. And the chicken smells great. You make the best roast chicken. I must learn how."

"Oh, just change the subject. And don't forget you still direct the graduate program which, in my opinion, makes three jobs." She moves to cut the chicken.

I step in front of her and put my arms around her. "But I love what I'm doing. And maybe it's making a difference."

"And you know I'm proud of you. Now do you want to eat or go upstairs?"

"Do I have to make a choice? I want both. Will the chicken stay warm?"

The lecture hall is graduated from front to back with desks and swivel chairs on each level. To avoid the steps I go in the front where the lecterns are. I quickly count at least fifty residents and see a few physicians who have been at University hospital for a few years, sitting behind the residents. They are in the highest row of seats and closest to the back door for a fast departure if the class is not to their liking. I notice that there is not one woman among them. Surely there are some women in this class of residents who will be treating HIV patients.

I step up to the lectern. As soon as they see me they all face forward and there's not another sound. I didn't say a word. "Good Morning. I'm Rose Walton, director of the AIDS Education and Resource Center in the School of Allied Health Professions. Welcome to our first HIV/AIDS education session for residents and physicians in University

Hospital. How many of you have encountered an HIV/AIDS patient in the hospital?" About half raise their hand. "How many of you expect to see an AIDS patient while you are here?" Almost all raise a hand. "And how many of you have had three or more hours of education about HIV/AIDS?" Very few hands go up. "Thank you."

"Dr. Buckeyser will begin. He is the associate director of the AIDS center and a challenging teacher who will engage you in an interactive kind of learning. You probably won't need to take notes. Our goal is to help you get in touch with your feelings, anxieties and perhaps a little fear about treating patients with HIV." As Joe comes to the front of the room, I tell them that refreshments will arrive soon. I leave to check on the refreshments. I need coffee.

Joe begins with, "Feel free to get refreshments anytime but not all at once. Let's get started. Please call out what you think when you hear someone say, "AIDS patient"." Joe picks up a piece of chalk and goes to the blackboard. There is an uncomfortable movement. "Don't hold back. Be honest."

Faggot

Queer

Promiscuous
Very sexually active

Don't know partners
Drug User

Home breaker
Started AIDS

Sick

Not Normal

257

Hair dresser
Child Molester

Sex crazed
Sissy

I can't listen. I want to shout. I'm glad I came to the back of the room when Joe started the class. I bow my head so they can't see my reaction. I admire Joe for his patience. And I think, in this case, it helps that he's not gay. His stomach is not turning over and over like mine. I get up and walk out of sight of the group. I can hear them but they can't see me. The words still fly. All negative. Their tone is negative. I kick at the wall. It's an ugly green. Everything in this building is a shade of green. I hate green.

Joe stops the words, says nothing about their descriptors. He simply says, "Please call out what you think when you hear "Straight Man."

Normal
Professional

Married
Loves women

Sports
Family

Normal Sex
No casual sex

Healthy
Like me

Who are these residents? Where are they from? Have they never known a gay man? Do they think there are no gay doctors? I can't believe this. Do they still believe that only gay men have AIDS? It's 1984 for God's sake. People were sick in 1978. I'm to talk with them about counseling all their patients, including the gay and bisexual ones about safer sex. I'll never be able to have a reasonable voice for this one. I wonder what they'd say about lesbians. I won't give them a chance. I look around to see if at least one lesbian physician came in late. I realize that I heard no female voices during the exercise. Why did the women stay away?

I signal Joe that I'm leaving. He frowns so I decide not to leave right now. I feel sick. My right ear's hot, and I know it is brilliant red. It gets this way lately when I'm upset. I take a few deep breaths. I get a drink of water from the refreshment table in the back and then pour myself a cup of coffee. I take a doughnut and walk back to the last row and sit down.

Joe starts a discussion pointing to the words and asks the group what they think is going on?

I listen to their responses:

"I've never known a gay man and don't know how to identify one."

"They're stupid for having sex with people they don't know."

"They can't all be hairdressers."

"I never think about them like normal men. I guess that's wrong."

"Gay men don't care about themselves like we do."

Then I hear one meek voice say, "My brother's gay and this discussion hurts, has been terrible for me."

Where were these physicians trained and where they have they lived? Maybe they're all the new residents who came from the Mid-West to be in NY but knew they couldn't handle the city. They came to the quiet suburbs on Long

Island, just sixty miles from the City. Now who's stereotyping? I don't want to believe my ears.

Without any judgmental remarks, Joe says, "Let's deal with these feelings. Choose a partner." So far they have had no reaction to the words from Joe or me. "Choose someone you don't know well. Spend the next ten minutes telling this partner that you, your brother, your father, your uncle or best male friend is gay."

There is much commotion and then everyone is speaking in a very low voice. I walk around to eavesdrop. One resident motions for me to come over. I go over and he says, "I know that no one in my family is gay. I can't do this."

I smile and say, "Try telling your partner that you are gay. Pretend. Remember this is about feelings." I turn my head and quickly walk away. My stomach does a flip.

I must remember that understanding difference is a process. My sister had a terrible time dealing with my relationship with Marge. It wasn't OK with her. She didn't want to talk about or hear about it. It was only after discussions with her teenage children that she had a better understanding that our relationship was very much like hers. Only gender differences. It took ten years. I tell myself to be patient with these young health care providers.

As I walk around the room, I begin to hear reasonable discussion. Some of these men are really getting into this activity. I think they understand a reason for dealing with their feelings. They had such negative descriptions in the first exercise but the tone is different now in this one-on-one exchange. I hear realistic conversation.

"I don't want to ask my partners to wear a condom."

"How many sexual partners do you have?"

"Well, maybe several every week."

Is there a chance these residents are educable? I suddenly realize that it is very late. We have been in this session almost five hours without complaint and only one break. I motion for Joe to end it.

Joe looks at his watch in surprise and says, "Well, how did that feel? Were you able to pretend? How do you think your feelings will affect your delivery of care to people with AIDS? I want you to think about these feelings and talk with your colleagues about them."

WOW a standing ovation. We didn't finish half the planned program but there's another session next week. They say they will make sure that all the residents attend. They thank us profusely as they leave. I drop into a chair and tell Joe he is wonderful. He quickly reminds me that next week is my turn.

It's a beautiful morning, bright sun, not much wind, and the birds are calling me to come and play. Marge rolls over. She looks out the glass sliding door and says, "Get up get dressed. Hurry! We're going kayaking." She gives me a kiss and is up like a shot, half-dressed before I roll over. I look at the clock. My god it's only 6:00. I jump up and try to be dressed before she goes downstairs. I'm never fast enough. Charlotte told me I'd never keep up with Marge. Charlotte was wrong. Marge always waits for me because she loves me.

Our neighbors, who always walk this early, smile as we go by with the kayaks; one on top of the other, on wheels and being balanced by Marge from her perch in the back of our station wagon as I drive slowly down the street to the bay. It's only an eighth of a mile. She jumps out of the car and rolls both kayaks over the rocks to the water as I lock the car and step slowly over the rocks and seaweed.

One man is watching as she expertly maneuvers both kayaks so they cannot float away before I get there. "Is it difficult to learn to kayak?"

"If you learned to canoe when you were a boy, it would be easy", Marge assures him. "I'll be happy to show you later if you want." He thanks her and tells her he'll think about it.

As we paddle side by side to the first inlet she tells me she wants to trade him a kayak lesson for time on his tennis court. I glance back and see he's still watching.

"Looks like your plan might work, he's still looking." She pulls ahead of me gliding around the bend. I doubt that she heard me. Oh, there's a kingfisher, my favorite bird. I stop to watch him dive for a little fish and then dart away; quick as a flash. I see little fish just ahead of my kayak. Maybe he'll come closer for another snack. Marge is turning her kayak around to see what happened to me. I wave for her to go ahead. I'm fine. I'm enjoying the morning sights and sounds. I'd tell her so but she can't hear me.

We investigate the little canals off the bay near our house. It's so peaceful gliding through smooth water. The big houses on the waterway sit like giant sleeping castles as we go by. Soon, mothers will rise to fix breakfast for fathers who go off to work and children who go off to school or play. Do the fathers ever fix breakfast for mothers who go to work? Later the housekeepers and the landscapers will come to brighten the place and manicure the lawns. Even the new houses have complete lawns and shrubbery when folks move into this neighborhood.

Marge is giving instructions. She's maneuvered around to be right behind me. "If you sit up straighter, it will be more comfortable."

"But I can't move my butt, it's stuck. And how can I lift myself with this paddle in my hand. You know I'm not as agile or comfortable in water as you are. And besides, I'm having fun even if I don't look exactly right to you."

"Rosie, I just want to help make it easier for you. The bay's only about two feet deep here, don't worry about turning over."

"I'm not! I know you want to help me but . . ."

262

We move back out to the bay and swing toward home. I pull in just ahead of Marge and she quickly gets out of her kayak to help me up. No neighbors waiting. Marge gives me a big hug as I get out of the kayak. "I'm so proud of you. Did you have fun?"

I let her help me over the rocks and say, "Of course."

The phone is ringing. Why doesn't Marge answer? Where is she? "Hello."

"Hi. It's Richard. I have some news to tell you but only you. You'll have to make all the announcements at the EEGO party tomorrow."

"Why? And is that the news?"

"Don't be in such a hurry, Love. I've lost some weight and just don't want to be up in front of everybody. They'll all gasp. And you know I'm the gasper in this group."

I have a sudden empty feeling. I know he's going to tell me he is infected. I don't want to hear it. We work so well together as co-chairs. He's such a queen but I don't mind. I think he's adorable and funny.

"How much weight have you lost? What about Lenny?" They've been together a long time.

"Lenny's fine. I'm positive but I don't have AIDS yet. And honey, I ain't gettin, it. This HIV is enough, like hives when I eat tomatoes. Sick all over."

"Oh, Richard, I'm sorry. Please take care of yourself. You know I'll do anything you want. Are you sure you still want to have the party at your house? We could put up a sign and move it or just cancel it."

"No. No. Everything's all set. It's the first party of the season. We can't change it now. See you tomorrow. Come early and remember you are the only one who knows." He hangs up.

263

DAMN DAMN DOUBLE DAMN Please God no more. Stop this sickness.

"Thanks for driving and coming early, Marge. I have to talk with Richard before the party."

"I know, you said that. Anyway, did you think I'd let you come by yourself? I see them on the side deck. Let's go in by the gate."

I'm almost through the gate when Richard grabs me in a bear hug. Tears are hot. He lets go and says, "Stop that. I'm the only one allowed tears."

"OH, you're the boss now?" We go up the steps to join Marge and Lenny. We stand hugging each other. Richard has lost a lot of weight and he looks pale. This disease is such a death sentence. If they could just find medication to keep people alive longer. "How can we help?" I know he will get care in the City where they live during the week. "If you need anything, please call."

"Thanks, but I'll be OK. I have a much better waistline now. Don't you agree?" He gets up a twirls around with his hands on his hips. He makes us smile and almost laugh with him. There is no time for serious talk. Lenny says nothing. Marge keeps her arm around him.

I hear people behind me. Within seconds people appear and set up tables. They must have been in the kitchen. Marge, Richard and Lenny go into the house. I stay to greet people as they come in. Everything's set up on the decks here and in the back of the house. It's good to be with friends. Our community has been hit hard with this epidemic. Some days are just plain heavy with the work I do and all the guys I know in the community who are sick, dying or already dead.

I find a group of women and join them to chat but I notice uneasiness. Talk is slow to begin. Finally one of them turns to me and asks if I'm still doing so much AIDS work. I feel proud and say "Of course." The bomb drops. It seems they all jump at once.

"WHY? The men would never help us. You think they would start hotlines, do education, and groups like you have? You're crazy"

I can't believe my ears. I'm suddenly very hot. My heart is racing and I'm not sure how to respond. We're all affected. Men and women, gay and straight. It's true that lesbians are the least infected but certainly the numbers of gay men we know, who are sick, dying or dead affect us. And lesbians who have sex with men or who share needles in drug use are at risk and many are infected. I shift uncomfortably and look around for Marge. She would tell them. Don't they have sick friends?

I try to explain. "The epidemic is affecting all people. Women, men and children are all getting sick."

"But we are not getting sick. And anyway we know if the tables were turned the men in this organization would not give a damn." They turn away and I know they aren't listening to me. As I walk away, I ask out loud, "Why are women refusing to learn about this epidemic?"

I sit watching Marge as she drives in this terrible traffic. She is beautiful. She seems to put on radar as we get close to the City. These drivers are crazy. Everyone is in such a damn big hurry. She looks at me, smiles, pats my leg and says; "Don't worry. We'll deal with it, no matter what."

"I know. But I don't have time for something to be wrong. And Joyce told me the same thing about this doctor as I heard about the one at Stony Brook. He's gentle, he listens, and he's very thorough."

"Rosie, she's a physician too and she worked in the City. She knows him. He's her neurologist. Relax."

I think, yea, easy for you to say. Your leg hasn't collapsed. You still run. But I don't say it. "You're right." She was upset that Dr. what's-his-name didn't order any tests. An MRI or myelogram or some scan. Still, I'm busy.

265

I teach, I direct an AIDS center and chair a department. I don't have time for this mess.

"Don't worry. You'll find a way."

"Of course I will." I turn toward the window. Traffic is slow, I hope it stays slow, then we'll miss the appointment and we can have a lovely time in the City and not worry about what's wrong with me. I'm speaking at a conference in Buffalo next week and have to get that speech ready. I don't have time for this. I just won't run. If my leg gets worse, then I'll do something about it.

I will not have anyone take care of me for the rest of my life. Wait on me hand and foot. I'll go away. Commit suicide. I will not live as a burden, not to her or any of my family. My family, that's a joke. Let's see which one would volunteer first. Nancy would say, of course you can come live with us, but Marge can't come. Right. Fat chance. I do know that Marge will be at my side no matter what.

We cross the 59th Street Bridge and I close my eyes. I hate this city traffic. Marge becomes a racecar driver with a different head. She's not about to let a taxi get ahead of her, much less a car from New Jersey. But the taxi is on my side of the car. I lean away from the door, like I think he'll hit any minute. She laughs and again tells me to relax.

"Yea, sure, the paint isn't coming off your side of the car." We pull into the parking lot of New York University Hospital. Dr. Jonas's office is just across the street. The parking attendant tells Marge, she can only park here for one hour.

"That's fine. If we're not finished, I'll come move the car."

That's a joke. I know she will not and he probably does too. Inside the building, we are directed to the offices on the right, on the main floor. Convenient, I hoped it would be on the 29th floor and that I could get lost on the way up. Not a chance.

I fill out the forms and wait to be called. The office is cluttered with magazines everywhere. Old ones, new ones, books for kids, and chairs all in a row. No one else is in the waiting room. It's nicely decorated. I sit down and leaf through a fishing magazine. Maybe the doctor is OUT. After fifteen minutes, the woman behind the glass says we can come in now. A very nice looking man greets us at the door. We shake hands but none of us utters a name. He is tall and slender. He moves with ease and I immediately like his approach. He is soft spoken and seems gentle. That's what I need.

"That's a nice airplane pin."

"I'm taking flying lessons. Somebody at the airport gave it to me."

"That's great. Will you take me for a ride?"

"That depends. I don't have my license yet. But maybe I will." I think he's an assistant killing time before Dr. Jonas gets here.

"Well, I'm Dr. Jonas. How is our friend Joyce? And tell me what brings you here today."

I look around, wait for Marge to tell him but she doesn't say a word. "Joyce is fine and I'm here because she says you are the best." I go on about running, my leg collapsing, and going to the "not so nice" doctor at Stony Brook. I feel my body getting very warm and I want to be sure he knows I expect better treatment here. "Dr. Morris said I had multiple sclerosis but that it was no big deal. He said that some people lived a long time but some died in six months." I bet he knows him, but I don't care. I wouldn't send my worst enemy to him.

Dr. Jonas smiles and says, "Well, let's take a look." He tells Marge that she may stay, asks her a few questions about what she does and when she tells him she's a PT, he wants to know if she has observed any changes in my walking, etc.

She shakes her head. I can see the wheels turning though. She's thinking back. She'll come up with a change that she's noticed but didn't want me to know.

He has me do some of the same things Dr. Morris did but adds lots more. I think I'm trying out for a motion specialist. I can do most everything he asks me to do, have a little trouble with some of the balancing acts, but I bet Marge might too. I know that's not true but I don't want to be the only one. When he's finished, he says he's not one to make quick judgments. "I'd like to admit you to the hospital and run some tests. It might be a brain tumor, a tumor in your spinal column, or **JUST** Multiple Sclerosis."

I look at the pictures on the wall. Nice art work, mostly modern, which I like. His desk is a beautiful antique. He doesn't sit behind it in his big comfortable chair but rather leans on the front side close to us. I'm running. Fast. I keep seeing in bright lights going on and off: YOU JUST HAVE MS, YOU JUST HAVE MS, YOU JUST HAVE MS.

I don't want just MS and I don't want AIDS for anybody. I see them alike. Both upset and ruin life. I don't want a brain tumor or any tumor for that matter. Thank you very much. We'll see you next year. Next century. I'm going home.

Way off I hear him talking to Marge. "This isn't an emergency. Wait for a bed. The hospital is full. It'll be about two weeks."

I'm right here. I'm back. He thinks he's planning this visit to the hospital with Marge. "Wait a minute. I have to have this over with before next week. I'm speaking at a conference in Buffalo. I can't be in the hospital then. We need to do whatever we need to do now."

He turns to me, "I understand your anxiety. I'll do my best but I know the hospital is full now. I'll have my office manager call you. You should go home, do anything you want. Act like nothing has happened."

Easy for him to say. I can't do anything I want. I can't run. I'm afraid I'll fall. No one understands. For them it's nothing. DAMN it's like a big elephant hovering over me ready to stomp on my leg. Marge puts her arm around me and squeezes me. "Come on, Rosie, everything will be OK. Let's go have dinner in a fine restaurant and see a show."

We walk out and across the street, arm in arm. I scream and begin to cry. What happens when I can't walk arm in arm with her? "Can we just go home? Everything is so black. I just want to be close to you. I don't want to go to a restaurant now. "

She says, "OK. But are you sure?"
"Yea. I need you to hold me very tight"

"That was a wonderful party. No one except you went in the pool but everybody had fun watching you. Three women came over to tell me 'how beautifully Marge swims'. I can't take my eyes off you when you swim. You are beautiful gliding through the water."

"That's nice. Who were the three women? It's early so let's stop at PC Richard's to look for a new stereo. OK?"

"I'm not telling but I'll be watching. Sure we can stop, why not? I'm sure glad they moved a store out here so we don't have to drive an hour west to shop. And I don't know the names of your admirers. "

As we go in the door a salesman pounces on us. "May I help you?" I hate that. They stand like vultures waiting for food.   .

I tell him we're just looking and Marge says he can help us with stereos. So, like dutiful women we follow him to the section of stereos and he begins to explain the brands and features. I'm only half listening when Marge gives me a nudge. I wanted to look first for myself and try to pick the one I thought best, and then I'd ask for help. She thinks

269

that's too time-consuming. I don't want to be pushed into **his** best deal. Bossy men. I always feel irritated. And I'm tired. I try to calm down and am glad to see two gay men walk in together. I nod hello even if I don't know them. I think I've seen them at EEGO and they greet me.

The men follow the first salesperson that steps up just as we did. I notice their salesman moves behind them and gives them a good once over. They're talking but I can't hear what they're saying and I'm forced to listen to our salesman go on and on about this receiver and these speakers. I don't want Bose speakers. They cost too much and my ear isn't that sensitive to tell the difference.

Just then the salesman helping the gay guys walks past our salesman and says, "I guess I should be wearing yellow gloves." I see the picture of the policemen wearing yellow gloves at the March on Washington. The rage builds.

I wheel around to see if the guys are looking or can hear him. I then turn on the salesman and blow my cork. "Do you know how ignorant that is? Do you have any idea what you're saying and how disgusting it is?"

My heart is beating very fast and I can feel the heat in my face. I am clenching my fists and wish I were brave enough to hit him in the mouth. The disgusting salesman has moved on to another part of the store as though he's looking for something for his customers. He doesn't even turn his head when I speak loudly to him. Other customers are looking at me and I know I must get out of the store. As usual, my anger brings tears to my eyes. My body stiffens. I bite my lip.

"C'mon Marge, I will not buy anything in this store. This is insulting and disgusting. They're bigots. I'm leaving. Get his name, if you can. I'll write a letter and let everyone know."

I stomp out the door and leave her open-mouthed. She's never seen me act this way. Neither have I. I cannot stand this blatant discrimination. I've worked for the last seven years in education to combat discrimination around this terrible epidemic and to establish the hotline, and to find referral services for those affected on Long Island. I will not stand for this in my presence. I fight this kind of thinking every time I give an educational session. I guess I never quit work. I shake my head as I walk to the car, kick the tires and hit the window. These salesmen should hear the calls on the hotline and get some idea of how many people just like them and their wives are affected.

On the way home, Marge tries to calm me. "Rosie, I understand how you feel but maybe if you were calmer they'd hear you. I don't blame you. He should not have said that. It's your work and I'm proud of you. Wish I had your nerve." She takes my hand and squeezes it.

"Please, just be quiet. OK?" I shake my head and crumble the information about speakers our salesman gave us and throw it on the floor. This is not over. I'll write to Mr. Richard and tell him what stupid bigots he has working for him. So insensitive. Tears streak down my face and I'm writing the letter in my head. "I'm sorry Marge. I hear this kind of stuff almost every day from all kinds of people. I guess I couldn't hear it again. I do try to answer others in a much nicer manner."

"You never have to apologize to me. I'm glad you spoke up. He deserved every word and more." She pulls me toward her and kisses my hand. "And I know your letter will be a masterpiece. You write the best letters."

I pound the keys on my computer very hard as I type. I write a letter to Mr. P. C. Richard and then one to EEGO members to tell them what happened. It will be in next month's newsletter. I see hundreds of us standing in front of the store. No one can get in. We'll hang the salesman in effigy. At least boycott the store. Marge reads and approves my language. I'll mail them tomorrow.

There is so much to get ready for the second site visit for our on-going mental health grant. I must finish this report and have someone make the slides before I leave today. The evaluators are at NYU today and will come to Stony Brook early tomorrow. I must also remember to order bagels, cream cheese, and all the trimmings. Maybe my secretary will do that. Oh, better not. It's too important. I write myself a note to talk with the cafeteria manager to order bagels, cream cheese, and all the trimmings. Maybe my secretary will do that. Oh, better not. It's too important. I should delegate. Not this time. Glad I came to work early today. No one is here. It is soooooo quiet. I love it.

The phone rings and rings just as I finish the report. I save it and check the handouts for tomorrow. DAMN. The phone still rings. It's too early for phone calls. Who could know I'm here. I answer, "This is Rose. How may I help you?"

"Dr. Walton, this is Roberta, in publications. I'm Ralph's assistant. Do you remember me?"

"Yes, does this mean my printing is ready early?"

"That's not why I'm calling. Ralph's in the hospital and I thought you'd want to know. I'm not sure about his room number."

My heart sinks. He didn't look good last week but he assured me everything was OK. He did say he was thinking about taking a leave. "Thanks, Roberta. Thank you for calling me. I really appreciate it. Do you need his room or phone number? I can get them for you. I'll call upstairs now."

"No, that's OK, but could I call you about how he is, say tomorrow or the next day?"

"Of course, you may. And don't hesitate to call if you want me to do anything else. If I find out anything today, I'll call you."

I hang up and write his name on a sheet of paper in front of me. It'll remind me to call before I go to the Unit later today. He's a real friend. He has gotten me out of several jams with brochures and grant reports and we were

272

co-chairs of EEGO last year. Not many at the University know that. I will sorely miss him.

I dial 4-1501 to ask Lynn, director of nursing on the Unit, about Ralph. My friend Roy, another nurse, answers, "I was just going to call you. Ralph's here. His mother just arrived. Can you come up?"

"I'll be right there." I bow my head and say a little prayer, thankful that I am in this position where I can teach about this terrible disease and be in the hospital for my friends who are ill. I know three of the fifteen on the unit now. I'll see them when I get upstairs.

Just as I walk out of my office, my secretary comes in. "Good morning, Rose. Good, you're here early. I have letters for you to sign."

"Not now. I'm going to the hospital. Leave messages on my door." I close the door and turn to go.

"But you have to sign the student class changes today. It will only take a minute." She gets to her desk and picks up a pile of papers. I do not want to deal with these now.

I sit in the chair beside her desk and sign three change forms and put the rest down. "Leave everything on my desk. I'll take care of it all when I come back. Thank you for doing all of the changes."

I walk out of the large room that houses the School and start down the hall. I stop at the AIDS office to tell them that my report is ready on my computer but that someone, hopefully Tad, will need to do the slides. I should be back in about an hour. I tell the secretaries that they can call me on the Unit.

I go toward the escalator, change my mind and keep walking toward the elevators. I'll do my usual tower hopping and walk through the glass walkway. This way I can stop in Dr. Steigbigel's office to ask about his new grant proposal and to find out when he needs our piece for the educator's salary. He's director of AIDS Research and the

273

hospital unit and always includes us in his grants and we include both his clinical and research programs in ours.

I get to the unit about an hour after I planned but that's pretty good timing for me these days. Nurse Roy, as I fondly call him, is waiting to talk with me about Ralph's mom. We hug, exchange pleasantries and sit in the conference room to talk. He fills me in on the latest. He thinks Ralph's mother is conflicted about Ralph's illness and his gayness. "She calls them choices but you and I know better." He tells me about other patients I sometimes visit. "By the way, Emily went home last night. And Steve is doing better than yesterday."

I walk into the single room, kiss Ralph, and turn to say hello to Mom. She's about five feet tall, has beautiful white hair and speaks very softly. She probably doesn't weigh a hundred pounds soaking wet. She has a beautiful smile.

"Ralph tells me you're wonderful. I'm so glad to meet you. Are you sure you can be here during your work day?"

"I'm very happy to meet you, and this is part of my work. How was your trip down from the Cape . . . right?"

"Yes. Pleasant, but I'm just so worried about him."

"Well, he's in the best place and with a very good, if not the best, physician on Long Island for his illness." I laugh and tell her that I'm not a bit partial.

We talk for a few minutes and I suggest she and I go have a bite to eat in the cafeteria. We tell Ralph we'll be back soon and I can tell from his expression that he's glad to have me talk with his mom.

I stick my head in Steve's room on the way down the hall and tell him I'll be back shortly. I introduce Ralph's mom and she takes his hand as she speaks to him. I am impressed with her ease with him. Visitors seldom show signs of comfort around AIDS patients. She continues to talk about Ralph's illness as we approach the elevator but stops as soon as we step inside. I face her and make small talk. She laughs as others get on and find me with my back to them. I like this lady.

I speak to several people as we go toward the cafeteria and she says, "Everyone knows you."

"Well not everyone, but I've been here a while and this AIDS work has propelled me into a limelight."

"Ralph tells me you've done so much."

I'm a bit embarrassed but appreciate that my colleagues think so. I thank her. We make our choices and go to sit at a table in the corner. I sit where I can see who is coming and going as usual. She says a little prayer before she eats her sandwich and again, I'm impressed and like the feeling I have about her. I ask about where she lives on the Cape and if she still goes to Florida in the winter? She tells me that Ralph always drives her down during his Thanksgiving break but she doesn't think he will be able to this year. She might just stay here.

I ask if she'd like frozen yogurt and she smiles. I get two cups and sit back down. There aren't many people in the cafeteria at this time of day - after breakfast and before lunch. It's the earliest I've eaten lunch in a longtime. It's usually around four when I'm starving. I could make this time a habit.

I notice a puzzled look on her face and wait for a question but she sort of shakes her head.

"What is it? Mrs. Chamberlain? Can I help with that question I see on your face?"

"Oh, I shouldn't feel like this but I just don't know what to do. I can't talk to any of my friends about Ralph's illness. I feel so alone. Even his sister doesn't want to know much."

I bow my head and wonder where to begin to be helpful. I've heard this so often and I try to be supportive. I don't want to show my anger. Gay men didn't go out looking for this God Damn disease. In those early days we didn't know about transmission.   They weren't doing anything wrong. It's not their fault. They're people dying before their time. It's a virus. How many times do we have to say it?

"Mrs. Chamberlain, Ralph is a wonderful human being, a really good friend, and you can be very proud of him. I'm sure you are. He didn't do anything wrong to get this disease. It can happen to anyone. It's not because he's gay that he's sick. He's sick because of the virus. And I know that he was infected long before we knew about GRID or HIV or AIDS."

"I know, but I can't tell my friends because then they'll know he's gay and they won't talk to me."

"Why?"

"They don't like gay people."

"Do they know Ralph?"

"Yes, and they all love him. Just as much as I do."

"So. . . . ."   I try to smile to mask my anger.

"But they don't know he's gay."

I look beyond her. It's a noisy cafeteria - banging trays drop as people leave. Just then someone knocks over a shelf of containers holding silverware. I jump and look around to see just where it was. I don't think she heard it and realize Mrs. Chamberlain is waiting for my response.

"I'll bet when you tell them he's very sick, they'll be sad. Maybe I'll bring you some things to read about the topic, if you want and when you're ready."

She says nothing to this and moves her chair and tells me she'd better get back to his room. Maybe I was too harsh. Maybe I can find a way to give her strength to seek support from those friends. Dig, Rosie, dig deep for that help. It's so stupid. They love him now because they don't know he's gay. I bet maybe they've figured it out and don't know how to talk about it or don't want to in fear of hurting her. How can that fact change so much? Parents disown their own children. They mind the gayness more than the illness. Makes me crazy.

We go back in silence. I thank her for our time together and suggest we meet day after tomorrow after the NIMH visit.

"I'd like that," she says with a faint smile.

Every time I visit the AIDS unit I check the names on the patient's doors. I try to visit the ones I know at least once a week. The population changes daily. They come and go and come back. Ralph is getting sicker by the day. Steve has gotten so much better that he's going home today. Bill is back after a few weeks at home. It's a crazy illness. What makes one sick doesn't bother another and one medication works for one and not for the other. Frustrating to watch. The safer sex message has not changed but everything else is moving at a fast pace. Of course not fast enough for most of us. I'm losing too many friends and feeling closer to their families and lovers and friends than ever before. I want it all to go away.

As I walk back across the bridge from the hospital I say a prayer of thanks that I only have MS. Never thought I'd pray that prayer but it's in my heart today. My fear of the unknown with MS is like their fear of what illness will weaken their bodies next. "And God, if you're in charge, stop this crazy virus. Stop the dying! And please let Ralph live long enough for his mother to work out this gay thing. Let me help." I look out over Long Island and wish I were in the small airplane I see in a distance. What peace that brought when I flew. To be up there all by myself, alert, in control, with only the voice of the radio and the hum of the engine. It was peaceful and exciting and a bit scary. It's wonderful. Those feelings belong to another life. A long cry from this day. OUT OF CONTROL. HELPLESS.

This is really a very steep bank. I think we should have stuck to our "Going in at the bay routine" but Margie wants to show me the Speonk River near our home. I stop the car right beside the road near the path down to the water. She jumps out of the car and tells me to go turn the car

277

around so it will be headed the right way on this side of the road and ready for us to pull both kayaks back home after our trip. By the time I do that she has both kayaks in the water. I hand her the paddles and a life jacket. I put my jacket on and stare at the bank to figure out how to get from here to there without falling. I take a step toward her and catch myself on the utility pole placed just right for a safe step. She takes my hand and I'm safe beside her at the water's edge.

"WOW, this water's cold."

"Oh, for Pete's sake, just sit down and swing your legs into the kayak. It's not that cold and only an inch deep. Hurry! The bugs are biting."

Off we go around grass flats and toward the birds, standing like statues in the early morning mist. They fly to near-by trees as we get closer. They glide like Jonathan Livingston and like I did when I flew the Piper Tomahawk.

It's quiet and peaceful. Where can I go? Anywhere but I can't stop for directions. And my instructor just got out and said, "Now do three more, I'll watch." I see him by the runway watching the rudder, the ailerons, and my flight pattern. I glide past him and pull the throttle to take off. Oops, I forgot to put the ailerons up. Keep going. Bring the nose down and level off slowly. He's still watching as I go round again. Just touch and go! This time it's perfect. A gradual descent with ailerons up, then ailerons down, and off I go into the sky, junior bird woman. Fantastic! I'll never land again. Just keep going. The earth is beautiful, colorful, and VERY BIG. Way bigger than this little tomahawk and me. Hold the nose up. Glide Glide Fly.

We paddle all the way to the next canal. This waterway is wider and has no houses right on the water. Just some docks and walkways to small motorboats, tied neatly waiting for the next fishing trip to the bay. I bet they catch the little green backs for bait. They're like baby blues and we can see them here swimming near the surface. I try to catch up with Marge as she skillfully glides past me and on to the end. She keeps her kayak straight as an arrow: I'll soon know how. I'm getting tired now but I don't want her to know. I reach the end and she holds the boat and takes my arm to help pull me out of the kayak. Oh boy, my left leg doesn't like that. I stand a minute to get my balance and then climb the bank to the car. I take the paddles, jackets and gloves from Marge and ask if I can help with the kayaks. I open the car and put everything away while she pushes both kayaks up the hill. She's very strong. We tighten the straps around the kayaks and the carrier and start our mile and a half journey home. It is so beautiful and I like feeling tired from activity instead of MS fatigue.

"Stop, Rosie, the wheel's coming off."

"What wheel?"

"Under the . . . STOP! PULL OVER!"

I pull to the side of the road and get out of the car to see what the problem is. OH my, we do have a problem. I can see that the left wheel is coming off the trailer. How are we going to get these home? It's really not far now but they are heavy.

"Maybe if we take the kayaks off, we can fix the wheel. It's just the rubber coming off the rim. Here, let's put them on the grass." Neighbors drive by and say "Hello". I see them laughing as they drive on. We are having fun although it will be a mechanical wonder if we get the wheel fixed.

"No, it won't go back on the rim. We'll have to put the longer one on top of the car and the other one in the back. But we'll have to tie the back down so the one on top will fit. I'm sorry, Rosie, I know you're tired. You can sleep when we get home. OK?"

"You mean we aren't going to eat breakfast?"

"Oh, yes, of course. I'll fix you a really good breakfast."

"WAIT, I can't walk that fast with this kayak."

"Just lift it to the edge and I will take it from there."

After some maneuvering, we get one on top of the car and the other balanced in the back. I drive very very slowly and we go down the street and to our driveway. I am very glad to be home.

"Let's clean them off so they are ready for tomorrow. Or maybe the next day."

I look at her like she has two heads. "It better be the next day, if you want me to go."

He was a terrific student   Taught me lots   Always cheerful except when someone was hurt   He majored in respiratory therapy   Already a nurse   So bright   fun loving   I hate this God Damn disease.   Now he has joined forty others I knew   Tears do not come   Just anger He educated so many at their bedside   Gave loving care Called me Aunt Rose   Said everyone needed an Aunt Rose   Brought me outrageous pins with gay sayings   His idea of making me hip.   I bought him a bright red boa for his fortieth birthday   What does it take   I hang my head   I hear a plane   I'll go far away   Away from this disease   And the other one   Granny said not to ask why but do or die   So many have   Bill   Roy   Emily Tom   Russ   Sue   Emily's daughter   Richard   Michelle Ed   Roy   Roy   Roy.

The summer opens with another EEGO party. I go over to tell Sandy how much I like her voice. She tells me she's singing at Ann's Place in Sag Harbor on the 29th. I try to tell her we can't be there when suddenly I can't get the words out right. What's happening? Having a stroke? Sounds like I'm drunk. I only had diet Pepsi. She takes my arm, says it's OK. You just got your tongue twisted. I know better. Something happened. Where's Margie? Have to find her. Sit down. I look around. There she is. "Mar.   Mar." She comes over. I'm having a stroke. Will I be paralyzed? Will I be able to get up? I don't want to go to Southampton Hospital. Take me to Stony Brook. Will they listen? I'm having a stroke. Marge is here. I'm OK.

"I don't know what happened. I just couldn't talk right. I slurred my words. Couldn't say them right. They sounded funny. Do I sound right now?"

"Rosie, here drink something."

280

"No, I'm OK now. Just let me sit here a minute." Other people are milling around and talking to each other. Did they see me? Do they know what's happening? They're watching a video about a gay television program. Maybe they didn't notice me. I don't want anyone to know something is wrong with me.

"I'll sing a new song for you, Rosie. Is that OK?"

I nod my head and she begins a song. Other people come over to listen. I keep my head down so I don't have to look at them. Is my face OK? Is it pulled to one side? Margie leans over asking if I'm all right. I don't know. Am I having a stroke or it's just an MS happening? Do people with MS have seizures and then can't talk right? I sit quietly and rub my face. My arms feel fine. I move my feet. They're fine. Granny had a stroke, so did Aunt Libby and maybe my mother when they died. Am I dying? I feel OK. I want to talk to see if the words come out right. What if they don't? Better go home. NO. I want to go out to dinner with friends. I whisper to Marge. I'm fine now. See I can talk. I sound OK. I can move everything. I'm OK.

I walk into Ralph's room and his Mom is sleeping in a chair. At least it's the comfortable one we brought in last night. I knew she'd stay. Ralph looks at me and I feel the pain. He looks ten years older than last week. He's all curled up on his side. I take his hand gently in my hand and say, "It's OK. You may let go." He closes his eyes and still has a faint smile on his face. I feel hot tears on my cheeks and turn away. He's forty + and just in the prime of his life. He has a partner who's here every day, who rubs his feet and legs, tries to get him to eat and makes him laugh once in a while.

Mrs. Chamberlain rallies and seems embarrassed about sleeping. She looks worried and sad. Ralph is happy that she is here and so is she. She sits up and looks around, smiles at us and asks, "How is he?"

"I think resting well. He did say a couple of words when I came in." I'm helpless. I smile but want to scream. He's young, filled with love and kindness.

281

"Dr. Steigbigel was in last night and started a new medication he hopes will do the trick. I pray it will give us some more time."

"That's great! Is it one of the new experimental drugs? That Roy Steigbigel is something. He tries so hard and cares so much."

"I love that man."

"So do I. He's one of a kind."

I give her a hug and tell her I'll see her later today. I turn to go back to my office.

"Rose, could you bring me those things to read that we talked about?"

"Sure. I'll send them up when I get downstairs. See you"

What a beautiful morning. The sunshine is streaming into the bedroom and birds sound like a symphony. I must get up and go outside. Two friends, Meg and Sherry, are visiting from California and they are probably already up and out running even if their clock is different. I hear Marge in the bathroom. I know she is getting ready to run. Everyone's running. I want to run with them.

"Can you wait two minutes for me? I want to go with you."

She's going down the stairs and calls back that she will if I hurry. I have my clothes on and I'm hurrying. I'm always been slow. I walk out and see her at the end of the driveway. I tell her to go ahead because I know she doesn't really want to walk.

"Oh, come on, Rosie, I'll walk a little way with you. Then I'll take a run."

We walk a few steps and she puts her arm around me. I'm on top of the world. The honeysuckle smells great. A pheasant walks across the road. We are so lucky. "Go ahead, Margie, run. I'll walk my mile."

She hesitates. I kiss her and push her ahead. I watch her round the corner of Cutler Lane and I want more than ever to run. I know I shouldn't but I must try. I hate this

Goddamn disease. I used to run five miles and now I can't run five steps. But I start anyway.

"Oh my God. DAMN DAMN." I'm stretched out face down on the pavement. I scream, "Margie. MARGIE. I'M HURT."

She is back in a flash and bends down to see what I've done. My face is bleeding. My knee hurts. She helps me up and wipes my face. She kisses me and we walk back to the house. How many more times will I fall? I just can't run. I must walk. Then what?

Suffolk County is having a hearing about gay rights today at the County Center in Riverhead. It's near the jail and other county buildings. The lawn is very spring-like with new flowers planted along the walkway. I arrive early to be sure I get my name on the list of speakers. I've been to so many of these hearings that I could just send a tape. But they want to make sure everyone has an opportunity to state their position. I think it should be simple to understand that gay men and lesbians need work related benefits just like non-gay people do. The gender of my partner should not have anything to do with it.

As I open one of the big, heavy doors to get into the building, I realize I'm in the middle of a large, noisy crowd. The high ceiling causes an echo so maybe it's not such a big group. There's still a loud murmur coming from the hearing room to my right that I can't see. What the fuck is going on? I sense an air of hostility in the crowd as people are jostling to get into the hearing room to sign up at the door. I excuse myself and go right in. Suddenly a sign comes into view: HOMOSEXUALITY = SIN = DEATH A SIN AGAINST GOD. I stop. Look around and see people with Bibles raised in the air. My heart quickens, I want to turn and run. I stand stiff. What the hell is wrong with these people? And they do it in the name of GOD. NOT MY GOD!

Granny and I discussed our beliefs about God often when I was home from college. She believed everything written in the Bible and what the pastor of the Southern Baptist church said was law. I could never get past the talk about "love thy neighbor" but if that neighbor is a different color, gay or lesbian or just different in any way, you don't really have to love him. But Granny did tell me that God loves everyone. From the looks of things today, you still can't be different if you want to go to their heaven.

I'm here to help a student tell his story about abuse in high school and in the community. He's a volunteer for the HIV/AIDS hotline and I agreed to be with him today. He's very shy. But I never expected this kind of a crowd. This is Suffolk County, New York, a community I always believed to be liberal and supportive. What's the big deal about adding "gay and lesbian" to the list of protected groups in the human rights statement for employment in the county? I hear them shouting about God's revenge.

In my head I hear my Grandmother talk about God's love of everyone and that I should love my neighbor and treat others, as I would like to be treated. I always believed that included me. She said it did, but I never told her I was a lesbian. That nags at me sometimes. Who are these people? What God do they hear speaking to them? Not the one my Granny talked about.

I bow my head, speak to Granny's God, and forge ahead through this angry mob to the door of the hearing room. A guard asks me my name and instructs me to sign in at the table at the back of the room if I plan to speak. I thank him and go into the room. I recognize several people and see that the aisles around the room are filled with people with "Hate" signs. Granny's God will have to be with me if I am to get through this meeting.

I go to the table, fill out a form for speaking, and find a seat near an aisle in the middle of the room. That way, I won't have to push through standing, angry folks to get to the speaker's stand. I take the notes from my briefcase and look over them. The hearing is about to begin. I listen to the first "born again" talk about how God hates homosexuals and how the legislature will be damned if they support this proposal of civil rights for all. That God did not allow for the sinful life they lead, and that the legislature should not give them special rights.

It's very hot in this room. I want to take my jacket off but know I'll look better with it on, when I speak. My blouse is soaking wet. I keep my head down and fumble with papers. I look around every now and then to see if I can find Andy. I sense that more people crowding into the room. They are filling the middle aisle beside my seat. I'll now have to move through them to get to the speakers stand. I want to scream. I have to change my testimony. No longer will I talk about the people who staff the hotline, those who are in the hospital, or those who have HIV. I will talk about me. I will let them know that there is one homosexual who has contributed to the community and who, like all gay men and lesbians, deserves equal rights with these crazies who are shouting hate. I try to gauge the reaction of the legislators but they sit stone-faced with no emotion or response or they whisper to the person next to them. Are they really listening? Have they already made up their minds? Not one of them tries to quiet the crowd.

The next speaker begins to talk about losing a job because his employer suspected that he was gay. The crowd claps and then boos. He is intimidated and his voice cracks. He sits down without having stated his case. My face reddens, my pulse quickens. Why the fuck can't the chairperson quiet the crowd so speakers can speak? I hear my name being called. Oh my God, it's my turn. I say a prayer to my God and hope Granny's is listening too. Maybe they are the same!

I stand and excuse myself. The person standing in the aisle doesn't move. I say excuse me again and push towards her. She steps a little to her right. I move in front of her and all the way to the speaker's stand I am saying excuse me while my heart is saying, "Get the fuck out of my way."

I thank the members of the legislature for conducting this hearing and for listening to all of us. I ask the crowd to listen as I have tried to listen to other speakers. I begin by telling them who I am: a professor at the University, a teacher for twenty five years, the director of the AIDS Education and Resource Center, a believer in human rights for all, a lesbian. As soon as the last phrase is out of my

285

mouth the crowd begins their chant about how God hates homosexuality. I stop, turn to the crowd and say, "I am also a Christian and my God teaches me to love my neighbor. So if you profess to be a Christian, please be quiet." They are still noisy but not as loud. I continue my comments. I finish, once again thank the legislators for listening and urge them to do the right thing. Facing this room full of angry faces I hear myself say, in a very loud voice, "My Grandmother would not call you Christian."

The legislators did not do the right thing that day.

For almost ten years Nancy and I have kept our promises to call that we made at mother's death. It was no surprise when my secretary says she's on the phone. She seldom calls here unless it's urgent or special. I know she has been feeling sick but insisted on taking the whole family to the Rose Bowl last month. I glance at the calendar and realize I marked today. She has a doctor's appointment today. That's what this must be her report. "Hi. Nancy. What did the doctor say?"

"Rosie, please don't be mad. I didn't tell you all of the truth. I saw the doctor before we went to California. I didn't tell anyone. Not even Ronnie or the kids."

"You sound awful. What's going on now? Never mind the lie."

"I had surgery yesterday. I have cancer. It's really bad. Can you come?"

"Of course I will be there as soon as I can make arrangements. I'll call you back. Give me a couple of hours. I'm sorry Nancy. Keep your chin up. I love you."

Damn. Cancer. Damn. First Mother, then Granny and now Nancy. Am I next? I have enough, God, leave me alone. I hit the save-key and leave the grant.

I walk in the dean's office and close the door. Edmund looks up with a perplexed look on his face. He knows it's serious for me to close the door. I do not hesitate. "Edmund, I can't finish this grant. My sister just called. She had surgery yesterday and she's upset. Things turned out worse than suspected. She wants me to come."

"Calm down. We'll get everything done. Relax. Do you have reservations? Do you want my secretary to make them? Can your staff finish the grant?"

"No to everything. None of them know about budgets or justifications. I'm afraid it will be up to you and Bob. Maybe I could call for an extension."

He moves some papers on his desk. I know he's busy and I feel guilty barging in this way telling him instead of asking. He asks, "Do you have time to go over the proposal or are you leaving today?"

"No. I'll outline the last section now and I have most of the budget figured out but it doesn't add up to the right amount. It needs a bit of an adjustment. You are the master of grant writing so it will be a piece of cake for you." I smile.

"From your record you're the master writer. I know this proposal is an extension of a grant we already have so I'll look at the first one."

"Thanks, Ed." I go back to my office to finish as much of the proposal as I can. I call Marge to tell her the news and before I ask she says she will make the arrangements.

Nancy is sleeping when I walk into her room. She looks very thin. As she begins to stir, I see the pain cross her face. She is definitely not comfortable. I give her a kiss and say, "Hi, Nancy. Your doctor Rose is here. Tell me how you feel. We may need to change medication."

She smiles and shows more pain. "It hurts to laugh. I'm glad you are here. I want you to ask some questions and get answers. I've warned everybody that my sister the doctor is coming."

"Did you explain that I'm not a doctor doctor? I don't want them to think I'm a medical doctor." I can tell by her look that she thinks what she said is right. She told me on the phone she told them I was at the Health Sciences center at the University.

She smiles. "I want them to be scared of you."

"Great! They'll think I'm a fraud. I wish you had not said that. But tell me what's going on." I sit on the side of her bed.

Tears well up in her eyes. I take her hand. "Rosie, I have a colostomy. No one has bothered to tell me why. How will it work when I go home? The nurses do something to it every few hours."

"Didn't the surgeon tell you that you might have to have a colostomy before surgery?" I feel the anger. I teach communications to health professionals and use this as an example. Patients need to know what to expect when they wake up. That is they need to know all possibilities. No surprises. "Do you know the surgeon? What do you know about him?"

"He's a good family friend. He goes to our church."

"Did you tell him I was coming and would want to speak with him?"

"Sure. I told him my sister, Dr. Walton, was coming today."

I knew it. She thinks it's cute. Now I have to explain that my sister didn't lie she just stretched the truth with her language and tone. "I wish you would stop calling me doctor." As I look around a man walks in the room and asks Nancy how she feels.

She says, "OK. I'm concerned about what's going to happen?"

"Don't worry about that. Let's get you stronger so you can go home. You must eat. I'll order anything you'd like. What's your favorite food?"

"My sister's cooking. This is my sister, Dr. Rose Walton."

I stand shake his hand and say, "May I speak with you sometime today?"

"Sure, I'll come back when I finish seeing my other patients. You must know that Nancy is very special. We've been friends for years." With that he leaves.

He did come back in about an hour and was very cordial until I ask why he would ever do surgery without first discussing all possibilities. I quickly added, "I teach a

288

communications class to health profession students and this example of a colostomy always raises much discussion. I'd like your reasoning, so I may use it in class."

He crossed his arms and turned slightly away from me. No more eye contact. "Are you a physician? How many patients do you see each day? I did not expect Nancy to need a colostomy."

I did not expect the defensive response. I pushed a bit more and thanked him before I ended the discussion. Nancy was more important.

Oh, DAMN. I have to pee. No store or restaurant in this City lets you use their facilities. You have to be a customer and then the bathrooms are downstairs, hidden away in dark halls. But this is the Upper East Side, where the richer folks live. Maybe they'll let me go. But it's too late. I feel the warm stream down both legs. DAMN. I hate this God Damn disease. My anxiety in the City always makes it worse. I should have stayed home. I had to be here for a Director's meeting of all the AIDS Projects in New York State. My friend Joyce suggested that I meet her at her place and she would drive me home. She knows I hate fighting the crowds at the train station. I'm not good at that.

It was a good idea but now my pants are wet, my slacks look two toned and I'm ashamed. I don't want to go to her apartment like this or let anyone in her building see me like this. Maybe my pants will dry before she gets here. I step up to the telephone on the corner, wedge my briefcase between the shelf and me and turn sideways so I can see how bad I look. My tan slacks are now brown and tan pants but clearly not an intentional design. I take Joyce's number out of my pocket and call.

"Lennox Hill Hospital, how may I direct your call?"

"Dr. Honor, please." Joyce is a best friend who also happens to be my doctor. She lived with Marge and me when she was practicing in Stony Brook. She's the best physician I know. She's also a really witty and a beautiful woman. I'm always teasing her that I want to run away with her. Her partner doesn't like that idea but Joyce and I joke about it.

I watch every face go by to see if they look at my wet pants. Some do and others don't even look at me. It begins to rain. I don't have an umbrella. What the hell, I'm already wet. Where the fuck is she? I wait and am ready to hang up when Joyce finally answers. We make plans to meet at her apartment an hour from now.

I walk toward her building and pass a little bar/restaurant that looks OK to me. I know nothing about the City. I guess everything in this neighborhood is OK. I back up and decide to check it out. I find a corner booth in the back and sit down. Spread my briefcase out beside me and try to look normal. I look around for the bathroom. It's right down the hall from this booth. Lucky me. Of course I don't know if there are steps behind the door or if it's on the same level. I'll wait for the waitress and order first then go to the bathroom. I order a glass of water and then a vodka and tonic. What if it is only three in the afternoon? I'm not driving, Joyce is and anyway that's later. I go to the bathroom and find a new roll of toilet paper. I press wads of paper against the cloth of my slacks and then stuff some paper in my pants. If they had one of those hand dryers, I could take my slacks off and dry them. I know this is not really helping but I do it anyway. I dry my feet and the inside of my shoes. UCK. I feel the seat of my pants and they feel pretty dry. If I sit a while, they'll be OK. No one will notice. I'll put on my jacket to hide my backside. I go back to the booth, sit down and take a paper out of my briefcase. I look busy and businesslike when the waitress brings my drink. I look around, to notice that there is no one else in the restaurant now. It must be a strange time of day; no one is eating or drinking. So What? I sip my drink and check my watch 3:12   3:17   3:21   3:23   3:28 I get the waitress's eye and ask for a check. She tells me the amount and I pay her and tell her to keep the rest. I'm the big spender from the country. I walk out and find the rain coming down even harder. I hurry up the street to Joyce's building. I walk in and shake the rain from my head. I'm glad it rained; no one will think a thing about my wet pants. As I walk into the lobby I see a familiar face. He's been at some meetings I attended. Where? He's about my height with graying hair. I can't remember his name but I know I know him. I remember, he's a Dean in Allied Health at a college in the City. I know he's a friend of Ed and Bob's. I've seen him at other meetings. He sees me and walks right over. He knows my name. How embarrassing. "Rose, are you visiting someone in my building?"

"Yes, Dr. Joyce Honor. Do you know her?"

"No. But why don't you wait in my apartment so I can catch up on what Ed and Bob are doing these days." Without waiting for my answer, he tells the doorman to have Dr. Honor call his apartment when she arrives. I protest but not enough. He has my briefcase and is leading me to the elevator before I have a chance to change his mind.

Now I'll have to sit someplace in his apartment in my wet pants. How do I get out of this? We have a nice chat going to the 16th floor. I keep remembering more about him. I even remember his name is Howard. He tells me that his partner lives in the next building. I guess he wants to be sure I know he's gay. His apartment is immaculate and filled with antique furniture. He directs me to a chair near the window in the living room. A straight, stuffed chair that looks like it just came out of the Queen's sitting room. A floral pattern with brass tacks holding the fabric on the polished cherry wood with its fancy scrolled back. I hesitate, and then sit as directed. "What can I get you to drink; *Vodka or Gin?*"

"Nothing, thanks. I'm sure my friend will be here soon and she'll be anxious to get going. She's going to East Hampton and will drop me off in Remsenburg." The phone rings. It's Joyce. He invites her up. He hangs up and says, "She is in a hurry. Sorry about that, I'd like to meet her. Maybe some other time."

I thank him for his hospitality and rush out the door.

This is going to be an interesting board meeting. I know that we are going to hear an amazing proposal for a major event like none other EEGO has had. I quickly call the meeting to order and announce that we have a guest who has asked to present an idea for a fundraiser. "He has asked to be first so that he can get back to New York City early. So, if there are no objections, I'm changing the order of the agenda. Mr. Bob Jacobson as some of you know is the editor of "Opera News" and is very well connected with both the New York City and the Metropolitan Opera. He has an exciting idea."

I know absolutely nothing about Opera. But others love it. At least that's what I'm told. "Thank you Rose. I want to organize a night of Opera as a fundraiser for the East End Gay Organization. I know I can get both City and Metropolitan Opera members to volunteer their time and talent. I'll do that part of it if you do the rest."

The board accepts his ideas enthusiastically. I appoint a committee to investigate the possibilities of space for the program, a committee to work with Bob on the final plans for the program, a committee to create, prepare and distribute invitations and a general committee to coordinate all aspects of the event. Everyone is excited about this end-of-year event and the rest of the meeting goes like clockwork.

We decide that the general benefit committee should meet next Saturday at ten in the morning. I promise to bring bagels and the fixings. I suggest if any on the board want to be a part of the committee that they should also attend meetings. As we leave, everyone is talking enthusiastically.

I stare at the computer screen. Justifying a budget is difficult. I've learned the things that must be included but finding the right words is hard for me. I hear the phone ring. I can't answer. This grant is due in Washington tomorrow and it must be finished in time to send it Federal Express before eight this evening. That's the last possible minute. We are joining the School of Public Health at Columbia University to submit a proposal to the Health Resources and Services Administration to continue as one of seventeen

AIDS Education and Training Centers in the nation. We will continue the NIMH project with NYU.

The phone rings again. Or maybe it's still ringing. I'm starving. I look at my watch. SHIT! It's nearly four and I haven't stopped to eat lunch.

My Associate Director, Tad walks in. "Your secretary doesn't want to bother you. They need you in the AIDS Unit."

"She should be afraid to interrupt me. I've yelled at her for lots of unnecessary interruptions today. She's driving me crazy."

Tad continues, "Bill is dying and his mother wants you there." I bow my head to hide the tears. Bill's so young. He was one of the first volunteers on the hotline when we opened in 1983. He took our stickers with phone numbers to every rest stop on the Island. He was always in the hotline office with a smile and a happy spirit. I love that kid. I see a sticker on my desk and reach for it. I crumble it and throw it across the room. DAMN! I say a prayer for his mother and wonder if his father's here. He disowned Bill shortly after he learned that Bill was positive. I tried to talk with him but to no avail. I look up at Tad and ask, "Can you finish this budget and then mail the whole grant?"

"Just go, Dr. Walton, you know I will. Does it go to Columbia University or Washington?"

"To the Health Resource and Services Association in Washington. Columbia has approved our portion even without this last section. But send them a copy. "Thanks."

As I get up the phone rings again. I answer, "Yes."

"Can you call a priest before you come up stairs?"

"Sure." I'm not even sure who that was. I make the call. Is Bill that close? I saw him yesterday and I thought he was rallying. Why, God why? Too many, too young. I take a piece of candy from the dish on my desk and walk out the door. Keep my chin up. I write grants, do education,

visit, pray, help feed, and still they DIE. STOP   STOP
STOP.

I walk to the elevator and go to the sixteenth floor so that
I can walk through the glass walkway from this tower to the
Hospital. I stop to collect my wits and look out at the acres
and acres of Long Island and the Sound to the North.

As I get to the Unit, I meet a priest. I've never seen
him so I introduce myself and ask, "Are you going to 1509?"

"Yes." I sense he sees my tears. He puts an arm
around my shoulder as we enter the room.

The stark green walls with their small mirrors, large
containers of hand washing soap and bright red canisters for
disposable needles so neatly attached to the wall bring me to
reality. I lean over and kiss Bill. I'm sure he doesn't
recognize me. I greet Bill's mother and then I think he
knows I'm here. He lifts his hand for me to take. His father
isn't here. I don't ask. I nod to the priest and he begins a
prayer. "Heavenly Father, bless this child of yours."

My eyes go around the room. Cards fill the bulletin
board at the foot of Bill's bed. I'm glad I'm here. His
mother looks lost. I'm relieved there's no one in the other
bed. I bow my head and add my prayer.

The priest continues, ". . . forgive this child his sin
of homosexuality and grant him peace and understanding."

I am stunned. Did I hear what I think I heard? Or
am I crazy? I look up and see Bill has opened his eyes. I
squeeze his hand as he closes them. I turn to the priest and
mouth "Get Out."

He looks puzzled that I would question him. I glare
at him and he knows he's crossed a line with me. He starts
to say, "But I must. . . ."

I point to the door and the priest leaves. I reach
across the bed and take Bill's mother's hand. She and I
hold Bill's hands and I say some kind of prayer. I hear
myself but can't make out the words. I feel a little squeeze

294

and then he lets go. I put my head on the pillow next to him and whisper that I love him. His mom comes around the bed and says, "Thank you. My Bill worshiped you." We hug.

In June, barely six months after her surgery, Nancy came to New York. She is bringing all of her records with her, including the slides of biopsies that had been done. I arranged an appointment with an oncologist and a pathologist to see her tomorrow. I really like and respect both of them and neither hesitated when I ask. They know me because of my AIDS work.

I drive to the door of the terminal and see her standing alone. She looks so thin and much older. Her hair came back white and a little curly. I park and go to get her bag and she is carrying a large file of papers. I hug her. She is all bones. I feel the tears and turn away so she can't see them. We walk slowly to the car. I open her door and she sits down with a sigh of relief.

"You are wonderful to arrange these appointments for me. I can't believe it has been ten years since I've been here."

"I'm glad it all worked out. They will see you at four and if we hurry we'll get there on time."

Both physicians are honest and straightforward with Nancy. They tell her she is very sick and that she may not be able to visit next year. She takes the news pretty well I think. Better than I do. I know it means death and she thinks just weaker. At least that's what I read from her body language. She smiles and thanks them. "Maybe I'll fool everybody and come see you next year just for fun."

I hang back and let her go out the door. "Now, tell me: How long?"

"You know none of us can be sure but I'd say six months. Tops."

I thank them and go quickly to catch Nancy. I know she doesn't have the slightest idea how to get back to my office. I put my arm around her waist and say, "Let's stop at the cafeteria for ice cream or a snicker. I need a pick me up."

We go by my office to pick up some papers. I know she is tired. It's been a long day for her. "How do you feel?" She looks terrible to me but her spirits are high.

"I feel really good most days. Of course I get tired quickly." She talks nonstop till I pull into the driveway. She thinks the house is beautiful and is very impressed with the deck Marge and I built around the pool.

I suggest a nap before dinner and she is asleep before I leave the room.

Getting to this evening of music on the East End has been an adventure. The air is electrifying. All around me people are hugging and kissing and congratulating each other that we did it. New York City Opera and Metropolitan Opera members have donated their time and talents for this fundraiser for EEGO. I'm very proud of all the members of EEGO who have worked so hard to make the evening a success. Most committees met weekly to secure places, arrange housing, and coordinate catering.

Last night after everything was ready, the tent erected, and green outdoor carpet with tables all around and even a dance floor in the middle of the area, we had a terrible wind storm: The first tornado ever to hit East Hampton. The tent blew down. The caterer said she would not continue. The ground was suddenly uneven with puddles everywhere. But some very dedicated members of EEGO worked almost all night and early this morning to put everything back in order and ready for this evening. Only those who saw it know the extent of the damage and the effort to fix it. Now it looks beautiful and everyone is ready for an evening of great music. There are hundreds here and all is well, even the caterer changed her mind after a little arm twisting. We will have a bountiful reception in the twice-erected tent after the program.

Just as I sit down, someone leans over and says, "Rosie, we need you at the door." I jump up, wonder what has happened and go quickly to the rear of the auditorium. I find my co-chair, having a tizzy. He has heard that my remarks, scheduled for intermission, are longer than three minutes.

"Rosie, we must not extend our speaking time. People will be eager to get out and talk about the wonderful music. They won't listen to us."

"Well I believe the audience will listen to what I have to say. I'm going to tell them just why fundraising is vital and that they are the most important people. Don't worry about what I'm going to say or how long it will take me to say it. You really shouldn't be so nervous. Enjoy the evening." I storm back to my seat. At least we spoke in hushed tones so others did not hear.

I can't believe he thinks he's in charge. I really like working with him. Most men always think they are in charge. I've always said, even in this organization of gay men and lesbians, the issue remains the same. Women constantly have to educate men about equality. It must be the evening and he knows I know nothing about opera.

As I sit down Marge wants to know what's wrong. I can't hide my anxiety from her. I say, "Nothing." I fidget in my seat. Take my notes out of my pocket and look to see if there is a word I can cut. It's what I want to say. I will not cut anything. It's only about four minutes. I'll talk fast.

Chills run down my back as I listen to the magnificent music. Beautiful! I've never gone to an Opera. These voices are wonderful. I look around and see hundreds of people sitting spellbound. I never dreamed that I would enjoy Opera.

Bob Jacobsen, the MC for the evening, announces intermission. I move quickly from my seat to the stage. As the house lights come up, I see that it is a standing room only crowd. The applause is overwhelming. It subsides as Stan takes the mike. He talks and then introduces me. I tingle all over. I adjust my bright blue hat. I have not heard a word he said. A little anxiety is a good thing.

I thank everyone for being here to support EEGO and our cause. "Never before in the history of fighting disease has a minority community responded with the dedication, the hard work, the love, the caring that the gay

297

and lesbian community has demonstrated in the fight against AIDS." The audience gets very quiet I can hear only my voice. I catch my breath. I continue with some statistics and facts about what the government has not done. I'm interrupted several times with applause. I end with "we must never allow ignorance and bigotry to pass us without our confrontation." Everyone is standing. The applause is tremendous. I tingle when Stan hugs me and says, "Thank you." I feel warm tears.

I walk down the stage steps and am met by many friends thanking me. Marge squeezes through the crowd and puts her arms around me. "Rosie, you are unbelievable. I love you." I'm on top of the world. I hope these thankful people dig deep into their pockets and help us raise money for this terrible crisis. That's what the evening is about. I look up and can't believe my eyes. I see the Associate Chancellor of the State University system coming toward me. He is smiling and grabs me in a very tight hug. He whispers in my ear, "You are great and you must come to Albany next week. We have work to do. I'll call, Monday." He lets go and is gone before I can respond.

There are rave reviews about the music and reports that we raised two hundred thousand dollars. As I read the account of Kathleen Battle coming from London to be here and barely making it because of a bomb scare I think of her beautiful voice singing, "He's Got the Whole World in His Hands." I tear the articles out of the paper, I highlight the names: Paul Pliska, Evelyn Lear, Aprile Millo, Roberta Peters and others. Can't wait to put these on the bulletin boards at the University.

This is going to be a very different Thanksgiving. Marge and I usually spend the day with her family either at our house or at her brother's in Boston. They are a family who love the holiday and make it special for all. There are usually about fifteen or twenty when it's in Boston. This year Marge and I are going to Nancy's to cook dinner for her family. Nancy is very sick and this will probably be her last Thanksgiving.

As the plane nears Pittsburgh I think about how few times I have landed here to visit Nancy. We have always stayed in touch, talking often but we have never seemed to visit with each other. She did bring the kids to New York that first year I was there. I remember so vividly that she told the kids not to mention that Marge was Jewish. And of course the first words out of their mouths to Marge were "Are you Jewish?"

Marge asks if I'm OK and I assure her I am. I fidget in my seat and look out the window. I see the airport to the right of our plane. It's like Charleston, WV. They sliced off the top of a hill and paved a runway. Here in Pittsburgh they have more than one.

I called Nancy the other day and gave her my list of ingredients for the dressing and the vegetables that I wanted. She called back to say that Robin, her youngest, did not want to buy chicken livers. "Do you really need them, Rosie?"

"Nancy, they won't even know they're in the dressing. But it is not essential to have them."

Of course she wanted to know how I learned to cook a turkey and all the trimmings. I said, "Marge and I are a great team. Your family is in for a real treat." I feel very sad that she won't even be able to taste anything. She now has a feeding tube.

We make our way from the plane to the baggage area. We go down two flights of stairs, around a major walkway and then down an escalator. I'm tired by the time I see Randy and Robin. They are the two youngest and look so much alike. Good thing one is a boy and one a girl or we might think they are identical twins. They rush over, give us both big hugs and kisses and grab our bags. We didn't bring much. I ask how Nancy is feeling. Randy says, "Fine." Robin hangs her head. Then Robin tells me she bought those disgusting things I wanted for the dressing and that she probably won't eat if I use them. I laugh and tell her she won't even know. Randy is about ten paces ahead of all of us and turns to tell us where the car is parked.

"Just wait for us." Robin turns to us and says, "His legs are so long he walks ahead of me all the time."

"That's OK. You are both very good looking. You must've gotten your looks from your mom. That's my side of the family." She laughs.

Nancy is thin and pale and looks very tired. She is happy we are here and thanks us for coming. I want to hold her and cry. Damn the cancer. First Granny, then Mother and now Nancy. When will it be my turn? Or is MS enough? Is there a God giving out these terrible diseases? Nancy's always been very devout and has gone to church much like Granny: every Sunday. Maybe it's a lottery. I won't buy tickets.

The turkey, sweet potatoes as well as the green beans and cranberry salads are fabulous. Marge made everything except the turkey and dressing. The kids keep asking for just a little more. Robin wants to know where the livers are. I just laugh and tell her, "I don't remember where I put them." Jennifer wants all the recipes. She is the oldest daughter and beautiful. She is quieter than the others and more sensitive. Ronnie, Nancy's husband, is shocked that Marge and I came to do this. He's over whelmed. I just say, "That's what sisters do."

Nancy sits with us while we eat. She asks to smell each dish. I am having trouble keeping the tears and my voice in check. I make several fake trips to the kitchen for imaginary things I have forgotten. I go to blow my nose. Marge is super. She keeps the conversation going and is so at ease. When I sit back down, her hand on my knee is a lifesaver.

I keep waiting for everyone to finish so I can bring the pies to the table. Jeffrey, who is playing football in college, keeps adding more food to his plate. I don't know where he puts it all. When he sees me waiting, he reminds me, "They don't serve this kind of food at college."

It's time for pie. I made pecan and bought an apple-blackberry. Nancy says, "This is the best pecan pie I've ever smelled. Thank you, Marge and Rosie. We love you."

We are on the corner of Christopher Street and Seventh Ave. in New York City. It's very cold and I think it might snow but Marge and I are celebrating. No special day just our special love. We've had a wonderful dinner and now are looking for a newsstand to buy a copy of the latest Time magazine It's a special issue about women and we are in it. Or we think we are.

We're on our bikes in front of the house. The Time magazine photographer is taking pictures as we position ourselves like we are riding. Then we're on the beach. The photographer runs ahead of us and turns to take our picture as we stroll toward her. Marge is acting crazy. She runs behind the photographer and when she turns around Marge is right in her face. They laugh and I walk faster to catch up with them. So many pictures.

Yes, they have the magazine. The man in the newsstand is just opening the bundle. "I'd like one of those, please." I point to the bundle in his hand.

"Jus wait a minit lady, I ain't got em open yit."

I stand and wait, shifting from one foot to the other. He slowly picks one up and says, "That'll be...."

I hand him a five-dollar bill. He gives Marge the magazine and I wait for change. We stand shoulder-to-shoulder, arm in arm flipping through the pages. Not there? It has to be.

"Let me see."

"Wait just a minute. I'll go slower."

"Right, you don't know how to go fast."

"Here it is and with our picture too. The first one the photographer took. Rosie, we're famous."

Marge kisses me and I hold her tight. I whisper, "Precious treasure, they call us the lesbians next door, in a special edition of TIME magazine! We're not just special. We're really something. How many copies should we buy?"

"Don't forget your nurse friend Roy and Frank."

"I have them."

I'm writing a list of all our friends who have died of AIDS as Marge drives us to the first EEGO memorial

301

service. She organized this event and got a minister and a Rabbi to conduct part of the program. I'm so proud of her. We should have done this in 1985 and 86. It's already 1987. We've lost so many in our community. Collectively we're sad beyond words.

Marge asked the other day if I were ever going to smile again. I've built a wall around me, trying to keep it all out. I look out the window and think how beautiful. The flat land with flowing grasses along the shore and row after row of corn or potatoes in field after field. A farmer is plowing under the last of the small potatoes. I used to pick them up in the fields near where we live, but now they plow them under the same day they dig the potatoes. I see that picture of the women in full skirts gleaning the fields and want to paint my own. Someday!

I add a few names. Now the list is at 13. Then I add Bill to make 14. We turn the corner in East Hampton and Marge asks about Emily.

"I don't think she's dead. She left the hospital the other day after her second stay in two months. But she's doing better." Then I remember that her little four- year old died last week. "I'll add Amy; Emily's daughter. Remember I told you about going to the hospital to be with Emily. That was a tough day." Surely these new drugs will help keep the babies alive longer. I'm not sure whether it's better for the mothers to die first or if they are more at peace if their children die before they do. Testing is still a big issue, but if the positive-HIV status of the mother is known during pregnancy some drugs have been successful in keeping the newborn from being positive

We walk into the church and greet many friends. I speak to Reverend Stuart and Rabbi Hirsch, and then quickly take a seat to be alone. I do not want to talk with anyone until this is over. Marge is greeting everyone as they come in. She's good. I should be there too; after all, I'm the co-chair of this organization. But I let her do it. I notice Lenny and Richard as they come in. Richard looks terrible but he's joking with everyone as usual. I smile at him and wave. I'll see them after. I have co-chaired this organization with both of them. They were so different in that role. I love them both.

The windows in this church are beautiful and remind me of my childhood church, but the stories I see in these don't match the playful stories my sister and I made up about ours. As I walk down the aisle with Lenny, to light the first candle, I'm looking forward. I shake my head. These candles pay respect to the past.

I am bombarded by names. Some I remember and can picture a face; some I don't know. I sink lower and lower into the pew. If I run out will anyone notice? I clench my fists and open them wide then clench. . . open. . . . clench. . . . . open. . . . clench. It ends. The rabbi asks us to rise and join hands. My fists won't fit.

We walk out of the church and Lenny leans heavily into my arms and sobs. Richard walks over and says, "Now none of that till Valentine's Day." We laugh and go arm in arm to the car. Next Valentine's Day we will light a candle for him.

"Thanks, Marge," I whisper as she starts the car.

I don't even look as the plane touches the runway. This trip is not like a month ago when Marge and I came to cook turkey. I wanted to come do the same for Christmas but Nancy wouldn't allow it. So Marge and I went to Florida just nine days ago and cooked turkey and all the trimmings for ten friends. Tomorrow is New Year's Eve.

The first person I see as I get off the plane is Randy. He's standing there with a big smile on his face and takes my bag as he puts his arms around me. He explains that the neighbor women wanted to pick me up so my dad could rest. We get to them just as he's explaining the whole thing to me. Nancy was taken back to the hospital about 10 this morning, just after she called me in Florida to let me know she thought the end was near. She told me not to come and ruin my vacation, but these neighbors called back to say that Nancy really wanted me there but could not ask. I just hope she's still alive.

"Do you want to go to the house or to the hospital?"

"I came to see my sister, so I guess we better go straight to the hospital. If she's OK after I see her for a while, I'll take a cab to the house. Randy, what do you think?"

"Mom was much better when we left the hospital about six tonight so you could just wait till morning if you want."

I saw Nancy a month ago. I knew then it was a matter of time and that the time was going to be soon. Where have these people been for the past year? She has gotten worse by the day. The physicians at Stony Brook who looked at Nancy's records and saw her for me said it would be 6 months to a year. Why aren't Ronnie and the kids at the hospital now?

"No, I'd rather go to the hospital."

Mrs. Ravasio turns to look at me in agreement. She said Nancy really wanted to see me but could not ask. I thanked her and slumped back in the seat. How do I say goodbye to my sister? We've just begun to care about each other as sisters after all those years of disagreement and surface level politeness. Now we've spoken to each other every day for a year. We know so much more about our beliefs and have found a real respect for our different lives. I doze thinking of the children. Will I lose them now? Why should they care about me? They have their own lives and their father will need them so much more. He has a hard time asking for anything. Robin will be the strongest. She'll probably come home from college more often to be with her dad. I'll call them often. Invite them to visit Marge and me. Jeff is working and living with his new wife, Kristi, in Eastern Pennsylvania, Jennifer is teaching and Randy is at Bucknell.

I sit up straight as the car makes a sharp turn and I realize we are in the parking lot of the hospital. It's midnight but I'm wide-awake now. "Thanks for the call and the ride."

Randy and I walk arm in arm. When we get to the door of the intensive care unit I see Nancy sitting up in bed. She looks alert and younger. But I know better. I'm glad I got here. She smiles and greets both of us with kisses. She quickly sends Randy on his way. "I want to spend some time with Rosie. Get some sleep. I love you."

For the next two hours we reminisce. "Remember the cherry tree. And all the times you were late getting home."

"And how you blamed me for doing everything?" She laughs. "You never did anything bad. Well maybe the time you cut mother's silk dress." We both laugh and hug each other.

"Rosie, I always wondered how you got through high school and maybe college without studying."

"Oh, I studied. I just didn't let any of you see me."

"Did our uncle abuse you? Did you ever tell anyone? Oh, Rosie, you are such a good person. I'm so glad you found Marge. I'm sorry we . . ."

"Now don't go there. We have to be happy with what we have. We can wish till the cows come home. It won't change the past."

"I know. I think I better rest. And you should sleep." We hug and cry together knowing that it's over. She tells me I'd better watch out for her kids.

I don't go far. Just to a lounge down the hall. The doctor comes to wake me about four and she calls the family. They arrive about four thirty. I kiss Nancy and step away from her bed. She peacefully leaves us at five.

Looking over the rail of the balcony in the gymnasium allows me to see and not be seen. The quilt, honoring those who have died from HIV and AIDS covers the entire floor and sections of the quilt hang from the balcony all around the gym. Each of these quilt pieces is made by loved ones of the person they represent. And all that we have here, more than ten thousand, are from New York with one section devoted to those from Long Island. When the quilt was displayed in Washington, DC it covered more than the area of three football fields. It is a national project that began in California.

I hear the names of people I knew being read. I want to run. I can't do this over and over. Next month will mark ten years since the first call to the hotline. It seems like yesterday but feels more like a lifetime. I find a chair on the empty side of the balcony and sit for a while. I fidget and wipe the tears away. I hope no one finds me hiding here. I must walk around to the other side where we have the microphone set up. People, including my staff of the AIDS Education and Resource Center, have volunteered to read for thirty minutes of the ten hours each day that names are read. Today, I'm responsible to see that the people are here and that names are read continuously. As I round the end of the track, I don't see anyone waiting to read at three o'clock. That means I must read. I look out over the railing at the gym floor and bow my head for strength. It feels like I carry three hundred pounds on my shoulders. And it's very hot up here.

I will read from the Long Island list. Many of them were friends, acquaintances, people I have met in the hospital or in education classes I conducted for organizations around Long Island. My voice shakes, sounds funny to me. I speak in public at least twice a week and never hear these quivers in my voice. Straighten up, Rosie, and read. Show your strength. Lift your voice and let the 100 or so people walking around the quilt pieces hear your respect for them and the ones they lost.

I read. I recognize many of these names and yet try not to let my voice say that. I add Ralph Johnston, Edmund McTernan, Ralph Chamberlin, Tom . . . . . .

One of my staff members, Dolores, steps up to let me know she's here to continue the reading. I acknowledge her and end my reading. I hand her the next list and go back to my chair. Out of sight and out of seeing. Tomorrow **I WILL** walk down on the floor to see quilts for Ed and Roy and John and Emily and Ralph. There are so many. I must do that tomorrow.

Today is a very special day for me. I am in Washington to testify before the National Commission on

HIV/AIDS. This commission was appointed by the President Reagan to make recommendations for a national response. It's about time. The federal government is way behind their responsibility in my opinion. But don't go there now. I am honored to be here with all these important people from around the nation. I feel like a little fish in a big pond. But I will make a ripple I hope. I walk up to the table just outside the hearing room. Several people standing around I recognize as leaders of gay and lesbian organizations like Lambda Legal Defense and Education Fund, the National Gay and Lesbian Task Force, and the Gay Men's Health Crisis. Suddenly I feel arms around me. I try to turn but whoever it is won't let me. I reach for a head near mine. Immediately I know it is my dear friend, Eric. I relax. "Eric, I didn't know you'd be here. Who is minding the project in San Francisco? Can we have dinner tonight or lunch when this hearing is over?"

He lets go of my hand and we kiss and hug. It has been months since we have seen each other. We met years ago at a gay and lesbian leadership conference and became dear friends. He is now the director of the Shanti Project, an AIDS community service organization in San Francisco. It is one of the largest. "I'm so happy you are here. Which hat are you wearing today, Rose?"

"I'm talking about the role of allied health professionals in the delivery of care for HIV/AIDS patients. Of course I'm sure to mention the discrimination in the delivery of that care and the need for more education. Who knows maybe they will recommend more money for us."

"I'm so proud of you. I tell my staff about you all the time."

"Sure you do. Now how about lunch or dinner to catch up with what you are doing?"

"I can't my dear. I'm flying back to the West coast as soon as I testify. In fact they moved me up the list so I could catch the plane. But it is wonderful to see you. Keep up the good work."

Just then someone announces that we should all take our seats. The hearing is about to begin. I look at the program and am pleased that I'm not so far down the list. I began to relax after listening to several testimonies. Mine is well organized and I've practiced reading it at least 100 times.

The "person with AIDS" on the commission said it best when I finished. "Thank you for telling us who all those people are who come into our rooms and do so much for us. I think you guys need a publicity campaign."

"But, Bob, we've had this conversation many times. I know I can't continue to do it all."

I sit at my desk and he sits on the other side. I look around at the paintings that cheer my day and at the mess on my desk. I want to wipe it clean. It's all in piles where only I know to find the notes for each project. How can I delegate? I'll give each person a pile and see if they can figure it out. That's a good test to see who should take over when I leave. One for the department stuff, one for graduate program leftovers, and a pile for each of the major funding agencies and projects in the AIDS Education and Resource Center. They're my piles and I know their workings. I look around at the stuff I've collected. The paper wasp's nest that a student gave me reminds me of the one Deh Deh knocked down a long time ago. It's beautiful. Then there's the table I just cleaned off to put my new jigsaw puzzle out. It's a wooden jigsaw of the color red. It will be a challenge and relaxing at the same time. That's what I do to make decisions. Sometimes Bob, when he was Associate Dean, would look for a piece and accuse me of hiding pieces. A puzzle clears my head. Deh Deh taught me that.

"So, that's what I'm trying to tell you. Give up some of it. Just teach one course and do the AIDS Resource Center."

He thinks he knows what's best for everyone. HE Should listen to his own advice. I look at him and want to tell him so but it won't help. He's as stubborn as I am. I think I know myself better. So I pick up a piece of candy from my desk and smile inside. I'll just leave when I'm ready and I know it.

308

"And be in my department with someone else as chair? I don't think so. I know I couldn't do that."

I gave the graduate program to the best qualified in the department and I still teach a graduate course. I believe that when there are questions, I can solve the problems and give answers more quickly and easily than anyone else.

"At least you admit that."

"I'll just retire."

"Then think about disability if you're intent on not working."

He stands to leave but pauses to say "if you're still here when I move into the department, you better leave me alone." I must look puzzled; he flashes his usual "I know all smile" and keeps going. I know it's a good thing we're good friends who can say almost anything to each other and be truthful in our feelings. At least until now that's been the case and for me, I think it still is. But I recognize that at work it is sometimes a love-hate relationship. When I don't feel like saying what I think, I keep my mouth shut. That's what Deh Deh always told me to do. He said, "If you can't say something good, keep your God Damn mouth shut."

I'll still teach this semester and next. I'm not ready to accept disability even though my neurologist suggested I do so last month. I'll show them, I always have. I want at least one more year.

Almost one year to the day, I walk out of the school of Allied Health for the last time.   The sky is like a painting; blue with wisps of white. The sun is bright and warm for late April. I can plant flowers all day tomorrow. No more school. No more work. I'm like a bird, just out of my cluttered cage. Flying high. Students left early and I sneaked out without good-byes. I'm not good at them and who knows maybe it won't be forever. No parties, I'm only taking sick leave.

I drive home singing at the top of my lungs. I stop at "Petals and Plants" to buy four flats of impatiens. Tomorrow the deck of the pool will be all dressed up.

As I turn into the driveway, Marge is just stepping out of her car. What timing. She turns and smiles and comes to take a box I'm carrying.

"Well, how do you feel? Are you sad?"

"Sad! What about? Are you kidding? Look in the car, and help me get all those flowers to the pool deck. We're going to have more color in our yard this year than ever before. I can't wait to get started."

"Well, my dear, we're going out to dinner to celebrate." She puts the box down and turns to give me a big hug. Her hair is so curly and looks as good now as when she left this morning. As I hug her, I feel her tight body. She's very fit. I'll get started on my own fitness level now without the interference of work.

"We're not going to dinner this early. I have an idea about celebration too." We take the steps two at a time.

Summer was wonderful. I biked with Marge and planted flowers and more flowers. I tried new recipes and read a lot of books. Now it is time for the beautiful leaves to change colors like a bright quilt. They will fall and snow will be right behind them. I'll leave before Christmas to spend the winter in Florida. Marge will follow to spend her winter vacation with me. I'll try to convince her to retire soon. She is very busy with her own private practice and her teaching. I don't miss going to work at all and think retirement is wonderful. I go to the gym two or three days a week and walk a mile each day. My cane and I are getting along much better than when I started using it last Spring.

"Marge, where are you? I need your opinion about this outfit."

She calls from downstairs. "You look fine. You're beautiful. Now hurry."

We are on our way to an AIDS fundraiser at Stony Brook. This one is in my honor. It's my big sendoff from the University. I am very proud of what I've done for the response to HIV/AIDS on Long Island. Today's proceeds will go to the pediatric AIDS unit in University hospital. I change earrings and then change again. I end up wearing the first ones. I try to hurry. Marge is getting impatient. I comb my hair again.

"Come on, Rosie, we can't be late"

"But I have to look good; I have to be on stage."

"Why? The Stonewall Chorale is singing, not you."

"I'll get to thank everyone for their support. Won't I?"

"If you don't hurry, you won't even get to hear the concert. Now come on."

I'm very excited. She is too, but doesn't want me to know. She acts like she knows something that I don't about today. I've asked her several times and she, as usual, says "Nothing." Marge can keep a secret better than anyone I know. It's very hard to surprise her.

I'm finally in the car. I lean over and give Marge a kiss as she pulls out of the garage. I ask again, "Are you sure Randy and Jeff are not coming?"

"They called you didn't they to say they could not be here and so did Robin and Jennifer."

"I know but I'm disappointed." Randy and Jeff live pretty close. They both called to congratulate me but had more pressing things to do today. I don't expect my nieces to be here. They'd have to fly and I know they can't afford to do that. They each called twice. I think Robin had a business trip. All four of them are so wonderful. Thanks, Nancy.

Marge lets me out at the entrance to the auditorium and I walk slowly to the door. Maybe she will catch up if she finds a close parking place. I look around for her. I say "Hello" to several friends and feel the excitement. As I get to the front of the Hall, I look in and the first person I see is my niece, Jennifer, and right behind her are Jeff and Randy. And right behind them are Marge's dad, her brother, and sister in law. They are the secret Marge had up her sleeve. I am speechless. The tears are warm. I have so many people to thank, mostly Marge. She joins us and says, "We really surprised the old girl didn't we?" We stand like family with arms around each other. It feels great. I'm so blessed.

There are so many friends here and so many people I've met during these ten years of AIDS work that I'm overwhelmed. I want to speak to each one to express my thanks for the support. I could never have accomplished all that I did at the University without so many of these people. I continue to greet people as we all go into the auditorium. My seat is right in the middle with the stage at eye level. I'm glad I'm not in the front row. It's below the stage. Bob arranged everything even my seat. As the singers walk on stage I whisper to Randy that they are a gay and lesbian group from New York City and are donating their time to do this concert.

Bob steps to the microphone to begin the program. He thanks the audience and asks me to stand. I am a bit embarrassed but so happy and proud that I smile from ear to ear. He introduces the director of the Stonewall Chorale and talks about the group. "This gay and lesbian singing group has been together since 1977. And, just a note of interest, that's the year Dr. Walton came to Stony Brook. The chorus is an all-volunteer group. They raise money from concerts, grants and donations. I welcome them and know that we will enjoy their program." As he walks off the director walks to center stage and the music begins.

My mind wanders. "Deh Deh, I wish you were here. You always made me feel like I was more than OK. You were the only one. If you were here it would not be OK for you to stand in the back like you did at Nancy's high school graduation. But I saw you before you sneaked out.

Today, you'd have to be right beside me. I speak in my head. 'I'd show you all my plaques and commendations. The one from the AIDS Collective is beautifully framed. A young woman, with AIDS, who spoke at some of my education programs, designed it. At New York University, I received an engraved plaque for my leadership and a few months later, one from Columbia University for my dedication to education. I worked with both Universities as part of the nationwide AIDS Education and Training Centers.

312

The staff of the center I created will continue our work. They are very competent educators and I enjoyed working with them. I'm very proud of them. The Suffolk County executive sent a proclamation and the Supervisor of Southampton proclaimed today, Rose Ann Walton Day."

The singing continues. It startles me. This is the first time I've heard them. Jennifer leans over and says, "This is your day Rosie and I'm glad I'm here. I have to thank Marge again. Do all these people know you?"

"Well, Jennifer they either know me or know my work. I want you to meet some of them, especially those who worked with me at the AIDS Center."

"Mom would have been so proud. And she'd be here. I think she knows anyway."

"I hope so."

I close my eyes and lean back in my seat. I still want to tell Deh Deh everything. He'd shake his head and remind me of the cherry tree. But I go back to tell him anyway. "Deh Deh, you'd be astonished at the money. Of course, the government never allocated enough money to do the job but I was responsible for more money than either you or I could imagine, and I remember, don't talk religion or politics to you. One day a group of us raised a hundred thousand dollars and a year later even more. I worked with the Long Island Council of Churches too. They did some very important education."

I suddenly hear "This song is about the beauty of roses. It is a special tribute to Dr. Rose Walton. Thank you for your tireless efforts."

I squeeze Marge's hand and whisper, "This is unbelievable. How can I thank everyone?"

She looks at me with a big smile and says, "I'm sure you'll think of something."

ABOUT THE AUTHOR

Rose's highest honor is the naming of the HIV/AIDS clinic at Southampton, NY. She has received many awards for her dedication to HIV/AIDS. She was named AN UNCOMMON WOMAN by the Legacy Foundation in New York in 1993 and in 2015 was granted a LIFETIME ACHIEVEMENT AWARD by Equality Florida.

Rose always wanted to live in Florida. She often talked to her chickens about moving. Education and teaching kept her in West Virginia and Pennsylvania until she went to Tennessee for her master's degree. She taught health and physical education the first 17 years of her career, 15 of which were in her adopted state of Florida. Rose became an avid fisherperson and could be found at water's edge with a pole in hand and fish in a bucket on any free day or night. Snook were her prize catch and best eating.

Life changed when she met Marjorie Sherwin. Love was a stronger pull than sunshine or fishing. Completing her Ed.D. Degree at Nova University, Rose moved to NY and began a second career at SUNY, Stony Brook as curriculum developer, graduate program director, department head and director of an AIDS Education & Resource Center which she created. AIDS education became her passion. She established the first information and referral hot line on Long Island, and developed a program to educate faculty leaders from SUNY campuses. Those faculty members trained other faculty on each campus and taught HIV/AIDS information to thousands of students. Rose traveled throughout the state and around the country lecturing about the epidemic.

With life filled with love and purpose, Rose thrived. She has been in a loving relationship with Marjorie for 39 years. In January there will be a remarkable 80/40 celebration.